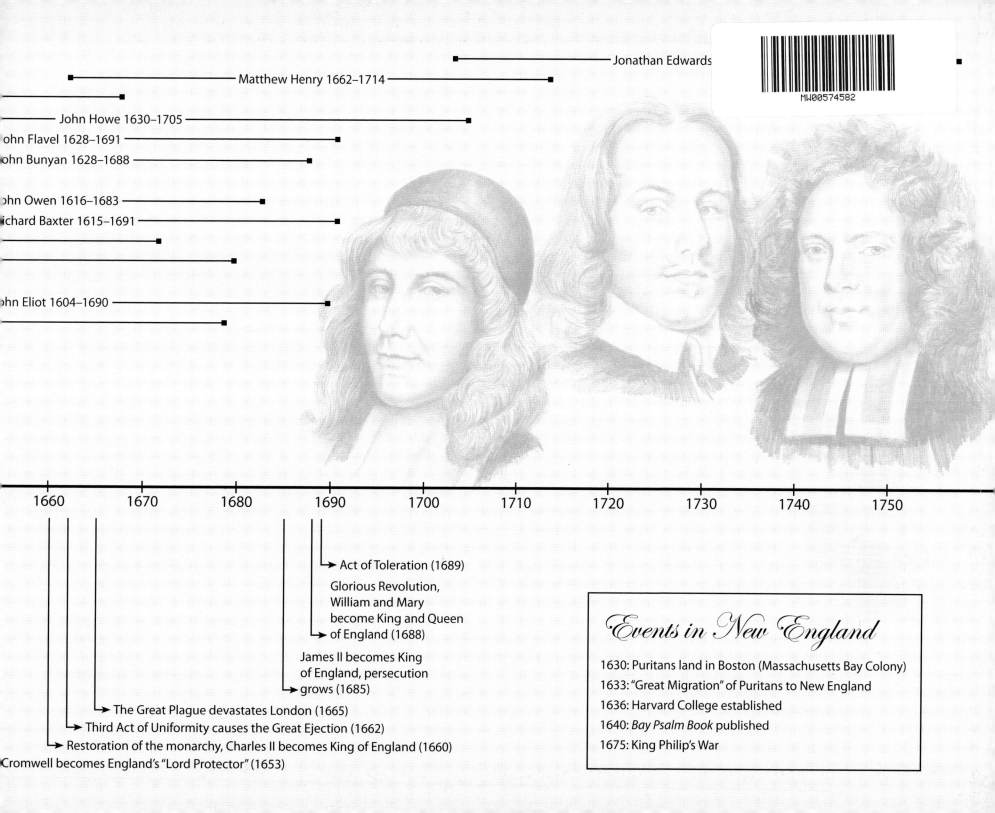

Jonathan Edwards

Matthew Henry 1662–1714

John Howe 1630–1705

John Flavel 1628–1691

John Bunyan 1628–1688

John Owen 1616–1683

Richard Baxter 1615–1691

John Eliot 1604–1690

| 1660 | 1670 | 1680 | 1690 | 1700 | 1710 | 1720 | 1730 | 1740 | 1750 |

Act of Toleration (1689)

Glorious Revolution, William and Mary become King and Queen of England (1688)

James II becomes King of England, persecution grows (1685)

The Great Plague devastates London (1665)

Third Act of Uniformity causes the Great Ejection (1662)

Restoration of the monarchy, Charles II becomes King of England (1660)

Cromwell becomes England's "Lord Protector" (1653)

Events in New England

1630: Puritans land in Boston (Massachusetts Bay Colony)

1633: "Great Migration" of Puritans to New England

1636: Harvard College established

1640: *Bay Psalm Book* published

1675: King Philip's War

How refreshing it is to step into the past. We need perspective and we need heroes. This book provides both. Richly illustrated, these brief but substantive biographies point us to faithful and fruitful servants. They remind us of our calling to be disciples. They encourage us to press on through trials and suffering. They remind us to be joyful and grateful for all that God has done. Above all, they remind us to keep our eyes fixed on the one Hero, our faithful Lord and Savior.

—Stephen J. Nichols, president, Reformation Bible College,
and chief academic officer, Ligonier Ministries

⟫◆◆◆⟪

A masterful summary of the pick of the Puritans, introducing a new generation to a gospel-centered, life-embracing, family-oriented people, and—yes—people who enjoyed life instead of the dour, sour, and twisted folk that a hundred years of prejudicial narratives have made them out to be. I wish it every success in dispelling the myths that plague these godly men and women.

—Derek W. H. Thomas, senior minister, First Presbyterian Church,
Columbia, South Carolina

The most obvious virtue of this book is that it is a triumph of scholarship. Although I am a published Puritan scholar, virtually everything in this book was new to me. I have known the Puritans through their writings; this book introduced me to the people. Still more scholarly excellence appears after the biographical chapters in the form of a glossary of the Puritan movement, a time line, and bibliographies of both the Puritan movement and the individual Puritans covered in the book.

The book is also a visual treat, with its abundance of photographs of places and buildings associated with people featured in the book and reproductions of contemporary materials such as people, buildings, and cover pages of documents. For me, the visuals made the book an instant page turner.

The book is also a Puritan primer ("first things" in the dual sense of being introductory and covering things of first importance). The introduction and conclusion provide an overview of Puritanism, and as someone who has published this type of material myself, I will record my opinion that it cannot be done better than it is done here.

The heart of the book is the portraits of twenty-one Puritan heroes. Three things stand out: all the major Puritans leaders are in the gallery; each one comes alive in a reader's imagination; and the combination of factual information, imaged dialogue, and a narrative thread makes the chapters accessible to any reader, including young people.

This book has something for everyone. For people who are new to the Puritans, this is the introduction they have been looking for. Study questions for the individual chapters make the book ideal for Christian schools and home-schooling families. On the other hand, I will speak for my scholarly guild and say that no Puritan scholar would want to be without this book.

—Leland Ryken, professor of English emeritus at Wheaton College
and author of *Worldly Saints: The Puritans as They Really Were*

Puritan
HEROES

Puritan HEROES

by Glenda Faye Mathes and Joel R. Beeke

Illustrated by Caffy Whitney

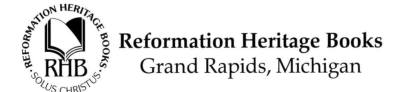

Reformation Heritage Books
Grand Rapids, Michigan

Puritan Heroes
© 2018 by Glenda Faye Mathes and Joel R. Beeke

Reformation Heritage Books
2965 Leonard St. NE
Grand Rapids, MI 49525
616-977-0889
orders@heritagebooks.org
www.heritagebooks.org

Printed in the United States of America
18 19 20 21 22 23/10 9 8 7 6 5 4 3 2 1

Library of Congress Cataloging-in-Publication Data

Names: Mathes, Glenda, author.
Title: Puritan heroes / Glenda Faye Mathes and Joel R. Beeke.
Description: Grand Rapids, Michigan : Reformation Heritage Books, 2018. | Includes bibliographical references.
Identifiers: LCCN 2018044953 (print) | LCCN 2018041662 (ebook) | ISBN 9781601786371 (hardcover : alk. paper) |
    ISBN 9781601786388 (epub)
Subjects: LCSH: Puritans—Biography.
Classification: LCC BX9323 .M38 2018 (ebook) | LCC BX9323 (print) | DDC 285/.90922 [B] —dc23
LC record available at https://lccn.loc.gov/2018044953

Cover artwork by Caffy Whitney: For additional artwork by Caffy Whitney, see pages 18, 23, 32, 59, 100, 108, 128, 162, 172.

For additional Reformed literature, request a free book list from Reformation Heritage Books at the above regular or e-mail address.

To
my children and their children,

in whom I have no greater joy
than to hear they're walking in the truth.

— Glenda Faye Mathes

———◆◆◆———

With much love
for our precious grandchildren,

Emma Layne, Edalette Wilma, and Tyler Joel,

with the prayer that you may grow up with Puritan heroes,
and follow them as far as they followed Christ.

— Grandpa & Grandma Beeke

Table of Contents

Preface

Who were the Puritans? Why are they heroes? Those may be your questions as you pick up this book.

The Puritans lived in the years following the Protestant Reformation. Like Olympic runners, they carried forward the torch of biblical truth lit by the Reformers to transform the church. Applying God's Word to every part of life, they joyfully emphasized the need for each individual to experience a changed heart and a personal relationship with Christ.

Although the Church of England was formed as a result of the Reformation, the Puritans believed it needed more reform. But they didn't all agree on how that change should take place. Because they refused to participate in some of the Church of England's unbiblical practices, they became known as nonconformists. The term "Puritan" was first used to ridicule them for their desire to be "pure" according to God's Word.

While some people still think of the Puritans as strict or narrow-minded, anyone who reads the timeless books written by them will soon see their love for God and His Word, their vitality, and their compassion for other people.

Puritan Heroes gives the reader a glimpse into the lives of the most well-known Puritans. Because sources sometimes recorded information differently and biographers were inclined to stress their own perspectives, we cannot always be sure about every detail. But these biographical sketches report the known facts as accurately as possible.

We have taken a bit more liberty with the first section of each story. Each introductory scene depicts how something might have happened. They are all based in fact, but some are more factual than others. John Eliot and Jeremiah Burroughs contain actual dialogue and actions that were recorded. Joseph Alleine and John Howe, however, are based on minimal information and contain more speculation. Most opening scenes are somewhere in between those two extremes. The purpose of these introductions is to draw the reader into the lives of the Puritans in a vivid way.

Winds of English political power blew in harsh blasts of persecution or dropped briefly into gentle breezes of favor during the lifetimes of the Puritans. England suffered through a bloody civil war, fueled by political and religious differences. Most people in these stories lived around the same time and experienced many of the same historical events. To avoid repetition, these events have not been described every time. The timeline at the front of this book and the definitions at the back of the book will help readers understand historical context. The Study Questions will help you retain more of these fascinating life stories in your mind and will also assist you to apply lessons from the Puritans' lives to your own life.

Now that you know a bit more about the Puritans and the times in which they lived, you may still wonder why they are heroes. Were they brave, like war heroes? Did they have special skills, like sports heroes? What does it really mean to be a hero?

Heroes are ordinary people who do the right thing in extraordinary circumstances. A war hero may be frightened, but he takes action that saves the lives of his fellow soldiers. A sports hero practices most of his life and becomes very good at the game he plays. Of course, saving lives during intense battle is far more important than playing a game well. When we talk about heroes, what really matters is the person's heart. Some men who received medals haven't always lived so well after the war. And quite a few of the people who earn millions of dollars for playing sports are poor role models for young people.

We can consider people as heroes when they have lived for the Lord, especially when their convictions cost them their livelihoods or even their lives. Many Puritans suffered a great deal for their faith and lived as models of Christian heroism. Hundreds were killed. A few had their ears cut off. Others were fined and imprisoned, and thousands lost their jobs and homes. Yet they chose to suffer rather than go against the clear teaching of the Bible.

The writings of the Puritans emphasize God's sovereignty over everything, the Holy Spirit's work in changing hearts and lives, and Christ's complete atonement for sin. Puritans stressed communing with God through Scripture reading and prayer. Their close union with the Lord led to godly activity in the world, and their understanding of the human heart and relationships grew so remarkably rich that they were called "physicians of the soul."

In the opening chapter of this book, we will go a bit deeper into the question of who the Puritans were before we tell their life stories. In the conclusion we provide ten important lessons we can learn from the Puritans. The Selected English Bibliography will assist those of you who are teenagers (and your parents!) to study these major Puritans in greater depth, where you will be sure to find great treasure.

It should also be noted that this book is a companion book to *Reformation Heroes*, published by Reformation Heritage Books a decade ago. God willing, we hope to also publish two other books in this series in the future, *Ancient and Medieval Heroes*—covering from the end of the New Testament age to the Reformation, and *Modern Heroes*—from the mid-eighteenth century until today. We are hoping that these volumes will be ideal for Christian schools and homeschoolers, as well as for teenagers and adults who want to become better acquainted with the heroes of church history.

Although the Puritans lived years ago and some of their writings may be difficult to read, their teachings and the examples of their lives can benefit Christians today. It is our hope and prayer that the biographical sketches in this book will awaken within each reader a desire to learn more about the godly men and women we call *Puritan Heroes*.

We express our heartfelt gratitude to the triune God for His abundant grace in the lives of these Puritan heroes, and for His work in our own lives and in the lives of those dear to us. We particularly thank our spouses for their patience and love shown to us as this book was being written. Finally, we thank our faithful editors, proofreaders, illustrators, and typesetter for their hard and careful work. You are all appreciated more than you know.

—GFM/JRB

~ 1 ~

Who Were the Puritans?

More than four hundred and fifty years ago, long before your great-great-grandmother was born, God raised up a people in England who loved His Word and wanted to live just as the Bible said. Because other people made fun of them as God's "pure" people, they came to be known as the *Puritans*. But they called themselves "Christians." They tried to live out the teachings of Reformers such as Martin Luther, Martin Bucer, Henry Bullinger, and John Calvin. People today still read books by the Puritans, especially books about what God teaches us to believe and to do in the Bible.

Who were the Puritans, and what were they like? Some people have strange ideas about them. They think the Puritans always dressed in black and white, never let anyone have fun, and were mean and cruel. Supposedly, "Puritan" means a religious person who is bad, dangerous, and perhaps even a bit crazy. However, none of those things are true.

In many ways, the Puritans were like other people who lived in England during the sixteenth and seventeenth centuries. They worked on farms or at their trades and callings, while their children played at home or studied in school. Some of them attended college to learn to be lawyers, pastors, or teachers. They enjoyed racing on foot or horseback, hunting, fishing, target practice with guns, and wrestling. They loved singing and music. They were interested in the latest discoveries of science and medicine. They believed that government should respect people's rights, and they fought in wars to defend those rights. They wrote poetry and kept journals and diaries about their lives. They loved their spouses and dear friends. In all these ways, the Puritans were ordinary people like you and me.

But the Puritans did stand out, for they worked to apply the Reformed faith to all things according to God's Word. In the middle of the sixteenth century, much of England knew very little about the Bible. For many years, English Christians had been part of the Roman Catholic Church with its false teachings, man-made rituals, and spiritual ruler, the pope. King Henry VIII had pulled the Church of England away from the pope's control, and though Queen Mary I put the English church back under the Roman Catholic Church, Queen Elizabeth I separated it from Rome once and for all. Nevertheless, the

The Westminster Assembly, 1643–1653
ASSERTION OF LIBERTY OF CONSCIENCE BY THE INDEPENDENTS OF THE WESTMINSTER ASSEMBLY OF DIVINES,
OIL PAINTING BY JOHN ROGERS HERBERT, © PARLIAMENTARY ART COLLECTION, WOA 652. WWW.PARLIAMENT.UK/ART

Reformation was only beginning to affect England. Queen Elizabeth did not want people to change too many things in the church, but the Puritans believed that God's Word must be preached throughout their nation and worship must be according to God's will. This caused the Puritans a lot of trouble from leaders in the government and the church. Some Puritans had to leave England and live in exile in the Netherlands, where they found friends in the Reformed churches. Others came over the Atlantic Ocean to plant the colonies of Massachusetts and Connecticut. For a short time (1649–1660), Puritan leaders ruled England as a republic and the nation had no king. The Puritans played an important part in English, Dutch, and American history.

How do we explain what made the Puritans who they were? The difference between the Puritans and most other people started with their *faith in the Bible as God's Word*. The Puritans believed that when they read or heard the Bible, God was speaking to them. Therefore, the Bible is perfect and should be believed and obeyed in all that it teaches. They taught their children to read, so they, too, could read God's Book. Many of the other books they read and wrote were about the Bible. They loved good sermons, which for them meant sermons that helped them to understand and obey the Bible, to hate sin, and to love the Lord Jesus Christ

The Word of God was the centerpiece of Puritan life and worship

as their Savior and Lord. Their favorite songs were the psalms of the Bible set to music. The Bible was the spiritual food they ate and drank every day.

From the Bible, the Puritans learned the *knowledge of the great and good God*. Their God is the majestic King who rules over heaven, earth, and all that is in them—for He made them. He is in control of all that happens, for even bad things are planned by God for good. God is not like a human king, for God is a Spirit who lives everywhere; He was never born and will never die. The Puritans believed that God loves sinners even though they hate Him. God loves them so much that God sent His Son to die for the sins of His chosen people and sent His Spirit to live within them. The God worshipped by the Puritans is the God of the Trinity: one God who is three persons, the Father, the Son, and the Holy Spirit. Many people say they believe in God, but the Puritans loved God and wanted to know Him and think about Him as much as possible.

This God, the Puritans knew, can be known only through *the person and work of Jesus Christ*. Whatever part of the Bible they were studying, the Puritans asked how it points us to Christ. They were amazed that God the Son would become a man like us, while remaining fully God. They taught that the Lord Jesus is the Prophet who teaches His people the truth,

*John Bunyan's character Christian, praying,
with a burden of sin on his back*

the Priest who sacrificed Himself for their sins, and the King who rules them by the Holy Spirit. He is the only Mediator, or middle-man, who can bring us to God. They spent time thinking about and rejoicing in each of Christ's many names and titles in Scripture. The Puritans believed that Christ is altogether lovely, and so they wanted to be as close to Him and as much like Him as they could. All of the Puritan hope hung upon Christ. Therefore, the Puritans had great hope because God the Father will honor His Son and Christ's kingdom will not fail.

Since people can receive Christ only by faith, the Puritans believed in *everyone's need for conversion*. People all start life as sinners because of Adam's sin. One of the first things Puritans taught their children was, "In Adam's fall, we sinned all." Sin is not merely a mistake or imperfection; it is evil, the worst of evils, far worse than the greatest pain. The most deadly sin of all is our unbelief. The Puritans did not believe that baptism or the Lord's Supper had the power to save sinners apart from an inward change of heart. They urged people to repent of their sins and trust in Christ alone to save them. Many Puritan sermons and books talk about what conversion is and how it happens, so that people could know whether they are saved. The Puritans thought the sweetest thing in the world is to know that you are God's child.

With conversion as the beginning of Christian experience, the Puritans pursued *godliness that involved their head, heart, and hands*. Since God has spoken, and we have His Word, we must learn about Him with our minds. Puritan Christianity was thinking Christianity and demanded that people meditate or carefully consider what they heard from the Bible. Their preachers filled their sermons with points of doctrine to understand and believe. However, it did not stop there. The Puritans sought to know God in the experience of their hearts. They warned sinners that they need to feel the evil of their sins if they are going to repent. They wanted Christians to taste a little of heaven on earth by the Holy Spirit given to them. They studied how the Holy Spirit kills evil lusts in God's children and makes them more like Christ. They also called Christians to put their faith into practical action, giving specific directions based on the Bible for how people should treat each other as husbands and wives, children and parents, pastors and church members, government officials and citizens, and so forth. They were convinced that God's grace in the heart produces fruit in good works. Holiness was not just for church meetings, but for the whole of life.

A Christian's pilgrimage to the Heavenly City

The Puritans viewed godliness and spiritual growth as *the Christian pilgrim's journey to heaven*. They knew that this world is not their home, but believers in Christ are citizens of a better country, the heavenly city of God. Life is a vapor, but Christians are headed for glory. The Puritans measured a man's life not by how much money he got in this life, but in this progress as a pilgrim through trials and temptations toward heaven. They often meditated on the everlasting rest of God's people with Christ in glory. As a result, they were bold in life and ready for death.

As pilgrims on their way to their heavenly home, the Puritans showed *patient endurance under trials*. Life was hard in the sixteenth and seventeenth centuries, and the Puritans experienced a lot of suffering. They suffered when disasters came, such as a terrible disease known as "the Plague" or the Great Fire of London (1666). They suffered when England was torn apart in civil war and thousands of men perished by sword, musket, and cannon. They suffered when they buried the many wives who died in childbirth in those times and many children who died young. Christians sometimes feel very sad even when life is good, what the Puritans called "melancholy" but we call depression. Through all these sorrows, the Puritans were teachers and models of trusting God's promises and submitting to His will.

The Puritans, however, did not try to overcome trials by themselves, but through *the help of the true church*. Though they knew that the Holy Spirit works when and how He pleases, they understood that the Spirit blesses what they called "the means of grace." These means are the reading and hearing of God's Word, worship with God's people, baptism, the Lord's Supper, and godly conversations with Christian friends. History had taught them, however, that not every church

A Puritan family

was true and faithful to God; many churches had replaced God's Word with man's ideas and traditions. Therefore, the Puritans said that the church, its leadership, and its worship must follow the pattern God gives us in the Bible, neither adding to it nor subtracting from it. Preaching must be plain, clearly based on the Bible, informing the mind and shooting straight for the heart. Though they had strong beliefs about the church, the Puritans were not a separate organization or denomination; what held them together were their shared beliefs and friendships between people who loved Christ and loved one another.

The place where Christian love was first lived out for the Puritans was *the Christian home*. They took very seriously the responsibility of fathers and mothers to raise their children in God's ways. They wrote books about marriage and family life to show how God's Word should direct each person in his relationships at home. They expected parents to lead

family worship, believing that the family that prays together enjoys the smile of heaven, and the family who reads the Bible together hears the voice of God in their home. Puritan pastors wrote many catechisms to help parents and children learn the basic truths of God's Word. Without taking away from the need to go to church, the Puritans wanted each family to be a little church where God was glorified through Jesus Christ. They understood that Christian families are a major way God raises up the next generation of leaders and members for the church, and trusted that their faithful covenant God would bless their efforts to raise their children in the Lord.

The Puritans did not hide in their homes and churches, but showed a real *concern for the welfare and righteousness of their nation*. Though they knew that this world was not their home, they longed for Christ to be loved and honored in their cities, towns, and countryside. They sought to model government and business on the Bible's teachings, while recognizing that God's laws for ancient Israel were not necessarily His laws for England. When disaster struck, the Puritans responded with prayer and fasting for God to be merciful to their nation. They wanted the Lord to be honored in the planting and gathering of the harvest, the buying and selling of goods at the market, and the judgments of the courthouse. In a word, the Puritans wanted all of life to be reformed by God's Word to the glory of God.

Though the great age of modern missions would not dawn until a century after the Puritan era, the Puritans had their hearts set on *the spread of Christ's kingdom throughout the world*. Their churches regularly prayed for the salvation of the Jews, the strengthening of the persecuted church in other nations, and the advance of Christ's kingdom among

The Pilgrims leaving for New England

all peoples. They trained and sent out hundreds of gospel preachers to places of darkness in their own land. They supported colonial missions to the Native Americans so that they too might hear of Jesus Christ and be saved, and entire villages became places of prayer.

Starting a new religion was not the Puritans' goal, but to follow *the old paths revealed to God's people in God's Word*. Today, people pay little attention to the past and think that the newest ideas are best. That may sometimes be true of inventions and machines, but the Puritans knew that when it comes to God, church, and how people live, the old ways are usually best because God does not change. Therefore, the Puritans saw themselves as part of a long line of godly men and women through the ages. They read old books and learned from Christians who lived many centuries before they did. In this manner, they followed in the footsteps of the Reformers such as Luther and Calvin, who also aimed to restore the church to a simple and pure devotion to God's Word that is not mixed or obscured by man-made traditions and rituals added to the church over the years.

The Puritans were Reformed Christians. Christianity had been deformed by teachings and practices not found in the Bible. It needed to be reformed by the Word of God. A special mark of the Puritans is that they realized reformation must begin with the application of the Bible's truths to the heart and flow outward into practical living in family, workplace, church, and nation. Hence they strove for *purity of Christian doctrine, worship, and life*. Although we do not live in sixteenth- and seventeenth-century England, and therefore cannot be "Puritans," we can learn much from them about what it means to live unto God by faith and obedience toward His Word.

~ 2 ~

Richard Greenham

1542–1594

Puritan Pioneer

"Why are you still sitting here, Richard? You'll miss the ceremony."

"Ceremony?" Richard Greenham looked up from the book he was reading in the college library. "What are you talking about, Laurence?"

"The ceremony honoring the great reformer, Martin Bucer. The students have been discussing little else," Laurence said. "I know you're new to Cambridge, but didn't you hear about it?"

"I saw his tomb, reconstructed at Queen Elizabeth's order." Richard laid his book on the table and quickly stood. "But I hadn't heard about a ceremony."

Laurence smiled, "I'm not surprised. Ever since you arrived at Pembroke Hall, your nose has been buried in these old books." He picked up the one Richard had been reading. "What's this? Augustine? We haven't even been assigned to read him yet."

"He's fascinating!" Richard spread his arms toward the shelves. "I can't get enough of all the wonderful reading this school offers."

"Believe me. You'll soon have enough of it." The young man motioned. "Come. Let's go."

Richard fell into step beside his friend. "Is the ceremony in the church?"

"Yes. Great St. Mary's. A memorial plaque will be placed on the spot where Bucer was originally buried."

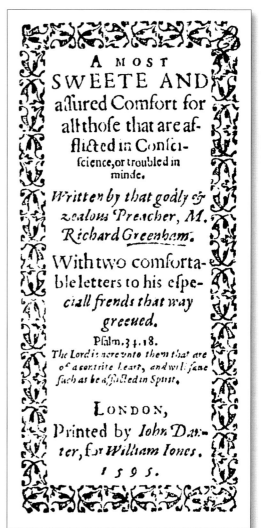

A MOST
SWEETE AND
assured Comfort for
all those that are afflicted in Conscience, or troubled in
minde.

Written by that godly &
zealous Preacher, M.
Richard Greenham.

With two comfortable letters to his especiall frends that way
grieved.

Psalm. 34.18.
The Lord is nere unto them that are
of a contrite heart, and will save
such as be afflicted in Spirit.

LONDON,
Printed by John Darter, for William Iones.
1595.

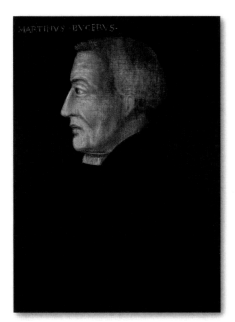

Martin Bucer

Great St. Mary's Church today

Less than ten years had passed since that day, and Richard easily recalled the news he'd heard about it. "They said three thousand people followed the funeral procession to the church."

"Where he rested in peace for too short a time." Laurence scowled. "Until Bloody Mary had his body dug up and tied to a post on Market Hill."

"And ordered it to be burned, along with his books," Richard added. "But she failed to stop the spread of his teachings."

"The Reformed movement only grew stronger, despite her killing over three hundred people."

"She wasn't satisfied with murdering the living but wanted to destroy even Bucer's dead body!"

As the two young men walked in silence for a while, Greenham mourned the many Protestants martyred under Queen Mary's rule during the previous five years.

"To think," Laurence said sadly, "she sentenced more leaders to be burned at the stake less than a week before she died last November."

"Only eight months ago."

"You know what their death register states?"

"What?"

"'Six days after these were burned to death, God sent us our Elizabeth.'"

Richard exclaimed, "God save good Queen Bess!"

"Amen," Laurence nodded. "The first thing she did was appoint a Protestant as our new university chancellor."

"And then she made a Cambridge man Archbishop of the Church of England."

Laurence clapped a hand on Richard's shoulder. "Things have improved tremendously for us Protestants in these last six months."

The two joined other students surging into the building, which was the oldest church on the grounds of Cambridge. Important reformers like Cranmer, Ridley, and Latimer had preached from its pulpit.

Laurence turned to Richard. "I suppose you know Martin Bucer was a Professor of Divinity at Cambridge?"

He nodded. "Before he became ill and died."

"And was buried here in Great St. Mary's with great honor."

Richard's eyes grew misty. "And even greater honor is being restored to his memory today."

Richard Greenham lived on the heels of the English Reformation and during the first strides of the Puritan movement that followed in its footsteps. People who would later become known as "Puritans" took the biblical truths rediscovered in the Reformation and applied them to their hearts and lives.

Greenham was never called a Puritan during his lifetime. The word "Puritan" was first used as a negative word to describe ministers who would not agree to certain rules of the Church of England. While Greenham didn't go along with some of those rules, he never promoted disobedience to authority in either church or state. He was a compassionate pastor, more concerned about the souls of people than the politics of the church. His beliefs and teachings, however, reflected a Puritan spiritual perspective.

That perspective was rooted in timeless biblical truth, but Greenham pioneered some practices that were new for his time. And during his life, common people could finally read an English Bible for themselves.

About a year after he arrived at Cambridge, the new Geneva Bible was published. It immediately became a best seller. Though not the first English Bible, it was easy to understand and the first translation to be widely available to everyone. Before this time, only priests or kings or wealthy people could own and read a Bible. One of the first English Bibles, ordered by King Henry VIII after declaring himself the Supreme Head of the church, was called the "Chained Bible" because most copies were chained to pulpits.

The Geneva Bible was produced by Protestant scholars who had fled from persecution to Geneva, Switzerland (where John Calvin lived). They made it very accurate by translating carefully from the original languages. They inserted verse numbers to help people find and memorize specific texts, and added notes to help readers understand and apply biblical truth. The new Bible was dedicated to Queen Elizabeth. Its preface spoke of two things necessary for the spread of the Protestant faith: First, "a lively and steadfast faith in Christ Jesus" who is the "only means and assurance of our salvation." And second, that "our faith bring forth good fruits…as a witness to confirm our election and be an example to all others." During Elizabeth's reign, many Protestants returned to England and brought the new Bible with them.

Because we learn to read the Bible at a young age and have so many copies in our homes, it's hard for us to

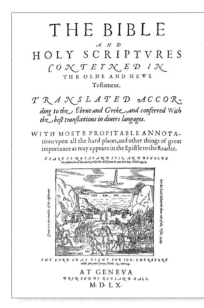

1560 edition of the Geneva Bible

understand how much the people in Greenham's day appreciated the opportunity to read God's Word for themselves. The memory of people who had died for this privilege was still fresh in their minds. This was especially true for Greenham and his fellow students, because many martyrs had been teachers or students at Cambridge.

Greenham took his education very seriously. In contrast to other students, he wasn't in a hurry to start earning money as a minister. He knew it was a weighty responsibility and thought young men should take time to prepare well and to mature. He believed a good education was not enough. Prospective pastors should also learn self-control over emotions and temptations before attempting to instruct others. They needed to enter ministry from a desire to proclaim salvation to the lost and to mature believers for God's glory, not out of a desire for self-advancement.

Although today's college students would find Pembroke's living conditions harsh and its food sparse, Greenham received a comprehensive academic and theological education. He earned a bachelor's degree and a master's degree and was awarded the opportunity for advanced study. For ten years, he was immersed in the Protestant community within and surrounding Cambridge University. His later writings show how thoroughly he had been trained in the reformational truths of Scripture.

In 1570, Greenham became a minister in the nearby village of Dry Drayton, England. Three years later, he married Katherine Bownd, a physician's widow with four children.

That same year, Church of England authorities issued a citation to him because he didn't wear priestly garments or use the *Book of Common Prayer* during worship services. He wrote a letter to try to smooth things over. He said his concern was to preach Christ and Him crucified, not to stir up arguments over clothing or ceremonies. He believed it was more important to unite around the common work of proclaiming Christ than to argue over external matters. Because the bishop needed ministers who promoted peace in the church, he did not take action against Greenham.

He even sought Greenham's help in identifying the errors of the Roman Catholic Church and a sect called the Family of Love. Despite such a pleasant-sounding name, this group caused disunity in the Protestant church. Its leader claimed to have a special indwelling of the Spirit of Love, which gave him personal revelations. He taught his followers that they could become perfect in this life. Just like Catholics paid more attention to what the Pope said than to what the Bible said, the Family of Love put their leader's words above God's Word.

Greenham saw the two groups as a double threat that might shipwreck believers. He encouraged Christians to stay on course by obeying God's Spirit and Word. They could "sail between" these "two rocks" of error by recognizing their need for "the stern of God" and His Spirit as well as the guidance

Dry Drayton village church, built in the thirteenth century

of the Word "to sail aright." A ship's stern is the back part, where the rudder controls the direction of the ship.

People caught up in these two belief systems needed to listen only to God and the Bible. Greenham said, "Where Scripture hath not a mouth, we ought not to have ears."

God and His Word formed the foundation of Greenham's teachings. He urged people to commune with God and glorify Him. He encouraged them to prize as their "greatest treasure" the Bible, which he called "the library of the Holy Spirit."

When asked if a person receives the Word first and then the Spirit, he emphasized that the Spirit comes before any response to the Word. The Bible reveals its truth through the work of the Spirit. He compared this to how smoke shows fire hidden in the ashes. We may see smoke first, but fire was present before the smoke arose. The Spirit first generates faith in the heart of a Christian, and then the Word comes alive for the believer. That person begins to live in a manner that reflects Christ, the Living Word.

In many ways, Greenham was a pioneer. He practiced spiritual counseling that was ahead of its time. He provided food for poor people through a unique distribution program. He established a system for training pastors, and he broke new ground in his teachings about observing the Sabbath.

Having experienced his own share of mental anguish, he cared deeply about people suffering with what was called "afflicted consciences." He comforted many visitors and traveled to homes throughout the countryside, providing spiritual counsel. Treating each person as a unique individual, he considered the whole situation: spiritual maturity, physical condition, particular problems, and special circumstances. But he said some of the same things to nearly everyone, reminding them that God was powerful to help overcome any difficulty and forgive any sin. He assured them that God often sends trials to strengthen His children. And he encouraged the sufferers to view their pain as an opportunity to grow closer to God and become more aware of His presence.

If people struggled with doubt or fear, he assured them that their act of seeking spiritual assistance showed the Spirit's work and God's grace in their lives. If they felt that God couldn't forgive their terrible sins, he reminded them that no sin was beyond Christ's pardon. If they were depressed about continuing to sin, he warned them not to judge themselves too harshly, remembering that only Christ was perfect in this life.

Greenham confronted sin directly but with gentleness, always examining his own heart and motives. He urged sinners and sufferers to dwell on the promises of God, remembering that His grace and love can overcome any obstacle. He taught that faithful meditation on personal union with Christ is the ultimate salve for emotional pain. Considering the time in which he lived, Greenham had an amazing understanding of human experience and was a remarkable spiritual counselor.

Greenham also cared about people's physical needs. Ordinary laborers could barely survive on their low wages and would sometimes starve when food prices went up. Greenham came up with a novel plan for a community granary, where poor people could buy enough barley for their family at half the regular cost. He sold his personal grain and straw for low prices. He was so generous to prisoners and other people that he sometimes had to borrow money for hiring workers to bring in his own harvest.

Living close to Cambridge allowed Greenham to implement another of his original ideas. He invited graduates to train with him prior to taking up their ministry. He taught them how to apply their academic education to pastoral duties. This internship program was very effective, and his students spread the concept all over England.

Greenham pioneered writings about proper Sabbath keeping, emphasizing the significance of the Trinity. God the Father established a day of rest at creation. God the Son rose on the first day of the week, marking Sunday as the day to be set apart. God the Spirit helps us rest in God every day by living for Him. A book he wrote on the subject became popular throughout England. Many people believe this was his most original and important contribution to Christ's church.

Although a naturally reserved and sober man, Greenham was an energetic and forceful preacher. After delivering a sermon, his shirt was often drenched with sweat. He preached twice each Sunday and taught catechism on Sunday evenings and Thursday mornings. On four other weekdays, he preached early in the morning, so people could attend the service before work.

Despite all his hard work, Greenham felt he saw little evidence of changed hearts. He sometimes complained how people seemed to forget his sermons as soon as they walked out the church door.

Some of his friends and family thought his gifts were wasted in such a little village. But he refused offers that would provide a better living, believing he needed to remain in Dry Drayton until he was convinced that God was calling him somewhere else.

After Greenham had served the church for twenty years, he was finally persuaded that the need for his work was greater in London. He helped choose Richard Warfield as the minister to replace him.

When Warfield arrived in Dry Drayton, Greenham said, "Mr. Warfield, God bless you, and send you more fruit of your labors than I have had, for I perceive no good wrought by my ministry on any but one family."

Most scholars agree his influence in Dry Drayton extended far beyond that one family. But Greenham may have felt that God was leading him to serve somewhere else by withholding His blessing.

Preachers who didn't follow all the rules of the Church of England were not welcome in London. Before Greenham could receive a license to preach there, he had to agree he wouldn't cause trouble. He also presented a statement, signed by an influential man, testifying to his good conduct.

At first, he preached in various churches throughout the city. Then he became the minister for Christ Church in Newgate Street, one of London's largest congregations. The people were eager to hear godly preaching and welcomed him warmly.

Soon great sickness called "the Plague" spread through London, and about ten thousand people died in one year. During this sad and frightening time, the Church of England told ministers to read from a book of lectures at worship services. Greenham didn't do that. Instead, he encouraged his congregation to pray, repent, and fast. People flocked to hear his sermons.

As he had at the very beginning of his ministry, Greenham tried to do what he believed was right without causing trouble. He believed it was important to keep peace within the church as much as possible. Although he didn't follow all the rules, he felt it would be better to go along with unimportant requirements than to be put out of the pulpit and deprive the people from hearing God's Word preached.

Greenham often talked about how life passes as quickly as a bubble, a sleep, or a vapor. He spoke of our bodies as booths or tents that do not last. He knew people don't like to give serious thought to death, but—like the psalmist—he encouraged them to number their days. He calculated that nearly half of the average life span of seventy years is spent in sleep, which leaves only thirty-five years. He subtracted another fourteen years for youth, because most children think primarily about themselves and do little to glorify God. Many of the remaining twenty-one years are taken up with sickness or business, which he believed left only about seven or eight years for wholehearted devotion to God. He encouraged people to make the most of every moment by delighting in God's Word.

When he was in his forties, Greenham's health began to fail. Whenever he was ill, he preferred to have no one around so he could commune better with God. But while he was only in his early fifties, he became so ill that other people came to assist him. He died in April of 1594 and was buried in Christ Church.

A friend reported that Greenham was very troubled the day before his death. He'd heard that the Queen's personal physician had plotted with the Spanish to poison her. To the very end of his life, he remained grateful to God for providing Queen Elizabeth as a means to further the truths of the Protestant Reformation.

Christ Church in Newgate Street

~ 3 ~

William Perkins

1558–1602

Father of Puritanism

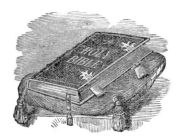

When William Perkins turned the corner, he saw a large crowd gathered around the gallows. He worked his way through the people until he stood before the scaffold.

A sturdy young man climbed the ladder. When he reached the platform, he turned toward the audience. His face shocked Perkins. The man already appeared half dead.

Perkins tried to encourage the prisoner, but his words had no effect. He asked, "What, man? What is the matter with you? Are you afraid of death?"

"Ah, no." The condemned man shook his head. "But of a far worse thing."

"Say you so?" Perkins motioned to him. "Come down again, man, and you shall see what God's grace will do to strengthen you."

When the prisoner reached the ground, Perkins took his hand and gently pulled him to his knees. The two knelt hand in hand at the ladder's foot. Perkins prayed, confessing sins and the bad choices that led to them. Then he spoke of the eternal punishment in hell demanded by God's justice. The prisoner sobbed beside him.

Perkins prayed about the Lord Jesus, the Savior of all sinners who repent and believe. He described Christ as stretching forth His blessed hand of mercy. He alone had power to save the distressed prisoner and deliver him from all the powers of darkness. The young man cried again, but with tears of joy.

Lifting his now beaming face, the prisoner looked out over people raising their hands, praising God for this amazing transformation.

Hurrying back up the ladder, the prisoner accepted the noose gladly with a lifted head. It was as if he already saw heaven opening to receive his soul.

William Perkins was born during the first year of Queen Elizabeth's reign and he died only months before she did. The stability of her reign allowed godly men to carry forward the truths of the Protestant Reformation. More than any other person, Perkins shaped the Puritan movement. He took theology beyond knowing doctrines in the mind to experiencing Christ in the heart.

William Perkins

Even though Perkins was raised in a Christian home, he lived wickedly as a young man. While a student at Christ's College in Cambridge, he delved into black magic and astrology. He drank, swore, and used foul language. Once he heard a woman threaten her misbehaving son, "Hold your tongue, or I will give you to drunken Perkins yonder!"

He was so shocked that he began thinking about his sin and his life. Before long he was converted. He then switched from the study of mathematics to theology, which he later defined as "the science of living blessedly forever." He studied under Richard Greenham and other godly men, learning a method for writing in a clear and organized way to make his preaching more meaningful. His own conversion made him long to bring gospel hope to others.

Even as a student, he was a great reader. His friends said he could read a book so quickly he didn't seem to read any of it, but he reported it so accurately that it seemed he must have read every word.

Perkins earned his bachelor's degree in 1581 and his master's in 1584. After he was ordained, he began preaching as a volunteer at the Cambridge Castle jail. Every Sunday, the prisoners gathered in a large room to hear his powerful sermons. When describing God's judgment in hell, he spoke the word "damn" so forcefully that it echoed in the ears of the hearers. Then he showed the beauty and hope of salvation in Jesus Christ. Some people called him the jailbird's chaplain. Others came from outside the prison to hear him. Both prisoners and free people were delivered from sin's bondage.

News of his preaching spread. Perkins soon was appointed as lecturer at Great St. Andrew's Church, where he preached for the rest of his life. His style differed from most Church of England ministers. They displayed their knowledge in their sermons, quoting numerous ancient authors and often using Latin or Greek phrases.

Perkins wrote, "In this kind of preaching, we do not paint Christ, but ourselves." He believed that for a minister to call attention to himself was a sin. His plain preaching focused on the Bible as God's very Word and the guide for all of life.

"The word of God must be our rule and square whereby we are to frame and fashion all our actions," he wrote. "And according to the direction received there, we must do the things we do, or leave them undone."

In other words, all things we do should be guided by God's Word. If they aren't, we would be better off not doing them. As Perkins explained each biblical truth, he told people how to apply it to their problems and the way they lived. He spoke calmly about doctrine, but became excited and quite animated when sharing application.

His sermons appealed to everyone. Scholars recognized his knowledge, while the uneducated found his messages easy to understand. He didn't memorize sermons. He reviewed the material until he was familiar with it, and then he preached from an outline. For Perkins, preaching was the most important part of public worship. He thought of it as the chariot on which salvation rides into people's hearts.

In contrast to his powerful preaching, his physical appearance may have seemed weak. He was short and stout, with a withered right hand. He struggled his entire life with pain from kidney stones. But he was always busy with the Lord's work. His words and actions testified to his love for God and other people. He believed a minister's life ought to be a visible sermon.

Perkins served at Dean of Christ's College from 1590–1591. As a fellow, he tutored students with both academic instruction and guidance in godly and responsible living. Thursday afternoons he could be found teaching catechism; and on Sunday afternoons, providing spiritual counsel.

In addition to students, people came from far away to seek his counsel about spiritual problems. When they experienced affliction, Perkins reminded them of God's control over everything for the good of His people. He believed that emphasizing God's sovereignty comforted Christians and glorified the Lord. When people struggled with guilt over sin, he guided them into a right relationship with God and encouraged them with His promises. He taught people to make biblical and prayerful decisions about the ways they lived. Perkins believed that God gave human beings a mind capable of understanding right and wrong, when guided by the Bible. In this way, he shaped Reformed thinking about the role of an individual's conscience in making godly choices.

Although Perkins didn't agree with many practices in the Church of England, he didn't try to change the church structure. Instead, he worked to transform souls. He trained godly pastors, clarified biblical teaching, and educated church people.

In 1586, however, university authorities summoned him to explain why he had called some practices of the communion service "superstitious" and "antichristian." Perkins admitted his comments may have been unnecessary and spoken at the wrong time. He didn't want to cause trouble in the church.

He didn't want to cause trouble for godly men either. When he was called as a witness against some Puritans on

Christ's College, Cambridge
MANNING FINE ART

trial, he answered questions as vaguely as possible, refusing to support the accusations against the men. Other than these two incidents, it seems most of his life was free from conflict with church officials.

Perkins was one of the most widely read authors of his time. He wrote more than fifty books, some put together and published by his friends after his death. Like his preaching, his writing was easy to understand but rich with knowledge. Also like his preaching, his writing explained biblical truth and applied it to people's lives. Because the Bible guides every area of life, he wrote about things of practical interest. His topics ranged from witchcraft to salvation, from family life to preaching, and from astrology to the end times. He described how to live for God in poverty or wealth, in eating or drinking, in working or playing, in personal appearance or corporate worship. He helped people connect God's Word to His world.

Similes and illustrations enlivened his writing. He wrote in language that appealed to average men and women. But his purpose wasn't just to capture reader interest. His purpose was to capture hearts for the Lord. His works were so popular that they were translated into several languages.

After the first eleven years of his ministry, Perkins gave up his teaching fellowship. He planned to marry and would no longer be able to live at the college. He and Timothye Cradocke, a young widow, were married on July 2, 1595. Six children were born to them within seven years, but three of them died. They were expecting their seventh when God took Perkins home.

In the fall of 1602, he experienced severe pain from kidney stones. He suffered intensely for several weeks. When a friend asked him what he wanted, he said, "Nothing but mercy." He died on October 22 at forty-four years of age.

A close friend, James Montagu, preached at his funeral from Joshua 1:2, "Moses my servant is dead." Perkins was buried in the churchyard of Great St. Andrews, where he'd preached his entire ministry.

His book, *The Art of Prophesying*, was published after his death. (The word "prophesying" in the title means preaching.) It was the first major English work on preaching and guided future generations of ministers. Perkins wrote out of concern about the lack of good preachers and the abundance of false teachers. He believed preaching was the most serious of all human tasks because of its importance for eternity. He wanted to train men in a plain style that focused on the Bible as the absolute Word of God.

In that book and others, he encouraged preachers to:

• Honor the Bible as God's very word.
• Study the text accurately and wisely.
• Present the text's truths, not personal opinion.
• Apply these truths to the hearts and lives of people.
• Speak with Spirit-given sincerity and power.
• Preach Christ and His saving work.

He concluded his book on preaching by writing, "The sum of the sum, preach one Christ by Christ to the praise of Christ." Perkins urged ministers to offer the "precious jewel" of the gospel promise in every sermon. These things still mark Reformed preaching today.

Perkins never considered himself a Puritan. The word "Puritan" wasn't widely used in his day, and he considered it a "vile term" when applied to godly people. Still, Perkins deserves to be remembered as the father of the Puritans. He is credited with making Cambridge a Puritan institution. Although his entire ministry took place within a few miles of the university, he influenced theologians in England, in several countries of Europe, and in New England.

Nearly one hundred Cambridge men led groups of immigrants across the Atlantic Ocean. Most families among the early colonists had a Bible or two, a copy of the works of William Perkins, and only a few additional books.

The primary characteristics of Puritanism are direct descendants of the teachings of William Perkins. He stressed the authority of Scripture and the Lordship of Christ. He promoted experiential piety, which means to experience biblical truth and love for God in every area of life. Both biblical and practical, his warm-hearted theology addressed people's problems with God's Word as it arose from his passion to see God transform souls.

~ 4 ~

William Ames

1576–1633

Calvinist and Congregationalist

William Ames

"Mr. Ames, you may wonder why I called you to appear before me today."

Richard Ames did not let his gaze waver from the stern face of Dr. Valentine Cary, the master of Christ's College at Cambridge University. Ames said, "I suppose it has something to do with the sermon I preached on December 21."

"Your sermon against Christmas revelries certainly showed poor judgment, scolding the students for such trivial things as playing cards and gambling with dice."

"Those things show the state of their hearts," Ames answered calmly. "The entire student body seems caught up in careless and ungodly living." He closed his lips before adding, *which reflects the state of the Church of England*. He'd heard that Dr. Cary himself had once administered the sacrament of the Lord's Supper and then walked down the hall to play cards. How he wished the College would return to the Calvinistic fervor of his student days, when he'd been converted under the biblical preaching of William Perkins. What a godly man and passionate preacher!

Dr. Carey recalled him to the moment by saying, "Regardless of your personal opinion about the students and their activities, preaching so sharply was not necessary. In fact, your sermon created quite an outcry. Every day I deal with new complaints and requests for your removal." He leaned back and put his fingertips together. "But I want to talk to you about something else."

Remaining silent, Ames had a good idea where the conversation was headed.

"You must realize, Ames, that you can't remain a Fellow at Cambridge while refusing to conform to the Church of England's requirements." Cary stiffened his back. "I summoned you to ask—no, to demand—that you immediately begin wearing the proper white robe when you preach."

Ames sighed. "Sir, you know my belief. Wearing such a garment continues ceremonies of the Roman Church that Protestants should have given up long ago."

"Nonsense!" Dr. Cary replied. "It adds dignity to the office of minister."

"That's just it, sir. I'm a minister—not a priest."

"No matter your views, Ames, the rules of conformity require you to wear it. We need consistency in the church. We can't have men all over England wearing whatever they like in the pulpit—it breeds discord."

"Still, sir," Ames said quietly, "I must obey God rather than men."

"Aha!" Cary rapped his desk with a knuckle. "But God's Word calls for you to wear the white surplice."

"It does?" Ames raised his eyebrows. "What Scripture text decrees that a preacher should wear a surplice?"

"Romans 13:12." Cary opened the massive Bible on his desk. "'The night is far spent, the day is at hand: let us therefore cast off the works of darkness, and let us put on the armor of light.'" He looked up and smiled. "I am sure you do not wish to argue with God's Word."

"But, sir, the armor of light hardly refers to a physical robe."

"Indeed it does. It clearly alludes to the white surplice." Cary shut the Bible with a thump, which seemed to indicate an end to the conversation.

Ames took a deep breath. "I don't believe the text mandates that I wear a white robe, Dr. Cary."

The college master leaned forward. "You will wear the robe—especially when you administer the sacraments!" His eyes blazed. "And that is the end of the matter!"

———— ◆◆◆ ————

The confrontation with Dr. Cary wasn't the end of the matter for William Ames. He didn't wear the robe because he couldn't in good conscience participate in practices he viewed as unbiblical. University officials suspended him from all his duties and academic degrees. Rather than wait to be expelled from his position, he left.

He moved to Colchester in Essex, where the city corporation had asked him to preach. But first, he had to be approved by the Bishop of London. The chief magistrates of the corporation and Ames appeared before Bishop George Abbot.

Bishop George Abbot, wearing a surplice

"How dare you choose a preacher without my consent?" The Bishop glared at the magistrates. "You are to receive the preacher I appoint, for I am your pastor."

Ames wondered how the man could consider himself the pastor of a flock he never fed.

Then Bishop Abbot turned to Ames. "And how dare you preach in my diocese without my permission?" He waved away the entire group. "You are all dismissed to await my pleasure." Twenty years later, Ames would write that he was still waiting. And he thanked God that was the only time he had to appear before a bishop.

Ames realized there was no future for him in England. His lot would soon be like that of his friend, Robert Parker. Ever since Parker had written a book against certain church ceremonies, he'd been hiding from the King's officers who wanted to arrest him and throw him in prison. Some wealthy merchants, who were Puritans, offered to help Ames and Parker flee to the Netherlands, where they could preach and write with more freedom.

Ames traveled secretly to meet Parker in a small village outside London. Late at night, the two men disguised themselves as fishermen and slipped out of the house. They walked down to the River Thames, where they waited in the shadow of a building. At the appointed time, the splash of oars carried softly across the water. A small boat bumped gently against the dock.

"That will be Richard Browne," Parker whispered. "Let's go."

As Ames followed his friend across the bouncing boards of the dock, a dim figure rose from the boat and wrapped a rope around a post. He whispered, "Hurry, but be as quiet as you can. I've heard you're being watched."

The boat rocked as the men stepped down into it, and Ames quickly sat on a wooden bench. Browne coiled the rope and pushed the boat away. Then he leaped over the water into it, landing on a piled fishing net. The narrow vessel rocked fiercely, and Ames clutched the sides. Browne scrambled to the middle and grasped the long oars. He maneuvered the craft away from land, and then bent to row with vigor.

He grunted, "We must get away before any watchers realize their prey has escaped."

When the boat reached the river's speeding current, it skimmed over the surface as quickly as a heron in flight. Ames tightened his grip and stared at the water, swirling within hand's reach. He gulped. "Thank the Lord we don't have to cross the English Channel in this tiny vessel."

Browne chuckled. "She's a fine fishing wherry, but I wouldn't want to take her across the North Sea."

"We only need to reach Gravesend," Parker said. "We'll sail on from there."

At the port city, Ames and Parker boarded a ship bound for Rotterdam. As the ship sailed out of the harbor, Ames and Parker gazed back at the shores of England. Neither knew it was his last glimpse of his native land.

Because the Dutch allowed freedom of expression about religious matters, many English Protestants lived in the Netherlands. Ames discovered that his fellow countrymen held differing opinions about the church. English ambassadors and a few others were Anglicans who accepted all the ceremonies and requirements of the Church of England. Some exiles were Separatists, who viewed the Church of England as very corrupt and thought people should have nothing to do with it. Presbyterians believed ministers and elders could work together in higher assemblies and cooperate with government leaders to improve society. Congregationalists, like Ames, thought the local congregation should have complete control over its own matters, such as choosing leaders and calling ministers. The Presbyterians and Congregationalists (or Independents) were still developing their ideas for church government, and most hoped for reform within the Church of England.

After only a few weeks in Rotterdam, Ames and Parker went to the university town of Leiden. There they plunged into theological writing and spirited debates. In his introduction to William Bradshaw's book *English Puritanism*, Ames explained that Puritans took Scripture seriously and tried to obey the teachings of Christ and the apostles in every area of their lives.

After about a year in Leiden, Ames became a chaplain for Sir Horace Vere, the commander of the English regiment in The Hague. Ames also preached to an English church in that city. But he hadn't completely escaped his enemies.

His old enemy, George Abbot, had become the Archbishop of Canterbury. He wrote to the English ambassador in the Netherlands, urging him to remove Ames from his new position, but Vere ignored him.

Ames was in his mid-thirties when he began working at The Hague. He became friends with a chaplain, John Burgess, who shared many of his ideas. Ames met and married Burgess's daughter. But neither of these relationships lasted long. Only a year later, Burgess returned to England and conformed to church requirements. He viciously criticized his son-in-law's views. Even sadder, Ames's wife died.

Ames spent considerable time writing against the teachings of Jacob Arminius. Arminius had died a year earlier, but his followers were causing discord in the churches. The year Ames arrived in the Netherlands (1610), the Arminians wrote a document promoting five false views regarding God's election, Christ's redemption, the Spirit's saving grace, man's conversion, and the Christian's perseverance in the faith. Many Calvinists united in opposition.

The two sides debated the issues at The Hague Conference in 1611, but compromise was impossible. Before Arminius died, he had written a paper attacking William Perkins and his view of predestination. When that document

Jacob Arminius

Leiden University building, founded by William, Prince of Orange, in the sixteenth century

was published in 1612, Ames was distressed to read this criticism of his godly mentor, William Perkins, and of a doctrine he held dear.

In 1614, the Dutch government supported the Arminians by declaring their views as "sufficient for salvation" and helpful for "Christian edification."

Seeing the conflict as a war for the souls of believers, Ames engaged in a fierce writing battle. He showed the errors of Arminian beliefs from the Bible as well as from the teachings of Augustine, Calvin, and other Protestant reformers.

A national synod was planned to discuss the Arminian problem. Shortly before it began meeting in 1618, an important book by Ames appeared in print.

This book, known as the *Coronis* (Crown), received high praise. Many Calvinists felt it demolished the arguments of Arminians so effectively that the Arminians couldn't respond and wouldn't dare to try.

In November of 1618, theologians from the Netherlands and eight other countries gathered in the South Holland city of Dordrecht (also known as Dordt or Dort). Ames served as a paid advisor to the Synod's president, traveling between

CORONIS
AD
COLLATIONEM
HAGIENSEM,

QVA ARGVMENTA PA
STORVM HOLLANDIÆ

Adverſus Remonſtrantium
Quinque Articulos

De Diviná Prædeſtinatione, & capitibus
ei adnexis, producta, ab horum exceptio-
nibus vindicantur.

Auctore GVILIELMO AMESIO.

Editio quarta.

Londini
Excudebat Felix Kingſtonus ſumptibus
Roberti Allotti. 1630.

Title page of Ames's Coronis ad Collationem Hagiensem

Dort and The Hague. The Synod continued meeting for seven months, from November 1618 until May 1619.

The Archbishop of Canterbury and other English churchmen, who had never stopped working against Ames, renewed their efforts. They implied that he was an enemy of England and warned the Dutch not to offend the English king. Vere gradually decreased the duties of Ames at The Hague and eventually dismissed him in 1619.

During this time frame, Ames married Joan Fletcher, an Englishwoman from a famous literary family. She was around thirty years old, and he was in his early forties.

Once the Synod was over and Ames no longer worked for Vere, he found himself with a wife and baby but no job. The University of Leiden wanted to hire him as a professor, but his old enemies again exerted pressure to keep him from being appointed.

A friend, Festus Hommius, allowed Ames and his family to live in a house he rented. He also arranged for Ames to oversee theological students at Leiden. Ames wrote a summary of Calvinism called *The Marrow of Theology*. "Marrow" refers to the heart of the matter (as we say), that is, to things of fundamental and central importance. The book later became the standard textbook for seminarians all over the world, especially in America.

Not content with what he'd already done for Ames, Hommius decided to plead for him in England. The Synod of Dort's actions were published in book form, and special editions were prepared for King James I, Prince Charles, and Archbishop Abbott. Hommius volunteered to deliver the books in person.

The English monarchs appeared delighted with the gifts, but the Archbishop was anything but cheerful when

Hommius met with him. Although Abbot said he was pleased that an Englishman was considered so favorably in the Netherlands, he called Ames a "rebel" who was not "an obedient son of his mother, the Church of England." He said Ames needed to repent. Then he dismissed Hommius. Later, the theological professors at Leiden received a letter from the Archbishop's chaplain, expressing the same thoughts. Everyone realized the situation was hopeless.

But the university at Franeker in the northern province of Friesland was not so concerned about the English church. The college asked Ames to be a professor of theology in 1622. He quickly accepted and moved his wife and family in July.

Still, the English attempted to thwart this appointment as well. Ames was not permitted to begin teaching until after an English colonel interceded for him with the Dutch Prince Maurice.

Life at Franeker had its challenges. The main one was his fellow professor, Johannes Maccovius, known for his sharp tongue. He and Ames clashed over many matters. The two promoted different schools of thought in philosophy. They also had opposite teaching emphases: Maccovius emphasized the theoretical, training students to militantly defend the faith; Ames stressed the practical, teaching students to live the Christian life.

Their most significant disagreement arose over student discipline. The college's rowdy students earned a bad reputation for the school. Many faculty members were concerned about student behavior destroying personal character. Ames, who had long ago spoken against student revelries at Cambridge, joined the professors calling for firmer discipline. But Maccovius headed up another group of instructors who promoted a hands-off policy.

Johannes Maccovius

While in Franeker, Ames continued writing. Ten years after the Synod of Dort, he found it necessary to refute another Arminian publication. That same year, he became rector of the college and was able to institute reforms that improved student behavior and the school's reputation. Serious students from other European countries began to attend.

But the damp northern climate took a toll on his body. He struggled so much with respiratory illness during the colder months that he thought each winter might be his last. His wife longed for fellowship with other English people in a larger city. Puritans in the New World often invited him to sail overseas and share in shaping American theology.

The idea appealed to Ames, and he planned to travel to America. Even though the plans fell through, he clung to that dream.

After Ames had been in Franeker for twelve years, he received a wonderful offer to work in Rotterdam, which was rapidly becoming the center of Puritan thinking. His friend, Hugh Peters, had formed an English church along the congregational model. The church was growing so large that it needed a second minister.

At the same time, a new Puritan college was being established in Rotterdam. When professors heard that Ames would be arriving in the city, they requested that this "very learned and distinguished man" teach some courses there.

In October of 1633, Ames and his family moved to Rotterdam. Although excited about the opportunities before him, Ames still hoped to sail for America someday.

One night soon after the family's arrival, the River Maas overflowed its banks and flooded a large part of the city. It crept into their house while they were sleeping and eventually impacted his health. His health had been poor before, and this setback weakened him further. His cold quickly turned into a serious illness.

A doctor came regularly to care for him, but it seemed little could be done. The fever could not be abated, and medicines proved ineffective. As Ames lay dying, he testified to his visitors of his faith in Christ and his hope for heaven. The doctor, who was a Roman Catholic, was so impressed with his Christian witness that he exclaimed, "Is this the way Reformed churchmen die?"

Ames died in the arms of his friend, Hugh Peters, and was buried on November 14, 1633. He was fifty-seven years old and left behind his wife and three children, the oldest not more than fifteen.

A few years later, the family fulfilled his desire by moving to America. Ames never returned to England and never set foot on the shores of New England. But by God's grace, his books made him even more influential in America than in England or the Netherlands.

~ 5 ~

Richard Sibbes

❖❖❖

1577–1635

Warm-Hearted Preacher

Steam hissed into Richard's face, and he blinked. He pulled another wheel shoe from the fire and quickly nailed the red-hot iron strip onto the curved wooden felloe. Then he plunged that section of the wheel into the water. As his eyes closed against the rising steam's heat, he thought again of a Bible text that seemed branded in his mind: "But his word was in mine heart as a burning fire shut up in my bones, and I was weary with forbearing, and I could not stay" (Jer. 20:9b).

Jeremiah's words reflected the longing of Richard's heart. How could he stay here, working as a wheelwright in his father's shop, when other desires burned like a fire within his very bones?

He grunted as he lugged the heavy wagon wheel out of the water. He set it on a wooden frame to cool and dry. Immersing the hot metal shoes had shrunk each one and fastened them securely to the hickory felloes. The felloes joined tightly to form the wheel's sturdy tyre. He picked up the circular tool, called a "traveler," and ran it around the cooling metal rim to measure the wheel. Exactly right.

Then he turned to the round bench, shaped like a huge stool with four strong legs and a center post. He slipped an elm hub, already banded with iron, over the post. Between the bands, a row of evenly spaced rectangular holes had been cut to seat the spokes. As Richard turned to pick up a sharp chisel, he wiped his sweaty hands on his leather apron, which reminded him of the leather breeches he'd worn to school as a young boy.

After grammar school was dismissed each day, the other boys ran outside to shout and play. But Richard would open a book and start the mile-long walk home. Sometimes the boys stopped him, teasing him about being too poor for better breeches. As soon as he was able to escape, he'd go his way, reading while he walked. Ever since he could remember, he'd loved to read and learn.

But books cost money. His father, with Richard and five younger children to feed, didn't see the need to purchase anything as unnecessary as a book.

Richard sighed and continued carefully smoothing out the holes with his chisel. Father had wanted him to begin working in the shop as a young lad. But someone—perhaps the grammar school teacher—had persuaded his father that Richard should continue his education. He'd been permitted to attend the school at Bury St. Edmunds.

Richard smiled as he remembered those happy years, learning so much at school and reading or enjoying creation while walking the few miles there and back. What a lovely trek in pleasant weather! Purple cornel blossoms poked through gaps in the hurdle fences, which lined the winding road like woven baskets. In May, the prickly hawthorn hedgerows burst into bloom. The blossoms were beautiful, but his nose wrinkled at the memory of their pungent odor. It reminded him of dead fish.

Then his education had come to an end. His father was tired of buying books.

Richard laid the chisel beside the drawknife and picked up the square hammer. His father had purchased these wheelwright's tools for him. He hoped to see his son go into the business for himself.

A wheelwright

A shaved spoke lay ready with a rectangular foot at its bottom and a round tongue at its tip. Richard placed the foot into a chiseled hole on the hub and hit the sturdy oak spoke. Again and again he swung the hammer. He pounded until the spoke was fixed as firmly as his father had ever done.

He glanced at the stacks of seasoned wood, neatly piled according to kinds and uses. Gleaming new wheels hung on

Richard Sibbes

the walls. Father was a careful workman. And a Christian man, raising his children in the Lord.

Richard wiped his sweaty face with his sleeve. Then he exchanged the hammer for the spoke shave. It took a lot of pressure to whittle wood curls off the hard oak of the next spoke. But every ounce of weight taken off meant that much less strain on the valuable horse pulling the wagon. The weight had to be removed carefully, without sacrificing strength. Carts often carried loads of more than five hundred pounds.

"Good day, young man." Mr. Rushbrook stood in the doorway.

Touching his forehead in a motion of respect, Richard straightened. "Good day, sir. Would you like a wheel made?"

"No, thank you, Richard." The attorney smiled and walked closer. He glanced around. "Your father is not here?"

"No, sir. He's delivering a cart to a farmer east of Thurston." Richard cleaned his hands with a scrap of cloth. "Is there something I can do for you?"

"Yes, there is." The man reached into his satchel and pulled out some papers. "Mr. Greaves and I have made arrangements for you to be examined by some of the fellows at St. John's College."

"St. John's? Cambridge, you mean?"

"Cambridge, indeed." He handed the papers to Richard. "Here are our letters of recommendation."

Richard's hand shook as he took the papers. "But, my father—"

"Won't like it."

"No. He won't." The young man gave the papers back to the attorney. "He's invested a lot of money in these tools for me. It's no use even asking him."

St. John's Cambridge, Second Court

Mr. Rushbrook cleared his throat. "That is why we do not intend to ask him."

Richard's eyebrows shot up. "Not ask him! I couldn't go against his wishes, sir."

"You are eighteen years old now, Richard. You are legally a man and can do as you like." The attorney peered into his eyes. "Do you want to go to Cambridge?"

"Of course! There's nothing I'd like better, but—"

The older man raised his hand. "Do you respect Mr. Greaves as your spiritual counselor?"

"Certainly, I do. He's a minister of God's Word."

"He and I think God is calling you to something other than crafting carts and wheels. God has given you academic gifts, and it would be a shame to waste them on a wheelwright's bench."

"But sir—"

"Mr. Greaves and I believe it is time for you to obey God rather than men." Mr. Rushbrook thrust the papers back into Richard's hand. "But you will need to be examined before you can be admitted. If you fail the examination, you can always come back and work as a wheelwright."

"I suppose…." Despite Richard's concern to obey his father, hope rose within his heart for the first time in many days. "Yes, I could do that—if I had to." His forehead wrinkled. "But even if I am accepted, how would I pay for my education? Father will not be able to support me."

The attorney smiled. "You leave that to your friends. Mr. Greaves and I aren't the only ones who want to see you succeed. Mr. Knewstub has already pledged his support."

"Mr. Knewstub? He's one of the principal benefactors of St. John's. What a good man!"

"He is." The attorney nodded and drew out another paper. "Here are your instructions for the time and place of your examination. See to it you're there." He closed his satchel. "Don't worry about the money. You have other friends who will help you. And I have a feeling your father will provide some financial support once he sees how suited you are to an academic life."

"I hope so." Richard scanned through the letters and directions. When he looked up, Mr. Rushbrook had gone. He carefully folded the papers and placed them deep in a pocket under his leather apron.

Tonight, he would start packing. Right now, he had a wheel to finish.

Shavings flew as he shaped another spoke. A warm feeling in his heart spread through his whole chest. For some reason, it reminded him of the disciples who walked and talked with Jesus on the road to Emmaus. They later said to each other, "Did not our heart burn within us, while he talked with us by the way, and while he opened to us the scriptures?" (Luke 24:32).

He didn't understand why his heart warmed him liked a banked fire in his father's forge, but he was eager to let it burst into flame.

—◆◆◆—

Richard Sibbes did well on his examination and in all his studies at St. John's College. His father eventually saw the wisdom of Richard's choice and contributed a small amount regularly for his education.

By the time Sibbes was twenty-four, he was teaching other students. But he was learning more at the college than academics. The preaching of Paul Baynes, whom Sibbes called his "father in the gospel," brought him into a personal relationship with Christ. He had been taught Scripture, but now he understood the Bible better and his Savior became real to him.

While still a student, he preached at Holy Trinity Church in Cambridge. Such large crowds flocked to hear him that a new balcony needed to be built. Spiritual renewal swept through the university. Several of the young men converted under his preaching would go on to become important Puritan preachers and teachers. Some people called him the "honey-mouthed" or the "sweet dropper" because he preached about Jesus Christ so richly and movingly. By showing others all that is lovely in Christ, the Holy Spirit used his sermons to persuade many to love Him.

Sibbes often wrote about how God's love flows between Him and His children. We love God because He first loved us, which Sibbes compared to being warmed by the sun. He wrote, "If cold and dark bodies have light and heat in them, it is because the sun hath shined upon them first."

When Sibbes was about forty years old, he became the minister at Gray's Inn in London. This was the largest of the four associations for training barristers or lawyers who argued cases in courts of law. Each one was housed in a complex of buildings, including a church. He developed a large network of friends, some of them important and influential people. Thousands, including visitors from other countries, were blessed by his preaching.

He preached the Bible as the only absolute and complete rule for

Holy Trinity Church in Cambridge

life, but taught that simply knowing the truth wasn't enough. He wrote: "Truth is no guide to us, being only in the book, but as it is seated in the heart." From his own experience he knew that biblical truth must be fixed in the heart as well as in the mind.

"Men of great learning know much, and so does the devil," Sibbes wrote, "but he lacks love." Perhaps images from his father's forge came to mind as he continued.

"In fire all things may be painted but the heat. So all good actions may be done by a hypocrite, but there is a heat of love which he has not." An artist can paint bright flames and red metal, but he can't depict the warmth of the fire. In the same way, people can do good things for show, but their hearts are cold without the warmth of God's love.

Sibbes wrote, "Many men are troubled with cold affections, and then they think to work love out of their own hearts, which are like a barren wilderness, but we must beg of God the Spirit of love. We must not bring love to God, but fetch love from Him." He realized that when we try to love God on our own, we can't do it. Love comes from God, and He draws it from us back to Himself. He said, "When you find the love of God in your heart, that your heart is taught by His Spirit to love Him, then surely you may say, 'Oh, blessed be God who has kindled this holy fire in my heart!'"

Sibbes encouraged Christians to develop an intimate relationship with the Holy Spirit. He called this process "entertaining the Spirit" in the soul. He wrote, "There is no one in the world so great and sweet a friend who will do us so much good as the Spirit, if we give Him entertainment." Just as welcoming a dear friend into our home and spending time with him helps us become closer to him, so our love for God grows as we grow in appreciation for the Holy Spirit and His saving work in our heart.

Not long before he turned fifty, Sibbes was appointed as the master of St. Catharine's Hall at Cambridge. He soon became a doctor of divinity. In his new position, he was able to help place Puritan ministers throughout England. While he worked as the director of the college, he continued preaching at Gray's Inn. Both upper-class and lower-class people from all over the country were eager to read his sermons,

and Sibbes became a popular writer. Because he helped Christians love the things of heaven more than the things of this world, he became known as "the heavenly Doctor."

Life was difficult during this time in England. Thousands of people died from great plagues and deadly wars. The country reeled with religious and political unrest. Kings and Parliaments couldn't work together, and even Puritans sometimes argued among themselves about politics. In all these struggles, Sibbes was able to remain friends with people who had differing opinions. Whenever possible, he tried to avoid conflict.

But his heart for spreading the gospel throughout the country once got him into serious trouble. Some leaders, especially Archbishop Laud, worked hard to keep Puritan men out of English pulpits. In response, Sibbes and others began a program of raising funds and setting up Puritans as lecturers in churches. Laud was furious about the effort, but he was too busy with other matters to do anything about it for several years.

Finally, Laud summoned Sibbes and his colleagues to trial. The men were called criminals and traitors. The verdict decreed that the funds be confiscated and the organizers be banished.

Some of the men fled to the Netherlands, while others sailed to New England. Because Sibbes had many powerful friends, nothing happened to him. He continued as Master of St. Catharine's college and minister at Gray's Inn. He even preached and published a sermon, in which he praised a man for the good he had done through the now-crushed assistance program.

When Sibbes was fifty-six years old, King Charles I appointed him as minister of Holy Trinity Church in

Gray's Inn, London
BY KIND PERMISSION OF THE MASTERS OF THE BENCH OF THE
"HONOURABLE SOCIETY OF GRAY'S INN"

Cambridge. This was the same church where Sibbes had lectured so effectively while a scholar. In addition to this position, he still directed the college in Cambridge and preached at Gray's Inn in London.

He kept writing his own books as well as introductions for at least thirteen works of Puritan friends. He greatly influenced the direction of scriptural theology, carrying forward the truths of the Reformation. His seven volumes of sermons and books continue to touch the hearts of believers today. One modern preacher, Maurice Roberts, described the theology of Sibbes as "the fuel of some great combustion engine, always passing into flame and so being converted into energy thereby to serve God and, even more, to enjoy and relish God with the soul."

A week before his death, Sibbes preached on the words of Jesus in John 14:1, "Let not your heart be troubled: ye believe in God, believe also in me." He urged listeners to meditate on such promises. "These comforts being warmed with meditation, will stick close to the heart," he said. "Warm the heart with these, and see if any trivial things can cast you down." He knew that memorizing and meditating on God's promises can keep a person from being brought down by the trivial things in life.

He soon became very ill. During his final week, someone asked how his soul was faring. He said, "I should do God much wrong if I should not say, very well."

The day before his death, he dictated his will, which began: "I commend and bequeath my soul into the hands of my gracious Savior, who hath redeemed it with his most precious blood, and appears now in heaven to receive it."

Richard Sibbes died on July 5, 1635, at Gray's Inn in London. He never married, but many friends and readers mourned his passing. Izaac Walton, a famous writer, had this to say about Dr. Sibbes: "Of this blest man, let this just praise be given, Heaven was in him, before he was in heaven."

Truly Sibbes did much earthly good while focusing on heavenly things. He always stressed the need for daily meditation. He wanted people to realize how thinking about God's love and praising Him for it make that love burn all the brighter within the soul. He encouraged Christians to foster a relationship with the triune God and contemplate "the infinite love of God in Jesus." He wrote, "Let us set some time apart to meditate of these things, till the heart be warmed." His heart, warmed by the fire of the Spirit, stirred the embers of faith in many other hearts.

~ 6 ~

John Cotton

1584–1652

New England Leader

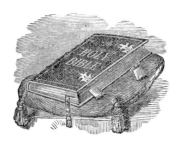

A bell's solemn ring rolled across the field, stopping John Cotton's long strides. His heart leaped with joy. He knew whose death the bell tolled—William Perkins, so revered by nearly everyone at Cambridge. Everyone but him.

He smiled in grim satisfaction and walked on with a lighter step. At last, he would no longer have to hear that man's convicting sermons about the state of his heart.

As Cotton crossed onto the college green, a student hurried past him. "What a terrible loss!"

Cotton composed his face and nodded. "A sad loss, indeed."

The young man's eyes shone with tears. "No one has ever done so much good for Cambridge as William Perkins. His influence has changed the entire university." He hurried off to join a mournful crowd gathering near the church.

By the time Cotton reached his room, the echoes of the tolling bell had faded. He picked up a book, but paused to look out the window at the church tower. He had feared the religion preached by Perkins might take away his dedication to his studies. Now he need not worry. His mind—so besieged by those sermons—was relieved; his academic career was safe. He ignored his thoughts and opened his book.

——— ✦ ———

But John Cotton could not ignore the Spirit's work in his heart. Before long, he found himself drawn to the sermons of another college preacher, Richard Sibbes. This Puritan taught that loving God with your heart was far more important than simply being "a good person." Cotton began to wonder: Had he been resisting the Spirit? He developed a friendship with Sibbes, and the two spent many hours in serious discussions about religion.

For three years, Cotton struggled with his feelings. He felt torn between focusing on his career or his faith. He was not only an excellent scholar, but also a popular lecturer at Cambridge. Well known for his witty rhetoric, students often responded approvingly to the worldly wisdom in his speeches. But the more he heard Sibbes speak, the more he began to consider that plain

John Cotton

eyes to show their displeasure. Some colleagues squirmed in their seats, while others covered their mouths to stifle yawns.

Afterward, Cotton went to his room to sort out his thoughts. Someone knocked on the door. It was John Preston, a fellow of Queen's College. He asked to borrow a book, but the real reason he came to see Cotton was that the sermon had touched his heart. Preston stayed a long time, and often returned. As the two discussed theology, they grew in their understanding of Scripture. Preston would later call Cotton his father in the faith. And Cotton would later recall with shame his joy at the death of Perkins.

style of biblical preaching as heavenly treasure. Perhaps the message mattered more than the method.

Finally, Cotton realized that his lectures had to change. Rather than seek personal advancement, he needed to follow in the footsteps of Sibbes and Perkins. Asked to preach at the largest college church, he knew he couldn't deliver his usual oratorical discourse. He decided to preach in a plain style about an unpopular topic: repentance.

As he spoke, he felt waves of disapproval from some in the audience. Many students pulled their hats over their

John Preston

Cotton was ordained and, two years later, began serving St. Botolph's parish church in Boston, Lincolnshire. Here he met Elizabeth Horrocks, the sister of a well-known minister. In July of 1613, the two were married.

On the day of the wedding, a conviction of spiritual assurance swept through Cotton's soul. He finally was convinced that God loved him and had applied His Spirit's saving work to his heart. All doubts and questions disappeared from his mind. For the rest of his life, he often told people about his wedding: "God made that day, a day of double marriage to me."

Although Cotton did not conform to all the rules of the Church of England, he avoided trouble for many years. Every Sunday, the impressive church building was crowded with people, some coming from far distances. He preached to huge crowds during the week as well.

John Preston, now influential at Cambridge, sent many students to train under Cotton. Students also came from other countries. Ministers and theologians from all over Europe sent letters to Cotton, asking his advice on difficult problems or theological matters.

By God's grace, Cotton's popularity and his ability to get along with other people kept him from being arrested during his twenty-year ministry at St. Boloph's. But in his continued nonconformity, he could not escape the notice of Bishop Laud forever. The Bishop of London, who would later become the Archbishop, was already making things difficult for Puritans. Some fled to the Netherlands and others to New England.

Cotton's interest in the New World developed gradually. He traveled one hundred miles to preach a farewell sermon to the members of the Massachusetts Bay Colony, who were preparing to sail under the leadership of John Winthrop and settle in New England.

Soon after that, he and Elizabeth became ill with malaria. They were sick for a year, staying with an earl who strongly favored colonization of New England. Unfortunately, Elizabeth died from the disease. While Cotton was recovering, he traveled through Europe and witnessed the increasing persecution of the Puritans.

About a year after Elizabeth's death, he married one of her friends, Sarah Hawkridge Story, a widow with a daughter. Not long after this, he received a summons to appear in Bishop Laud's court. He went into hiding in London, staying with friends who tried to persuade him to conform to church regulations. Instead, he convinced them that not conforming was the only righteous response. After Sarah and her daughter joined him, Cotton and his friend, Thomas Hooker, made plans to sail for New England.

To keep Puritans from fleeing the country, Bishop Laud ordered all ships searched when arriving at the Isle of Wight, which lay just off the coast of Portsmouth. In July of 1633, a ship called the *Griffin* set sail for New England. Someone persuaded the captain to pick up a few more passengers after the ship had been searched. He stopped at a nearby location, where Cotton and Hooker came aboard in disguise.

Once well out to sea, they discarded their disguises and preached to the passengers every morning, afternoon, and evening. A month into the voyage, Sarah gave birth to a son named Seaborn. The Cottons arrived in Boston, on the shores of New England, on September 4.

Cotton was called to the First Church of Boston, the largest congregation of the colony, and soon became the

Anne Hutchinson on trial

most influential minister in New England. While he was a respected leader, he also struggled with major conflicts.

A woman named Anne Hutchinson and her family had followed Cotton to New England. She criticized all the ministers except Cotton and her brother-in-law, claiming they were the only two preachers with the right view of grace. She was an intelligent woman and a persuasive speaker. She held meetings in her home, where sixty or more women gathered each week while she reviewed sermons and added her own interpretation. Many of the people within the Boston church became her followers, and the church asked her husband to become one of its deacons.

Anne Hutchinson's practices and teachings caused a great deal of trouble in the colony. Church leaders and civil magistrates held many meetings, trying to resolve the situation. At first, Cotton supported her, but he eventually realized how far she had strayed from biblical teachings. She didn't believe it was necessary to do good works as evidence of a changed heart. She also paid more attention to what she thought the Spirit was telling her than to what the Bible said.

Cotton attempted to correct her teaching and restore unity among the pastors. Although she had signed a document expressing repentance, she seemed unrepentant when speaking in her own defense. Church leaders banished her from the colony, giving her a year to reconsider her views. Her family moved to Rhode Island, where her husband died. Later she moved to a Dutch territory in New York, where she was killed by Indians.

Another conflict arose with Roger Williams, who believed the Church of England was the Antichrist and all true Christians should separate completely from it. He felt the government had no spiritual authority, while Cotton

Roger Williams

Cotton's ability to see both sides of issues enabled him to be a successful moderator in theological debates. While he never compromised on matters of conviction, he accepted admonishment with a humble spirit. He was a compassionate man who was quick to help others. Because he wanted the Native Americans to hear the gospel, he supported the work of John Eliot, a well-known Puritan missionary to the Indians. He also raised funds for a group of Puritans who had been forced from Bermuda and were stranded on an island.

Cotton worked hard to shape New England into a godly society, writing a law code that reflected God's sovereignty and provided for churches and magistrates to work together in governing the people. Although this code was more lenient than England's in many ways, it was never adopted.

Cotton was more successful at establishing a congregational form of church government in New England. He viewed congregationalism as a good compromise between the Independents and the Presbyterians. Some would say his most important books were on church government.

He also wrote a catechism for children, *Milk for Babes*, in 1646. This was published with the popular *New England Primer* and was a standard teaching resource in the colonies for more than two hundred years.

Cotton continued to maintain an active correspondence with people who sought his advice, including members of the English court and such notable leaders as Oliver Cromwell. He became an overseer of Harvard College and provided important leadership on many levels throughout New England.

While traveling by ferry to a preaching engagement in November of 1652, he became soaked and chilled, and fell

believed the government should restrain evil and suppress heresy. Williams also didn't believe in praying after any meal, not even the Lord's Supper.

Cotton initially attempted to prevent the banishment of Williams. But when he recognized how reports carried back to England were endangering the colony's future, he agreed that banishment was necessary. Williams fled to another area, where he founded a settlement he called Providence. Later this settlement would develop into Providence, Rhode Island.

ill. Believing he had little time left, he preached the following Sunday and then put his study in order before taking to his bed. Civil officials, ministers, and many friends visited him to seek his final blessing and advice.

On December 9, a meteor flashed across the night skies, which many people of Boston considered a sign of something bad about to happen. Someone asked Cotton what it might mean. He said he thought it signified "great changes in the churches."

As his health continued to fail, the elders of his church gathered in his room for parting instructions and prayer. On December 23, his friend John Wilson prayed at his bedside: "Lord, lift up the light of Thy countenance upon this, my dying colleague."

Cotton said, "He has done it already, brother."

Sarah and their children expressed goodbyes. He committed the children to God's never-failing covenant, and then he asked everyone to leave the room. A few hours later, the Lord took him to his heavenly home.

Many people in Boston thought that Cotton's death was the change he had anticipated in the churches. But he most likely would have reminded them that he was only a humble servant of Jesus Christ, who rules over the whole church and works everything for its good.

John Cotton's body was laid to rest in the New England soil that had sprouted a new form of church government

Cotton's Tombstone
MICHAEL KRUSE

through his efforts. Despite much conflict in his life, he always tried to persuade people of the truth without personal attacks. The tombstone marking his grave reads:

> *Could wound at argument without division,*
> *Cut to the quick, and yet make no incision.*

That little poem testifies to his ability to argue without creating discord and cut to the heart of a matter without hurting his opponent. God had used the keen intellect of John Cotton not for his own glory as a witty speaker, but for God's glory as a powerful preacher and a leader in a new land.

~ 7 ~

Thomas Hooker

1586–1647

Connecticut Founder

Screams pierced the night. Thomas Hooker threw aside the bed covers and ran out of his room.

He met Susanna Garbrand in the hall. She held up her candlestick, the flame wavering in her trembling hand. "It's my mistress again, sir."

He nodded. "Another terrifying dream, no doubt."

The two rushed into the room of Mrs. Joan Drake, who sat rigid on her bed, grasping her head and shrieking. "No, no! Not the fires of hell!"

Susanna handed the candle to Hooker and hurried to the bedside. "There, there, mistress. Please don't distress yourself so." She put her arms around the stiff woman and rubbed her back.

"My brain feels ready to burst." Mrs. Drake leaned her head on her hands. "How it hurts!"

"Shall I get your medicine?"

"No, don't leave me." The frantic woman clutched Susanna's arm. "Don't let me suffer alone."

Thomas walked forward. "You are not alone, Mrs. Drake. We are right here. And even if we weren't, God is always with you."

"The wrath of God. Fire and brimstone!" She sobbed on the younger woman's shoulder. "Woe is me! What can I do? My doom is sure."

He pulled a chair close to the bed. "Dear Mrs. Drake, don't allow your mind to dwell on these dreadful dreams." He lifted the candle and saw dark circles under her eyes. "Think instead of God's comforting assurances in Scripture. Do you remember what He promises?"

She shook her head. "No. I don't recall a thing." She groaned and crossed her arms over her stomach. "Oh, it seems the very fires of hell burn in my belly."

The young man spoke calmly. "Turn your mind to the love of God."

"How can God love me?" Tears poured from her eyes. "I have committed the unpardonable sin. I will be damned for all eternity!" Her words turned into an incomprehensible wail.

Susan gripped her shoulders, and Thomas leaned forward. "Now, now, Mrs. Drake, take a deep breath and listen to what I'm saying." He took hold

Thomas Hooker

gleaming in the candle's flickering light. "God's love for you is as real as this hand. Just as it is always in front of you, your name is always before God. You are safe in His hands, and He promises that nothing—not even the devil himself—can ever snatch you from Him."

Susanna wiped Mrs. Drake's tears with a corner of her shawl. "Yes, mistress, that's all true."

"I suppose so." The older woman sighed.

Thomas continued. "How often God assures us that He is always with us! What does He say over and over in the holy Scriptures? 'I am with you always. I will never leave you or forsake you. Be strong and of good courage.' Isn't that right, Mrs. Drake? Isn't that what God says to you?"

"Yes. Yes, He does." The woman's eyes closed, and Susanna eased her mistress's head gently onto her pillow. Her eyes fluttered open briefly. "Thank you, Mr. Hooker. I think I'll rest now." She rolled to her side and began to breathe deeply and evenly.

Susanna and Thomas nodded to each other and left the room. She closed the door quietly behind them. "Thank you, Mr. Hooker. Ever since you became Vicar of Esher and moved into this house, Mrs. Drake has been improving. She is far less short-tempered with everyone."

As the two walked down the hall, she laughed a little. "You should have seen how she acted about the other ministers Sir Francis brought to try to help her. She refused to see them, shouting and throwing things at the door." Susanna turned to Thomas. "Truly, you have been a gift from God."

"My own past struggles with assurance help me understand hers." He handed the candlestick to her. "And God graciously equips me with the words she needs to hear."

of her tight fist. "Your very concern shows that you have not committed the unpardonable sin. If you truly had rejected the Holy Spirit, you wouldn't worry about heaven or hell."

Mrs. Drake sniffed. "Do you think so?"

"Yes, I'm sure of it." He felt her fingers relax. "We've spoken of this many times before, haven't we? Concentrate on Scripture's comfort. The names of believers are engraved in the palms of God's hands." He held up her pale hand,

She nodded, her eyes shining in the candle's glow. "Blessed be His name forever."

"I have just one question."

"Yes? What is it?"

The young man cleared his throat. "Will you marry me?"

———◆◆◆———

Thomas Hooker and Susanna Garbrand were married on April 3, 1621, in Amersham, the town where Mrs. Drake had been born. That woman, plagued for years by physical pain and spiritual despair, had become so much better that she was able to pray and sing psalms with her family. By the time she died, four years after the Hookers were married, she had finally experienced peace in her soul. Thomas and Susanna named their first daughter, Joanna, after her.

Following Hooker's ministry to the people of Esher and the Drake family, he became a preacher in Chelmsford. Its citizens were known for rowdy drunkenness and ungodly living. Most shops were open on Sunday. Hooker's sermons drew huge crowds and changed the hearts of many people. The town and surrounding countryside became orderly and people observed the Sabbath. Hooker met every month with other local ministers, and they learned how to preach the plain truths of the Bible to needy souls.

As a Puritan, Hooker didn't observe some Church of England requirements, which he believed were not biblical. A local minister, jealous of Hooker's success, reported him to church officials. London's Bishop Laud threatened to bring Hooker before the church's highest court.

Hooker offered to leave the country quietly if no charges were filed against him. But he was dismissed from his position and forced to pay a bond to guarantee his court appearance. He moved to a nearby community, where he became the master of a school. Many men and ministers came to ask his advice and hear his teaching.

In 1630, Bishop Laud summoned Hooker to appear before the high court. Friends convinced Hooker to give up his bond money and flee the country. He sailed secretly to the Netherlands.

During the first two years he spent there, Hooker helped minister to an English congregation in Delft. Then he worked for another year with the famous William Ames in Rotterdam. Hooker became convinced that congregationalism was the best form of church government, and decided to go to the New World with his friend, John Cotton. Hooker returned briefly to England, where he and Cotton finalized their plans and boarded a ship in disguise. Another Puritan preacher, Samuel Stone, traveled with them.

After the three ministers arrived in New England in 1633, people joked that they now had Cotton for their clothing, Hooker for their fishing, and Stone for their building.

Hooker became the first minister at New Town (later named Cambridge). The church was officially named the Church of Christ at Cambridge, but his congregation was known as "Mr. Hooker's Company."

Hooker and Stone didn't always agree with Cotton, especially about the best form of government for the new colony. They considered starting a new settlement some distance away. Less than three years after coming to the New World, Hooker and Stone had their opportunity.

Thomas Shepard and many other Puritans landed in Boston, eager to purchase land. Hooker and Stone and one hundred of their followers sold their property to the new arrivals. Then they headed west to a wilderness area in the

Hooker and Company journeying through the wilderness from Plymouth to Hartford, in 1636

Connecticut River valley. Susanna Hooker, whose health was poor by this time, they carried on a cot with poles strapped to horses. Other women and children rode in carts pulled by oxen. Ahead of them, men drove 160 head of cattle, goats, and pigs. Sometimes the travelers needed to fell trees to get through dense woods, but other times they camped in pleasant meadows. Although the journey was difficult, they ate wild strawberries and drank fresh milk. It took them two weeks to travel the hundred miles. When they arrived at their destination, they sang praises to God. Previous settlers had built a small chapel there, and on the first Sunday, Hooker preached and administered the Lord's Supper.

The group named their settlement Hartford, after Stone's hometown of Hertford in England, and Hooker established a church. Hartford joined with nearby planta-tions called Wethersfeld and Windsor under the authority of one general court. Dutch people had settled in the area earlier, and their fort stood some distance south of Hartford.

Although many Native Americans in the area were friendly, the Pequot tribe became violent. They attacked Europeans and committed a series of murders. The settlers took action against the tribe after its warriors attacked Wethersfeld, killing nine people and carrying off several girls.

In an attempt to retrieve the girls, the Dutch neighbors tried to negotiate with Pequot tribal leaders aboard a ship in

Hooker's Company arrive in Connecticut

the harbor. When that effort failed, they took several hostages and secured the return of the girls in exchange.

The governing council ordered the militia to enter Pequot territory and attack them directly. But the captain wanted to sail past that area and double back over land for a surprise attack from the rear. The soldiers couldn't agree on whether to obey the council or the captain. Samuel Stone, the army chaplain, spent all night in prayer. The next morning, he announced that God's divine will was to follow the captain's leading. With no more argument, the militia followed the captain's plan. That night the Pequot held a wild celebration in anticipation of their victory, and then they collapsed into sleep. The English soldiers surprised the sleeping warriors and won the battle. This action turned the tide in the war against the Pequot threat, and the tribe was eventually conquered.

The first two winters in Hartford were harsh. Food became scarce, and the settlers lost much of their livestock. A number of people died. Then exploring parties came across a friendly tribe that was willing to sell corn to the settlers and deliver it by canoe. And a ship arrived in the colony, carrying fresh provisions. Hooker called these events "miraculous deliverances of God."

In addition to being a powerful preacher and a kind pastor, Hooker was a capable leader. Still respected in Massachusetts, he participated in the trials of Roger Williams and Anne Hutchinson for their unbiblical views. Puritans remaining in England also admired him, and he was one of a few ministers invited in 1643 to represent New England at the Westminster Assembly. By that time, Hooker was fifty-seven years old. Declining to travel back across the ocean, he decided instead to contribute to the church by writing

a catechism, a book about the Lord's Prayer, and numerous books about how the Holy Spirit applies Christ and His work of salvation to the souls of sinners. For most of his life, Hooker's focus as a leader was establishing the government for the Connecticut colony.

He was the primary author of a constitution called the "Fundamental Orders of Connecticut," which some people believe was the beginning of American democracy. This document differed from the style of government in Massachusetts by allowing more classes of men to vote for magistrates and laws. While the document was intended to protect and promote the church as well as the community, it did not base voting privileges on church membership and land ownership. It introduced the idea of people electing civil rulers and limiting their power instead of a small group of people appointing magistrates with unlimited power.

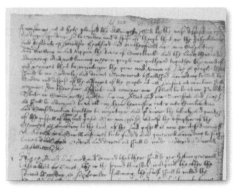

Title page of Fundamental Orders of Connecticut

Hooker preached a famous sermon on Deuteronomy 1:13, "Take you wise men, and understanding, and known among your tribes, and I [the Lord] will make them rulers over you." Hooker pointed out how God decrees that people choose public magistrates, not according to personal wishes but according to His will, and how citizens have the right to limit the power of elected officials. He declared, "The foundation of authority is laid in the free consent of the people."

Although the government in Connecticut differed somewhat from that in Massachusetts, ties between the two settlements remained strong. Thomas Shepard married Hooker's daughter, Joanna, in 1637.

Hooker was also a compassionate man who often gave money to widows and orphans. He paid special attention to the families of deceased ministers, and very likely supported the widow and children of his old friend, Dr. Ames.

An epidemic swept through Connecticut during the summer of 1647, and the disease struck Hooker. A friend, who stood weeping by his bedside, told him, "Sir, you are going to receive the reward of all your labors."

Hooker replied, "Brother, I am going to receive mercy!"

He died on July 7, at the age of sixty-one. His long-time friend, Samuel Stone, told Hooker's son-in-law, Thomas Shepard, "He has done much work for Christ, and now rests from his labors and his works follow him, but our loss is great and bitter." He added, "I can never look to have the like fellow officer in his place. There are but few such men in the world."

While most people remember Hooker as the founder of Connecticut, he probably would want to be remembered as a faithful minister of the Word of God and a man of prayer. He prayed for hours daily and devoted one day each month to private prayer accompanied by fasting. He believed that those who neglect prayer will find sin increasing in their lives, while their love for God will grow cold.

~ 8 ~

Jeremiah Burroughs

1600–1646

Gem of Contentment

As the room filled with townsmen, Jeremiah Burroughs scanned the faces of the six officials of Bury St. Edmunds in England. His financial welfare was in their hands. The congregation had supported him for some time, but laws had changed and now the city was responsible. Some ministers in England were not being treated fairly. Were these councilmen still upset he had preached against the sins of one of their council members?

The room quieted, and Burroughs began speaking: "I called this parish meeting because I have been offered another position, but I wanted to speak to you men before I give my answer."

He took a deep breath. "As you know, the people of the congregation have been paying me as well as my fellow minister, Mr. White. Now it has been determined that the city will pay our wages. And the amount has been limited to only one hundred pounds for the parish with no additional contributions from individuals."

The municipal men nodded. If only they would agree to everything he said! He was afraid they'd try to force him out by giving Mr. White the whole amount. A nearby village recently had given the entire wage to only one of the two ministers. Even if one shared fairly with the other, fifty pounds was barely enough to live on.

Burroughs continued, "I am willing to refuse the offer of the other position and stay with you here at Bury. All I ask is for your promise that I might have the same wage as the other minister who does the same amount of work."

The officials shuffled their feet and mumbled excuses about a wage increase not being given yet.

"But promise that when it does happen," Burroughs said, "I may have my means as well as the other shall have his."

One of the aldermen said, "Perhaps the sole power will not be ours."

Burroughs persisted, "Promise that if you shall have any power, you will use it for this end."

"Remember your sermon," one official shouted, shaking his fist at him.

Another spoke up: "We will wait to see what the rest of the parish desires."

"We must not see our chief governor abused," a third alderman added.

Jeremiah Burroughs

A fourth said they should take appropriate action for the sermon he'd preached.

All six officials sided against Burroughs. Only one of the twenty-four other townsmen spoke in his favor. The meeting broke up, and Burroughs walked home.

What was God's will for him? Were financial considerations a good reason to leave his ministry in Bury? Should he give it up just because some men wanted to get rid of him? It seemed he could accomplish more for the Lord in this large congregation than in a smaller church. And if he left, who would care for the souls of the people?

⸺ ◆◆◆ ⸺

Conflicted about what to do, Burroughs sought the advice of John Cotton, who was still in New England at this time. Burroughs was so fond of the older man that he addressed his letter to "Great-Grandfather Cotton." Cotton's reply encouraged Burroughs to seek the counsel of godly ministers in his area more familiar with the situation. Burroughs may have discussed the matter with his close friend and mentor, Thomas Hooker. Burroughs had studied under him in college and at his home seminary.

Whatever advice Burroughs received, he left Bury and went to the small village of Tivetshall in Norfolk. There he preached and had sole responsibility for the spiritual care of two congregations.

He soon began taking turns with other Puritan pastors to preach at a church in Norwich on Fridays. The twelve ministers met for the service and ate their evening meal together afterward, advising and encouraging each other. Later, Burroughs enjoyed a similar preaching rotation at Mendlesham.

Archbishop William Laud visited Norfolk and found many ministers were not conforming to the prescribed usage of the Church of England. He asked Bishop Matthew Wren to straighten things out. Intending to trap the Puritans, Wren made a long list of questions ministers had to answer. That list led Burroughs to study what the Bible said about worship. He realized that many Church of England practices had no basis in God's Word and were "merely man's inventions." He refused to read the king's *Book of Sports* from the pulpit and did not bow when the name of Jesus was mentioned. Rather than reading printed and approved prayers, he prayed to God from his heart.

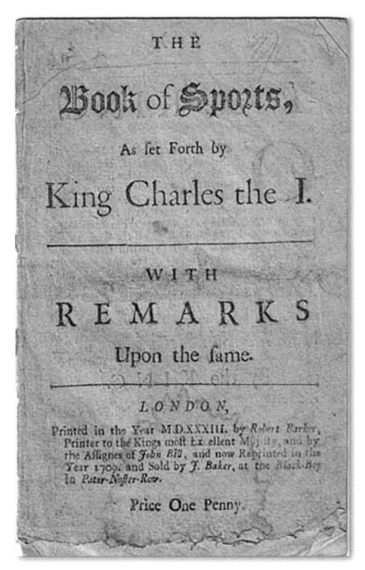

Book of Sports

Wren suspended Burroughs and fifty other pastors from preaching in their churches.

Burroughs moved to London. He lived in a house owned by the Earl of Warwick and served as a chaplain to his son-in-law, Viscount Mandeville. Even though Burroughs ministered to only one family, he enjoyed peace and fellowship.

But Wren wasn't finished with Burroughs. He wanted to prohibit him from preaching anywhere. Because Burroughs had many influential friends, Wren decided to try his case before a private church court. Some powerful friends of Burroughs requested an investigation of the matter, but that didn't work. They tried to persuade the court to allow Burroughs to resign, but that effort also failed. Burroughs was removed from the ministry, although he continued to serve the Mandeville family.

A number of persecuted pastors fled to the Netherlands, where they enjoyed more freedoms. The Netherlands was a common place for printing Puritan literature. In October of 1637, Burroughs and a friend visited the Dutch city of Breda, which recently had been freed from the Spanish army. They agreed to help bring Puritan publications into England. Disguised as soldiers returning from the war at Breda, they sailed back on a ship whose master had consented to carry Puritan literature in unlabeled barrels.

Unfortunately, English officials stopped the ship at Yarmouth and searched it. The literature was discovered. Burroughs and his friend managed to escape, but the ship's master was arrested for importing rebellious material.

Burroughs once rode seventy-two miles to preach in Dedham. Although he was not arrested, charges were brought against the vicar who had invited him.

Despite such constant danger, the Earl of Warwick continued to support Puritan preachers by inviting them to his homes in London and Essex. The ministers would preach to the Earl's many houseguests.

Archbishop Laud

Oliver Cromwell

In the spring of 1638, eight ships were loaded and ready to sail to New England. The Archbishop ordered that all the passengers be put on shore. Puritans throughout the country were concerned. It seemed even the hope of religious freedom in the New World was taken from them.

Soon after that, Burroughs preached at one of the Earl's houses in London. The large crowd included Oliver Cromwell, who had been removed from one of the ships. Using Psalm 56:11 as the text, Burroughs preached about courage in evil times.

The sermon greatly encouraged the audience. Cromwell said, "Who is Laud, that I should obey him? Or Strafford, that I should fear him?" Archbishop Laud and the Earl of Strafford were two of the king's chief advisers, who encouraged his policies against Puritans. Cromwell would later rule England as its Lord Protector.

The Countess of Warwick asked Burroughs to be her chaplain in Essex. While he was there, he walked in the garden with a man named Michaelson. They spoke at length about Scottish politics and the authority of the king—dangerous topics in those days! Burroughs was careful not to express personal opinions, but to speak about things only in theory. Still, Michaelson thought he was treasonous and reported the conversation. Burroughs went to Michaelson and reasoned with him. Thinking he had been successful, he assumed he would not be charged with a crime.

Meanwhile, Burroughs struggled to know God's will for his ministry. While praying for guidance one day, he looked through his window and recognized an approaching man. From Norwich, but now living in the Netherlands, he told Burroughs he had been sent to ask him to serve the English church in Rotterdam.

"When I heard him say this, I stood a while, amazed at the providence of God," Burroughs later wrote, "that at such a time a messenger should be sent to me about such an errand. My heart, God knows, exceedingly rejoiced in this call of His."

But Burroughs wanted to be certain this call was truly from the Lord. He asked the messenger to return with a written letter from the church.

Several months after the conversation with Michaelson, the Earl of Warwick became ill. Fearing the worst, he asked Burroughs to come to him in London. As the Earl improved over the next few weeks, Burroughs walked freely about the city.

A messenger from the Rotterdam church brought Burroughs a letter of call, signed by the elders. He agreed to meet with church representatives in Norwich and finalize the arrangement.

Then he heard that the accusations against him had not been dropped. His arrest appeared certain. He traveled to Norwich and sailed from there to the Netherlands.

Harbor of Rotterdam

The Netherlands

Burroughs was hired as a teacher for the English congregation in Rotterdam, which William Ames had once served. Burroughs instructed the people in biblical doctrine and the Christian faith, but he also ministered to many souls in private with pastoral love and wisdom.

He learned a great deal about the congregational system of church government. When differences of opinion led to a church split, Burroughs focused on his preaching and the people. His sermons were often published during these years, including one written for mariners. Rotterdam was an important port in Europe, and Burroughs cared about the constant flow of sailors who visited the city.

While he was in the Netherlands, things were changing in England. After the Long Parliament invited exiled ministers back, Burroughs quickly returned.

London

At some point during this time frame, Burroughs married. The wedding may have taken place in the Netherlands or in England, but it was not recorded. Although his wife's name is not known, she appears to have been a supportive and wise woman.

While Burroughs didn't accept a ministerial call to a specific church, he was hired to preach for the two largest congregations in London. Other churches and groups often invited him to speak. He

*Queen Anne addressing the House of Lords,
in the early eighteenth century*

Early publication of
Rare Jewel of Christian
Contentment
LOGOS

on Philippians 4:11–13, printed as *The Rare Jewel of Christian Contentment*, became popular even to the present day. His former suffering and his newfound success had taught him how to be content in both poverty and prosperity.

After many years of preaching to small congregations or private households, his longing to accomplish much work for the Lord was finally fulfilled. Burroughs took an interest in the city's merchants and assisted them in various ways. He helped establish the Corporation for the Propagation of the Gospel in New England, which supported John Eliot's mission work to the Indians. Burroughs cared more about people's souls than political issues.

But he couldn't avoid politics completely. Conflicts between the king and Parliament led to the outbreak of civil war in 1642. What a sad time for England! Christians fought against fellow Christians as Royalist forces and the Parliament's army battled for control over political and religious matters. Not even all Puritans agreed on politics. Although most supported Parliament, many maintained loyalty to the king.

Christians debated with one another whether it was biblical to take up arms against their king. Burroughs preached a sermon showing that it could be justified if men

even addressed the House of Commons and the House of Lords on several occasions.

Burroughs's printed sermons were widely read. A friend wrote that these sermons were "twice printed," once in this godly man's life and again in his books. A series based

were not permitted to worship God freely. He said the Creator gives men their rights, and a king must rule according to godly laws. This sermon was printed and distributed all over England, encouraging those who supported Parliament and the cause of the Puritans.

Westminster Assembly

King Charles I had been waging bloody religious wars against Scotland, but Parliament wanted to sign a treaty with that country. Scotland urged Parliament to work toward religious unity by developing four things in common with the Scots: a confession, a directory of worship, a catechism, and one form of church government.

On June 12, 1643, an assembly was called to work on these matters. Burroughs was one of 121 ministers invited. Thirty men from Parliament were also to attend: twenty from the House of Commons and ten from the House of Lords. The first meeting was held on July 1, 1643, in a chapel of Westminster Abbey. That is why the meeting was called the Westminster Assembly.

Six weeks later, some Scottish ministers arrived in London to advise the Assembly. And ten days later, Parliament signed the "Solemn League and Covenant" as an agreement to work toward the "Four Points of Conformity" with Scotland.

Because of the civil war, it was sometimes difficult for the Assembly to meet. The ministers who attended were expected to be present every day during the week and continue their regular preaching schedule on Sundays. It was stressful and exhausting.

About sixty men attended regularly. Of those, only twenty-five or so contributed substantially to the discussions. Burroughs was one of them. He served on multiple committees, including one writing a confession of faith and another which presented a directory of worship to Parliament. He helped write two catechisms, the Larger for adults and the Shorter intended for children between the ages of five and thirteen. Concerned about the many congregations without pastors, he worked hard to speed up the process of ordination.

Thomas Edwards's "Gangræna," beginning the Pamphlet Wars

Although members of the Assembly agreed on matters of doctrine, conflict arose about the form of church government. Most Puritans favored Presbyterianism. Several others were Independents who supported a Congregationalist form. Burroughs was one of five who became known as the Five Dissenting Brothers. They were not mean-spirited, but they were persistent. Burroughs made every effort to get along with those who disagreed with him. The motto on his study door read: *Opinionum varieta et opinantium unitas non sunt* ασυστατα. Most of the sentence is in Latin, although the final word is Greek. The motto means, "Difference of belief and unity of believers are not incompatible." He thought Christians could hold differing opinions about some matters, as long as biblical truth was not compromised.

Burroughs and his friends wrote a document defending their view of church government, which they presented to Parliament in 1644. A man named Thomas Edwards attacked Burroughs personally for this. He even criticized his wife. While Burroughs and his colleagues chose not to respond, others did. Accusations flew back and forth in what came to be known as the "Pamphlet Wars."

Believing the root of the problem was a matter of the heart, Burroughs preached a sermon series about loving truth and peace in order to heal divisions. He wrote, "Peace is precious to me. I feel the sweetness of it and am willing to do what I can to honor it."

Many people saw his view as the remedy for conflict within the church. But Thomas Edwards continued to attack Burroughs. Fearing that Edwards was causing people to stray from the faith, Burroughs finally wrote a response. His tone was kind, but he expressed the truth honestly.

Last Days and Death

On the morning of October 30, 1646, Burroughs got on his horse and rode from home. Because it was a Friday, he most likely planned to attend the Westminster Assembly. On the way, the horse threw him, and he severely injured his back.

The following Sunday, he was unable to preach. His fever spiked, and his lungs filled. On November 11, the Westminster Assembly voted to send two men to visit him. They showed their appreciation for Burroughs and his peacemaking efforts by sending men who were Presbyterians, but also his friends.

Burroughs was ready to face death and clung to God's promises during this time of intense suffering. He had once written, "If Christ may be magnified in me, if I may be of any service for Him in any way, then I am content to live. But if it be so that He may be no more served by me here, let me die, and I shall lose nothing by that either; for that same thing you call 'death,' the thing that people make such a stir about, and are so scared about, that 'to die,' it's nothing to me, but that which will be gain." For Burroughs, like the Apostle Paul, to live was Christ and to die was gain (Phil. 1:21).

On Friday, November 13, 1646, only two weeks after his fall, he raised his eyes as if looking into heaven and said, "I come, I come, I come"—and then died.

Although Jeremiah Burroughs sometimes struggled to know God's will, he learned to trust God for whatever happened in his life. Through sermons and books, he taught thousands of people (and is still teaching them today through his reprinted books) how to enjoy genuine worship, contentment, and peace.

~ 9 ~

Thomas Goodwin

1600–1680

Overwhelmed by God's Love

Alone in a room at Christ's College in Cambridge, Thomas Goodwin closed the book he'd been reading and smiled. Skimming through John Calvin's *Institutes of the Christian Religion* was a great way to get ready for the sacrament of the Lord's Supper. How sweet to think about God's love for sinners and Christ's death for them!

Young Thomas stood and stretched. He had prepared well for his second time of participating in the Lord's Supper. He'd gone to hear Dr. Sibbes preach. The Puritan students always attended his lectures, and they seemed very confident of their salvation. He longed to share their firm assurance.

He stared at the wall, recalling the times as a little child when he'd wept over his sins or felt great love for God. Those feelings must have meant something. And when he'd participated in his first Lord's Supper at the college, he'd felt such joy and comfort when everyone sang the 103rd Psalm. He returned his book to the shelf, singing softly, "Bless the Lord, O my soul, and all that is within me, bless His holy name." This second Communion was sure to be an even better experience.

When the day of the sacrament arrived, Thomas filed into the chapel among students who towered over him. He had entered college a year younger than most and was the smallest boy in the entire university.

As he was about to receive the elements, someone tapped his shoulder. He turned in surprise. An older student leaned forward and whispered in his ear, "You must go out. Your tutor says you are too young to partake."

His face red with embarrassment, Thomas walked out in front of the assembled people. With stiff legs and a burning heart, he marched back to his room. See if he'd ever go back to hear Dr. Sibbes preach! And what was the use of studying divinity? Why even bother to pray?

For a long time, Thomas didn't pray. He avoided Puritan preachers and students. He developed friendships with boys who believed that God's grace could come and go in a person's life. After all, that seemed to be his experience. He and his friends admired Dr. Senhouse, whose less spiritual sermons demonstrated his wit and learning. Thomas decided to learn to speak like him.

Thomas Goodwin

Thomas Goodwin may have thought he was finished with Puritanism, but God wasn't finished with him. Over the next several years, the Holy Spirit gradually worked in his heart.

Goodwin sometimes felt strong emotions about God. He once heard a sermon that moved him so much, he couldn't get on his horse afterward. He stood beside it for a full five minutes, grieving his sin and weeping into the horse's mane. Another time, he and some friends headed to a party. On the way, they heard a funeral bell, and his friends persuaded him to go into the service with them. The last thing Goodwin wanted to do was listen to a sermon, but he reluctantly went along with their whim. The minister stressed that "today" was the day to believe in Christ. He seemed to speak directly to Goodwin, and the words affected him deeply.

He turned to one of his companions and said, "I hope to be the better for this sermon as long as I live." Refusing his friends' urging to go on to the party he wrote, "I thought myself to be as one struck down by a mighty power."

These occasional feelings and thoughts, however, didn't reflect a truly changed heart. He spent seven long years examining himself, searching for signs of grace in the things he did. Only when a wise man advised him to look to Jesus instead of himself did Goodwin finally experience a measure of the assurance of grace he craved. He stopped depending on himself and began trusting only in Christ and His finished work of salvation.

Goodwin's manner of preaching changed. Rather than trying to impress people with his wit or frighten them about their sins, he focused on the love and grace of Christ. He followed the advice Dr. Sibbes had once given him: "Young man, if you ever would do good, you must preach the grace of God in Christ Jesus."

Goodwin became lecturer at Trinity, received his divinity degree, and then became Trinity's vicar. But his growing Puritan convictions had not escaped the notice of Bishop Laud, who

Fourteenth-century church in Rollesby, Norfolk—
Goodwin's birthplace

brought pressure for him to resign. He wrote that he "cheerfully parted" with all because Christ had given him "the comforts and joys of his love." In God's providence, Dr. Sibbes was appointed in his place.

Goodwin moved to London and preached to Independent congregations. He kept up a lively correspondence with Independents in the Netherlands and New England. In 1638, he married Elizabeth Prescott. A year later, Goodwin was threatened with arrest for his preaching, so the Goodwins fled to the Netherlands. There he pastored a congregation of English families and settled disagreements between other English preachers.

When the Long Parliament invited Puritan exiles to return, Goodwin came back to London and formed a church. As an educated and influential preacher, he was often asked to preach before Parliament and was appointed to serve as a member of the Westminster Assembly. He became the leader of the five men known as the "dissenting brothers" and wrote most of their documents. These men had practiced an Independent form of church government in the Netherlands and favored it over the Presbyterianism proposed by most of the delegates. Goodwin is said to have written fifteen volumes of notes on the Assembly, although only three remain.

As the Assembly's work on the Westminster Confessions neared completion, Goodwin considered what to do next. John Cotton persuaded him to join the Puritans in New England. Friends and members of Goodwin's congregation begged him not to leave. By the time he finally decided to stay in London, his books were already loaded on the ship!

When Oliver Cromwell became the ruler of England, he promoted Independency as the official type of religion. Cromwell asked Goodwin to serve as one of his chaplains and as a preacher at Oxford. Parliament soon appointed Goodwin as President of Magdalene College. His greatest desire was to train godly young men

Westminster Abbey

to serve in ministry, and he worked joyfully and tirelessly in that effort.

His wife, Elizabeth, died, leaving him with a little girl, also named Elizabeth. Two years later, he married Mary Hammond, a young woman who was a helpful wife and good mother. He and Mary had two daughters, who died as infants, and two sons, who grew to adulthood. One son died on a sea voyage, but the other became a minister who would eventually take over his father's congregation.

While at Oxford, Goodwin was a colleague of John Owen. The two took turns preaching on Sunday afternoons and spent much time teaching students about God's Word. Goodwin's publisher later called the men "living and walking Bibles."

Owen was known for his bright clothes and tall boots, but Goodwin was known for his unusual hats. Sometimes he appeared to be wearing more than one, earning him the nickname "Dr. Nine Caps"!

Goodwin established an Independent congregation at Oxford. Owen shared this perspective and helped Goodwin write the Savoy Declaration. This document largely restated the Reformed theology of the Westminster Assembly, edited according to the distinctive ideas and preferences of the Independents.

After the monarchy was restored under King Charles II, Goodwin lost his position at Oxford. He and many members of his congregation moved to London.

In 1665, the Great Plague broke out there, killing about seventy thousand people. While the king and court fled the city, Goodwin and other Puritan pastors stayed to minister to the suffering. Less than a year after the Plague subsided, fire spread through the city, destroying more than thirteen thousand homes and almost ninety churches.

As the raging flames roared closer to Goodwin's home, he packed more than half of his precious books and moved them to the home of a friend, far from the fire. But the wind shifted. Goodwin's home was spared. His friend's house and Goodwin's boxed books were burned.

This great loss caused him to write a book, based on James 5, about patience under sudden and difficult trials. He continued to preach and write for twenty more years, publishing numerous books with rare biblical insight and a warm devotional tone. They have often been reprinted and are available today in twelve volumes.

When he was eighty years old, he became ill with a fever. He faced death with an assurance stronger than the longings of his youth.

Great Fire of London, 1666

"I could not have imagined I should ever have had such a measure of faith in this hour," he said. He spoke about having not his own righteousness, but the righteousness of God by faith in "Jesus Christ, who loved me, and gave himself for me. Christ cannot love me better than he does. I think I cannot love Christ better than I do. I am swallowed up in God…. Now I shall be ever with the Lord."

Goodwin died on February 23, 1679, and was buried in Bunhill Fields in London. The long Latin inscription on his tombstone praises him as a man who knew the Bible better than anyone else, who was blessed with both rich imagination and sound discernment, who could calm troubled consciences and clear confused minds. It extols his knowledge, wisdom, and eloquence, and calls him "a true Christian pastor."

Thomas Goodwin began his university education as a short boy who struggled with assurance. But he ended life as a pastor and theologian of tall stature, firmly convinced of his salvation in Christ. His focus on himself had been swallowed up by the great love of God.

~ 10 ~

John Eliot

1604–1690

Apostle to the Indians

As John Eliot and his companions rode through the woods, the cold wind swirled fallen leaves around their horses' hooves. A gust penetrated Eliot's coat, and he shivered. How would the Indians react to his preaching in their own language? Would they even understand what he was saying? He calmed his thoughts. The interpreter riding beside him could help, if necessary. Eliot prayed quietly for God to bless the day's efforts.

The weathered logs of a stockade surrounding the Indian village appeared. A few men came out to meet them, speaking words of welcome in English. They led the way to a large wigwam in a central clearing. Several Indians stood in front of it, but two caught Eliot's eye: the chieftain, Waaubon, wearing a headdress flaring with feathers, and his son, dressed in European clothes.

Waaubon had asked for his son to receive formal instruction, so he could learn about the white man's God. The young man now attended school in a nearby town, but had come home to be present for this first worship service in his father's village.

Eliot dismounted and greeted his friends in the Algonquin language. Waaubon invited the Englishmen inside the wigwam. As his eyes adjusted to the dimmer light, Eliot saw many men, women, and children sitting on the ground. The air was warm, and some had already shaken off the blankets they'd wrapped around themselves to protect against the cool fall wind.

Standing before the gathered people, Eliot began the service by praying in English. Although he had studied and translated Algonquin for many years, he didn't dare try to pray in that language.

But he felt confident enough to conduct the rest of the service in the native tongue of the listeners. He read his translation of the Ten Commandments, pausing after each to explain it briefly and simply. Then Eliot preached. He described God's creation of the world and everything in it. But the first people sinned, and God was terribly angry with all sinners. Eliot lovingly showed his listeners ways they broke the commandments every day. He told how Jesus came to earth to save people from God's wrath and eternal death. He said Christ was now in heaven but would return one day to judge all people. The earth and everything in it would burn up in fire.

John Eliot

The Indians listened intently. Eliot assured them that those who truly repented of their sin and believed in Jesus alone for salvation would be forgiven their sins. They could live forever with the Lord Jesus in the joy of heaven.

After an hour and fifteen minutes, he stopped preaching and looked at the people. "Do you understand what I've said to you?"

They answered all together, "Yes."

"Do you have any questions?"

One man asked, "How may we come to know Jesus Christ?"

"If you were able to read God's book, the Bible, you would learn all you need to know about Jesus. But because you cannot do that yet, think about what you have heard me teach out of God's book. Think about it when you lie down on your mats in your wigwams, and when you rise up. Think about it when you go alone into the fields and woods. If you meditate on it, God will teach you more, especially if you pray to Him."

Someone said, "We do not know how to pray."

Eliot replied, "Even if you only sigh or groan in your heart, God will hear you. But you can pray simple prayers. Ask God to help you know Jesus. Confess your sins and ask God to forgive them."

Another man asked, "Does God understand Indian prayers?"

"God made all men, both English and Indian. He knows all our thoughts and understands our prayers." Eliot picked up a woven basket. "This basket is made of both black and white straws. Perhaps other things that I don't know because I didn't make it. But the one who made it knows everything about what it is made of and how it was made. So God knows everything about each one of us."

The Indians asked more questions. The discussion went on for another two hours. Sometimes Eliot turned to his friends for advice or asked the interpreter about unfamiliar

John Eliot's home in England
PETER KIRK

words. But he had a good grasp of the language, and it was clear that the Indians thought highly of him.

Finally, Eliot asked, "Do you not grow weary?"

"No," they replied.

"We will come back another time," he promised. Then he closed the service with prayer.

The Englishmen gave apples to the children. They agreed with Waaubon to return in two weeks for another worship service.

The crowd was even larger for the second service. This time the Indians provided seats for their visitors.

After again opening with prayer in English, Eliot asked the children, "Who made you and all things?"

They stared at him, and he taught them to say together, "God."

Next he asked, "Why did God make you and all things?"

The children learned the answer, and repeated it: "For His glory."

John Eliot, the first missionary among the Indians

Then he asked, "How can you glorify God?"

They learned the answer: "By loving Him and doing what He commands."

Then Eliot turned to the whole group. "We are come to bring you good news from the great God Almighty, maker of heaven and earth. And to tell you how evil and wicked men may be saved and learn to live holy lives in Jesus, so that while they live they may be happy. And when they die, they may go to God and live in heaven."

At these words, an elderly man struggled to his feet. "Is it not too late for such an old man like me—who is about to die—to repent or seek after God?"

Tears shone in Eliot's eyes. "In the Bible, God tells us that we may still come to Him at the end of the day. He also tells about a father whose son had been disobedient many years, but came to his father and begged for mercy. The father forgave him and loved him. How much more God will forgive and love His children who repent and seek forgiveness in Jesus Christ!"

He looked at all the people. "Now is the day the Lord is calling you to repent. If you are truly sorry for your sins, you will surely find God's favor, even if you have lived many years in sin." He pointed to the old man. "It is not too late, as this man fears. But if you do not come when God calls you, He will be very angry with you."

The Indians wept. Eliot read from the Bible about the Valley of Dry Bones, and how the Spirit of God made them come alive. Then he preached. The meeting lasted for hours, with the people again asking many questions.

Someone asked, "Why has no white man come before to tell us these things?"

Eliot considered his answer carefully. Finally, he said the only thing he could say: "I am sorry."

———◆◆◆———

By the time Eliot conducted these worship services, he had been in America fifteen years. He'd arrived in Boston on November 3, 1631, as a single twenty-seven-year-old eager to obey God's call. His fiancée, Hannah Mumford, soon joined him in the New World, and the two were married in October 1632. It was the first wedding to take place at the church where Eliot taught in Roxbury, which was about two miles south of Boston.

A goal of the Massachusetts Bay Colony had been to share the gospel of Jesus Christ with the Indians. The colony seal even showed a Native American with outstretched arms, saying, "Come over and help us." (These words are from Acts 16:9, when God, through a vision, called Paul to missionary work in Macedonia.) But early settlers found little time for evangelizing. They initially struggled to survive harsh winters, and then they worked hard to establish churches, schools, and communities.

As the settlers lived among the natives, their views of them began to change. Indians who caused trouble or begged for handouts made some people think they were all wicked or lazy. Sadly, not many of the early ministers cared a great deal about missions to the Native Americans.

Eliot never forgot about the colony's seal, however, and his heart was touched by the poor who begged at his door. He viewed the Indians as lost souls who needed a Savior. Although he regularly preached in Roxbury and was just as busy as any minister, he traveled far each week to tell native groups about Jesus.

In fact, Eliot may have been busier than most ministers. He was highly respected and provided leadership on many civil and theological matters in the Massachusetts communities. He wrote several manuscripts and assisted in preparing the *Bay Psalm Book*, which was the first book published in New England. But Eliot is most remembered for his Algonquin translation of the Bible.

1676

Massachusetts Bay Colony Seal

Translating something into another language is always difficult and time-consuming, but it is even more difficult when the language is only spoken. And no Algonquin words had ever been written down.

A young man who had been taken captive during the Pequot War was the first Indian to help Eliot. As they spoke together, Eliot puzzled out word sounds and wrote them down. He learned more phrases each time he visited the Indians. He hoped they would remember what he told them about Jesus, but he knew they needed to

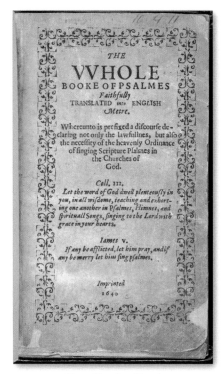

Bay Psalm Book

read God's Word for themselves. So he kept working year after year on translations. He translated the Lord's Prayer and the Ten Commandments, and then other parts of Scripture as well as simple catechism questions and answers.

When he knew the language well enough, he conducted entire worship services in the Algonquin language. God used Eliot's preaching to change the hearts of many Indians. As their hearts changed, so did their lives.

The people in Waaubon's village were first. They fenced in fields to raise crops to support their families. They set up a school for their children. Women learned to spin and weave.

Eliot advised the people to govern themselves with a system of leaders in levels, like Moses used in Exodus. They wrote laws that punished sins, such as working on the Sabbath. Eliot especially encouraged them to pray, and this new Indian community became known as a "Praying Town."

Other tribal groups asked Eliot to come and teach them. Soon a second Praying Town was formed, and then a third. Eliot traveled far and wide to bring the gospel, riding through the wilderness alone, sometimes coming into danger.

A young warrior once stopped him in the woods, threatening the minister with a drawn knife. Eliot looked him in the eye: "I am about the work of the great God, and He is with me, so that I fear neither you nor all the sachems [chieftains] of the country. I'll go on, and do you touch me if you dare."

The warrior sheathed his knife and went away. Reports of Eliot's bravery and his message of hope in Jesus spread to other tribes throughout the region. In one village, the leader encouraged his people to accept Eliot's teaching. The leader asked, "What have you gained while you have lived under the power of the higher sachems, Indian fashion? They only sought to get what they could from you." Then he added, "But the English, you see, do no such thing. Instead of taking from you, they give to you."

Some settlers did take advantage of Native Americans, and early missionaries are often criticized for making them live like Europeans. But the Indians appreciated godly men like Eliot. He loved them and treated them with respect, caring about the welfare of their souls.

Eliot was not in a hurry to gain converts. He made sure the people's faith was genuine before he baptized them. He and other English ministers listened to their personal accounts of what they believed. Then they asked questions to see how well they understood what they had been taught.

As more and more natives were converted to Christianity, word of Eliot's success spread back to England. People formed a society and raised money to help support his work. He was able to help Indians buy land and set up more Christian communities.

Despite being very ill during 1657, Eliot finished translating the entire Bible. The publication process took a long time. Political upheaval in England slowed financial support for the project. Finally, in 1663, one thousand copies were printed.

The *Mamusse Wunneetupanatamwe Up-Biblum God* became the first Bible published in the Americas. Once Native Americans could read God's Word for themselves, more and more of them came to truly believe in Jesus Christ alone for salvation. Additional Praying Towns were formed. Eliot often traveled as far as seventy miles from Boston to preach to them. It's easy to see why people called Eliot "the Apostle to the Indians."

By 1674, more than a thousand natives lived in fourteen Praying Towns. Twenty-four men had been trained as pastors. A few communities even sent out their own missionaries. Some people think as many as four thousand Native Americans were Christians. The future of Eliot's missionary efforts looked hopeful. Then disaster struck.

Tensions between colonists and natives had increased, especially with settlers taking over native lands. Sometimes treaties were ignored or the Indians were deceived. The Wampanoag tribe especially suffered. One of their leaders, calling himself King Philip, raised an army of warriors to drive the English out of the country. His men robbed and burned settlers' homes, killing entire families.

Eliot personally knew Philip. He had traveled to share the gospel with him more than once. But Philip's heart had remained hard, and he always responded with anger. One time, Philip cut a button from Eliot's jacket. He held it up and glared at the minister. "I care about your gospel as much as I care about this button," he said.

John Sausaman, a man who lived in a Praying Town, was accused of a petty crime. He left his position as schoolmaster and became Philip's trusted adviser. But his conscience and

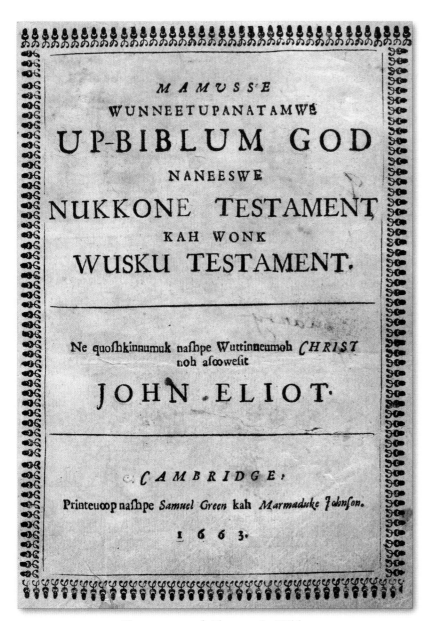

Cover page of Algonquin Bible

Eliot convinced him to return to the Christian Indians. He repented of his sins and was baptized, beginning to preach more powerfully than any other native pastor.

Philip was enraged by what he considered a terrible betrayal. Under his orders, some of his men killed Sausaman.

The Praying Indians were caught in the middle of the bloody King Philip's War. Indian forces feared they would join their English friends in battle, so the warriors wanted to kill them. Many Englishmen no longer trusted any Indians, and some of them murdered Christian Indians.

Eliot once witnessed a young colonist open fire on a Christian family, killing a child and wounding four others. The mother cried out, "Lord, Thou dost see that we have neither said nor done anything against the English, yet they thus deal with us."

One group of more than a hundred men, women, and children were ambushed as they attempted to flee to safety. No one ever heard if any survived.

About 350 inhabitants of Praying Towns were put on an island in the harbor. Some people said it was for their own protection. They suffered from a lack of food and supplies, and many died during the harsh winter. Eventually, some of the men were permitted to fight with the English, and King Philip's warriors were overcome.

But the losses were huge. Nearly six hundred English soldiers died and men, women, and children were killed in raids. About ten percent of the towns in Massachusetts were obliterated and others damaged. But no one suffered as much as the Christian Indians. Most of them died. Only four of the Praying Towns survived. Copies of the Algonquin Bible were lost or destroyed.

John Eliot preaching from his Indian Bible

Hatred for the Indians became so strong that captives from the war were sold into slavery. One vessel that could not find a buyer for its slaves left them stranded at Tangier, on the coast of Africa beside the Strait of Gibraltar. Eliot tried to arrange for their rescue, but his requests fell on deaf ears.

People in the colonies and England gave little support as Eliot tried to help the Praying Towns recover and reprint the Algonquin Bible. He had begun his missionary work on his own, and so he continued it.

No doubt he believed more than ever what he had written in an earlier letter: "I am resolved through the grace of Christ, I will never give over the work so long as I have legs to go…. If the Lord stir up the hearts of men to help me, blessed be His name and blessed be they that help me. If no man help me, yet mine eyes are to the Lord who said He will never leave or forsake me."

He continued to preach and teach in the few remaining Indian communities as well as in Roxbury. Translations still occupied much of his time. Eventually a second edition of the Algonquin Bible was printed. His famous *Indian Grammar Begun* helped English speakers learn the Algonquin language. At the end of it, he encouraged readers: "We must not sit still, and look for miracles. Up and be doing, and the Lord will be with you. Prayer and pains, through faith in Christ Jesus, will do anything."

Although Eliot is known as "the Apostle to the Indians," he also accomplished much in his colony, community, and family. He worked hard to protect the charter government of Massachusetts and Puritan theology in the New World. He established a school that accepted both black and Native American children, which was unheard of at that time. And he served as overseer at Harvard College from 1642 until 1685.

He and Hannah raised their daughter and five sons in the Lord. Three sons became ministers who were active with missions to the Indians. Sadly, all five died prior to their father. The Eliots were married for fifty-five years before Hannah died in 1687.

As Eliot grew older, he grew increasingly weak. When he could no longer preach every Sunday, he asked the people to call another minister and give him Eliot's salary. They called the man he chose, but they continued to support Eliot.

In May of 1690, Eliot became ill with a fever. He reflected on the work he most loved: "There is a cloud—a dark cloud—upon the work of the gospel among the poor Indians. The Lord revive and prosper that work, and grant it may live when I am dead." Then he said, "Alas that my doings have been poor and small and lean."

Eliot died on May 20, at the age of eighty-six—an age that very few reached in the seventeenth century. His last words were, "Welcome joy!" Then, "Pray, pray, pray!"

Though King Philip's War seemed to have brought all of Eliot's work to nothing, he saw the importance of each saved person. While he deeply grieved the lives lost during the war, he knew the souls of the Christians were eternally safe. The Indian ministry suffered a huge setback, but it was not destroyed. Who can know how many souls are now in heaven because of the way God used Eliot's decades of preaching in Roxbury and beyond?

~ 11 ~

Thomas Shepard

1605–1649

God's Story

A sudden motion nearly thrust Thomas Shepard from his bunk in the hold of the ship. Shouts and thumps sounded overhead. Leaving his wife and son below, he hurried onto deck. The dawning light revealed the danger. A fierce wind was blowing the ship straight toward the shore.

Shepard grasped the railing and struggled to keep his footing. Had he misunderstood God's will in taking his family to New England? They'd planned to leave before winter, but the ship's departure had been delayed many weeks. When it finally sailed two days earlier, storms had blown it off course. Now it appeared they would all perish.

Sailors raced about and clambered in the ropes above, shouting and straining as they tried to change direction.

"Man overboard!"

Shepard turned and scanned the ocean. A bobbing head rapidly grew smaller as the waves swept the seaman farther and farther away. The other sailors, trying frantically to turn the ship, could do nothing to save him.

A harsh sound echoed through the timbers, and the entire ship trembled. Its keel was grating against sand.

Thomas trembled too. What would happen to little Thomas and to Margaret, who was expecting their second child?

A sailor carrying a hatchet ran past Shepard. He swung it to cut a taut rope, and the ends flew apart with a loud twang. The ship groaned and shuddered free from the sand. It turned and sailed farther along the coast.

Thomas Shepard

Rescue boats arriving

An hour later, excited shouts erupted from the men high in the rigging. They had sighted their lost companion! Sailors lowered a boat with three men in it. When they reached the man floating in the water, he appeared dead. They hauled him into the boat and forced water from his lungs. He gasped and began breathing. By the time they returned to the ship, he was able to speak and walk.

The ship sped in the wrong direction all night. The next day, the captain was finally able to anchor it. Then another, even stronger, wind arose. More anchors were cast out, but the cables broke. The ship again flew toward shore.

The shipmaster cried out, "We are all dead men!"

A sailor near Shepard pointed ahead: "There will be our graves."

Two of the ship's guns were fired to signal for help. Thousands of people crowded the walls surrounding the city of Yarmouth, looking down on the vessel about to wreck. The wind and waves were too strong for any of them to attempt a rescue.

A man onboard eventually persuaded the sailors to chop down the mast. The last small anchor was thrown out, but the wind still drove the ship toward shore.

"I have done what I can." The master threw up his hands. "You must pray."

Another minister prayed with the two hundred passengers below, while Shepard prayed with the seamen on the deck. He committed their "souls and bodies unto the Lord who gave them." Immediately after prayer, the wind lessened. The anchor caught on the bottom, and its cable stretched tight. The ship slowed to a stop just short of running up on the sand.

Shepard thanked God that the small anchor and its narrow cable held the large ship in the great storm.

A man of faith pointed to the thin cable: "That thread we hang by will save us."

That night many passengers lay ill and weak on board. The following morning, the sea had calmed somewhat. Rescue boats arrived from Yarmouth. Margaret and little Thomas departed in the first. Still, he became terribly sick and suffered for two weeks before dying. He was only a year old. In a private ceremony he was buried at Yarmouth, but Shepard could not attend the funeral because men lay in wait to arrest him.

Although Shepard was crushed by the loss, he still trusted that God was in control. He used the tragedy to examine his heart and repent from his sins.

Thomas and Margaret spent the harsh winter in a vacant home provided for them in a Norfolk village. They didn't know whether to try sailing again to the New World or to remain in England and risk persecution. But God renewed their conviction that He was calling Shepard to New England. Other Puritans felt the same way and had decided to go with them.

Friends in London offered to shelter the Shepards until after their baby was born. On the way, they stayed for two weeks with their friend Jeremiah Burroughs. At his house, Margaret tumbled down the entire length of a long staircase. Her back hurt so much, everyone believed the baby had been injured. But after all seemed well, they continued their journey to London.

A boy was born on April 5, 1635, and named Thomas after the older brother, who had died. The baby soon became

House of Thomas Shepard

ill. Fearing he would lose his second son, Shepard spent all night in prayer. Little Thomas was much better in the morning.

A short time later, their hiding place was discovered. Their pursuers entered the house to find the Shepards gone. They had fled by night to another home.

On August 10, 1535, the family boarded a ship bound from London to Boston. Shepard traveled in the disguise of a farmer and under the name of his brother, John. Baby Thomas was so sickly that few of their friends expected him to survive the voyage.

The old ship's rotten timbers sprang a leak during the first storm. The captain was ready to attempt a return to port when the sailors managed to repair the ship, but the entire voyage was plagued with storms and rough weather.

Margaret cared tenderly for her sick baby day and night. Once, a violent toss of the ship threw her, with Thomas in her arms, toward a post. She was about to strike her head on an iron bolt, when it seemed as if an unseen hand pulled her back.

Worn out, Margaret became ill and steadily grew worse. As she weakened, the baby gained strength. Some nights she cried and prayed, asking God to glorify Himself through her son and to help the boy not dishonor God by a sinful life.

After fifty-four days at sea, the ship landed at Boston. The passengers soon went on to Newtown. Thomas Hooker and his company, eager to travel to the Connecticut River valley, were happy to sell their homes and properties to the newcomers.

Shepard's group settled in and formed a congregation. But Margaret was so ill that another woman cared for little Thomas. Soon after he was baptized, Margaret died.

Years later, Shepard wrote that she died at peace, having fulfilled her heart's desire to see her husband safe from his enemies while he and her son lived among God's people and under His precious rule.

For Thomas Shepard, everything that happened to him—even the bad or sad things—showed how God was writing his life's story. And his whole life was full of difficulties. Even before these voyages, he had suffered a great deal.

His mother died when he was only four years old, and his father died six years later. He endured an unkind stepmother and a harsh schoolmaster until an older brother took him in. His brother was like both father and mother to him and guided him until he attended Emmanuel College.

Although Shepard was proud and rebellious during his college years, he came to a humble and trusting faith before he graduated. He was ordained in the Church of England and preached in a small town. Shepard was not as yet committed to Puritanism, but Bishop Laud thought he was. He summoned Shepard to appear before him.

Laud didn't bother to ask about Shepard's views and barely let him speak. As he shouted at Shepard, his face grew red and he shook with anger. He pronounced his sentence: "I charge you that you neither preach, read, marry, bury, or exercise any ministerial function in any part of my diocese. For if you do, and I hear of it, I'll be upon your back, and follow you wherever you go, in any part of the kingdom, and so everlastingly disenable you."

Shepard begged him to consider his little town that would be left without a minister, but Laud cut him short and accused him of stirring up trouble. Shepard asked if he could teach catechism on Sunday afternoons, but Laud shouted: "Spare your breath." He added, "Get you gone," and told him to go complain to someone else.

Most men would be bitter at such treatment, but Shepard viewed Laud as God's tool to discipline His people.

Archbishop Laud

Instead of blaming the bishop, he blamed his own sins and thought he must be unworthy to continue preaching.

With no pulpit and no home, Shepard took up a friend's offer to live with him. People of Shepard's congregation appreciated him so much that they contributed to his support, even though he was not permitted to preach.

Having time on his hands, Shepard read the church's liturgy carefully and studied all the issues. The more he learned, the more he became convinced that the Puritans were right. Laud had been determined to stop a Puritan preacher, but what he really did—by God's providence—was create one.

Bishop Laud later visited the area and ordered Shepard to leave. During the same visit, Laud excommunicated one minister and suspended another.

Shepard agreed to go with those two men and a couple of other ministers to attempt to reason with the Bishop while he was preaching in the area. The man who had been excommunicated did not go into the church until after the service was over. But when Laud caught sight of him, he had him arrested and fined. He ordered him to appear before the Court of the High Commission for desecrating a church by his presence.

Several people urged Shepard to flee, but he wanted to help his friend. One man pulled Shepard away, just as his name was called. Laud sent a soldier to find and arrest him. But he and his rescuer mounted horses and rode away in the nick of time.

Shepard agreed to become a chaplain in a private home in Yorkshire, far from London and Laud's men. The journey took six days in cold and stormy weather. Shepard and his guides had to cross a flooded river that surged over its bridge. The two other men were swept into the water and nearly drowned. Shepard's horse slipped off the bridge, but regained its footing and carried his rider safely to the other side.

By the time Shepard reached the house in York late that night, he was wet and cold. His dismay grew when he found several people gambling there. The first night he felt he had never been "so sunk in spirit" and so far from friends.

Although his enemies had brought about what seemed like a dreadful setback, God blessed Shepard more than he could have imagined. His ministry changed many hearts within the household. One woman, Margaret, would become his wife. He later wrote that she was "a most humble woman, full of Christ, and a very discerning Christian," who was loving to him and showed a "sweet spirit of prayer."

Thomas and Margaret were married in 1632, but found no place where he could preach in peace. They moved all over the country, often staying in homes of friends, until Shepard felt the Lord calling him to ministry in New England.

Once the Shepards made their plans, they traveled in disguise to Ipswich. They remained hidden in the home of a friend for nearly two months while waiting for the ship to be ready to sail. The entire time, their pursuers prowled the town, hoping to find and arrest Shepard.

It finally appeared they would have their chance. They enlisted the aid of a young man who lived in the same house, offering him a large sum of money to open the door at a certain time one night.

But the more the young man heard Shepard speak and pray, the more he regretted his agreement. His distress became apparent to members of the household, and they questioned him. Breaking down, he tearfully confessed the whole plot.

The Shepards were whisked away to the safety of another home, with the door bolted and guarded on the appointed night. When the enemies attempted to break in, they were confronted by strong men. They fled into the night.

Perhaps Shepard hoped for some relief from trouble when he finally set sail. But those difficult voyages resulted in the deaths of his first son and Margaret. Although discouraged, Shepard trusted that all things work for good to those who love the Lord.

His trust was put to the test when little Thomas became as sick as he had been after his birth in London. Once again, Shepard feared he would die. The baby's sore mouth healed, but a white film covered his eyes. Shepard believed his poor son would be blind. He prayed with bitter tears, but finally accepted whatever happened as God's will.

After an ointment made from white paper was applied to his eyes, the child's sight was suddenly restored. Many years later, Shepard referred to this incident when he addressed his autobiography to Thomas:

> Now consider, my son, and remember to lift up thine eyes to heaven, to God, in everlasting praises of him, and dependence upon him; and take heed thou dost not make thine eyes windows of lust, but give thine eyes, nay thy heart and whole soul and body to him that hath been so careful of thee when thou couldst not care for thyself.

Shepard soon found himself facing new difficulties in the colonies. Like other ministers, he helped confront false teachings. He recommended that people who were not wholly committed to Christ should not be permitted to join existing churches.

Observing the need for higher education, he became influential in establishing Harvard College. Once the school was started at Newtown, the village name was changed to Cambridge. A man named John Harvard contributed half of his estate and his entire library of two hundred and sixty books. Although that doesn't sound like many books now, it was a huge amount for those days in New England. No wonder the college was named after him!

Harvard's first instructor wasted money and treated students cruelly. Shepard had such a trusting nature that he was not at first aware of the man's true character. He took his side in a few conflicts. It wasn't long, however, before Shepard realized how the man had deceived him. He confessed his lack of wisdom in the matter and agreed that the man should be excommunicated.

In October of 1637, Shepard married his second wife, Joanna. She was the oldest daughter of his friend, Thomas Hooker. Their first child, a boy, died at birth.

Over the next few years, the entire colony experienced severe financial problems. Colonists had earned money to feed their families by selling cattle and other products to a steady stream of new settlers. But events in England put a stop to arrivals. In 1640, King Charles I allowed Parliament to meet, ending his eleven years of personal rule. Rather than leave the country, Puritans stayed and hoped for more religious freedom.

This made money scarce in the colonies. Prices for their products dropped, and people couldn't pay their debts. Everyone suffered, especially the ministers. They were paid in grain, but not all members contributed.

Some colonists considered returning to England, while others planned to move farther south. Shepard's father-in-law, Thomas Hooker, urged him to take some families from his congregation and join him in the Connecticut River valley. Although it would be a lot of work to start over, he would have friends and relatives eager to help. Shepard's congregation, however, voted against going to Connecticut.

Harvard College in 1726

Although some people may have cheated him, Shepard didn't blame others for his problems. During this time of great financial difficulty, he and Joanna were blessed with the birth of a son, Samuel. Thomas was six years old when his brother was born. Sometime later, another son, John, was born. But he died at only four months of age. Joanna's parents, the Hookers, asked if Samuel could come and live with them. Perhaps the Shepards agreed because food was so scarce. Samuel's grandfather was very fond of him, and often wrote about him with deep affection in letters to the boy's parents.

Because some families could not afford to send their sons to Harvard College, Shepard developed a plan to fund poor students with the sale of grain contributed from throughout the colonies. Every household was asked to donate one peck of grain. People responded with enthusiasm, and his plan was a huge success.

Shepard also worked hard to establish the congregational form of church government. Some people in England misunderstood the churches in the colonies. Shepard prepared a book that corrected false assumptions and explained the biblical basis for New England beliefs and practices. He tried to show that what many had called a "New Church Way" was actually the "Old Church Way" of the Bible and godly reformers.

Shepard assisted John Eliot in his mission work among the Indians, sometimes traveling with him. He wrote an account of Eliot's work that was later published as "The Clear Sunshine of the Gospel Breaking Forth upon the Indians in New England."

Native Americans from all over New England attended the first meeting of a synod held in Cambridge because they wanted to hear the opening lecture by Eliot. Those synod meetings eventually resulted in a confession of faith known as the Cambridge Platform, which was reflected in the laws of the Commonwealth of Massachusetts and is still influential in many Congregational churches today.

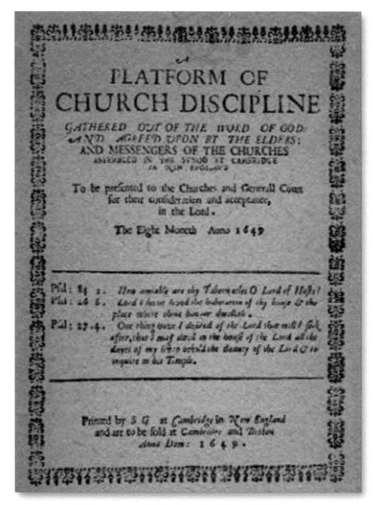

Title page of the Cambridge Platform

On April 2, 1646, Shepard suffered another heavy personal loss. Joanna died after giving birth to a son they again named John. "This affliction was very great," Shepard wrote. "She was a woman of incomparable meekness of spirit, towards myself especially, and very loving; of great prudence to care for and order my family affairs." He continued, "She loved God's people dearly, and…loved God's Word exceedingly, and had a spirit of prayer, beyond ordinary."

Shepard married one more time. On September 8, 1647, he and Margaret Boradel were united in marriage. Their son, Jeremiah, was born on August 11, 1648.

Only a year later, Shepard caught a cold when returning from a meeting of ministers in another village. His fever spiked and he developed quinsy, an abscess of the tonsils.

Knowing the end was near, he dictated his last will and testament. In it, he left a few things to friends and provided for his wife and four sons. At that time, Thomas was fourteen, Samuel was nearly eight, John was three, and Jeremiah had just turned one.

Shepard also wanted to provide for the spiritual welfare of the church he was leaving behind. He urged his friend, Jonathan Mitchel, to take over that ministry.

He told another pastor at his bedside, "Your work is great and calls for great seriousness. As to myself, I can say three things: that the study of every sermon cost me tears; that before I preached a sermon, I got good by it myself; and that I always went up into the pulpit, as if I were to give up my account to my master."

Shortly before he died, he told those gathered around him, "O love the Lord Jesus Christ very much! That little part which I have in him, is no small comfort to me now."

The Lord delivered Thomas Shepard from all his troubles on August 25, 1649. He was only forty-four years old.

Thomas Shepard's impact lived on in the New World, particularly through the influence of Jonathan Edwards and through Shepard's well-known books: *The Ten Virgins*, *The Sincere Convert*, and *The Sound Believer*. These books examine the reader's conscience very carefully, but also demonstrate the Holy Spirit's work in reconciling sinners to God. They have often been reprinted down to the present day.

Although Mitchel felt unqualified to replace Shepard as the church's minister, the congregation eventually persuaded him to do so. They appreciated him because he was so similar to Shepard in his humility and godliness.

Margaret, Shepard's widow, must have also appreciated Mitchel's good character. She later married him.

John apparently died when he was only twelve or thirteen; their other three sons graduated from Harvard and became ministers. Samuel died when he was twenty-seven, and Thomas died at forty-three. Jeremiah served as a minister for forty-one years and died when he was seventy-two. Shepard would have rejoiced to see his sons in the ministry. His desire had always been for God's covenant promises to come to fruition in the lives of his children.

Shepard's journal describes almost continual sorrows and trials. But it also shows how much he saw God's providential hand in every event. He often grieved over his sin or felt unworthy, but he also expressed great joy in God's mercy and grace. As he recorded his thoughts and circumstances, he demonstrated a keen awareness that God was writing his life story and all of history.

~ 12 ~

Thomas Brooks

1608–1680

Soul Servant

The ship lurched, and Thomas Brooks steadied the inkwell in its holder on his desk. The calls of the sailors on deck filtered down to him in the hold. But no one shouted that another ship had been sighted. Not a fight this time. He relaxed. It was probably only a stronger wind filling the sails.

He dipped his quill's tip into the pot and continued writing:

Satan loves to sail with the wind, and to suit men's temptations to their conditions and inclinations. If they are prosperous, he will tempt them to deny God (Proverbs 30:9). If they are in adversity, he will tempt them to distrust God. If they know little, he will tempt them to small thoughts of God. If their conscience is tender, he will tempt them to be too strict. If their conscience is lenient, he will tempt them to fleshly security. If they are bold-spirited, he will tempt to presumption. If fearful, to desperation. If flexible, to inconsistency. If peaceful, to be unrepentant.

Brooks paused. The ship rocked and creaked. It seemed so tiny, bobbing over the immense depths of the ocean. But how much greater were Christ and heaven!

He wrote, "It is as easy to contain the sea in a nutshell—as to relate fully Christ's excellencies or heaven's happiness."

Heaven was often on his mind during these days of civil war. The naval vessel in which he sat might be attacked any moment. Cannonballs could splinter wooden timbers or human bones. He shuddered. The threat of sin was every bit as real.

"The only way to avoid cannon shot is to fall down," he wrote. "The best way to be freed from temptation is to keep low." He thought of the sailors who wasted their money on drink and riotous living when they went ashore. They would be much better off to avoid the temptations of such places.

And how frightened they became during storms! A recent tempest had raged all through one long night and into the next day. Some of the sailors were so terrified they looked like dead men. If only they had the assurance of salvation and the hope of heaven! Compared to eternal happiness, life on

Thomas Brooks

earth was as short as a stormy night. He inserted his quill into ink and wrote once more.

This short storm will end in an everlasting calm. This short night will end in a glorious day that shall never end. It is but a very short time between grace and glory, between our title to the crown and our wearing the crown, between our right to the heavenly inheritance and our possession of the heavenly inheritance.

Brooks leaned back and closed his eyes, filled with thanks to God for the comfort and help of His wonderful promises.

———❖◆❖———

Most of what we know about Thomas Brooks is what can be gleaned from his writings. His parents were likely Puritans of moderate means, who sent him to Emmanuel College when he was about seventeen. At that time, John Preston was Emmanuel's headmaster, and Richard Sibbes preached there. Brooks probably knew three classmates who later became important leaders in New England: John Cotton, Thomas Hooker, and Thomas Shepard.

Brooks enjoyed studying the Bible in Hebrew and Greek, the languages in which it was first written. He said, "I am a lover of the tongues, and do by daily experience find that knowledge in the original tongues is no small help for the understanding of Scripture."

Chaplain on Land and Sea

Soon after his years at Emmanuel, Brooks spent time with the English fleet and the Parliamentary army. He once wrote, "I have been some years at sea, and through grace, I can say that I would not exchange my sea experiences for England's riches." He obviously enjoyed and valued this nautical time period, traveling to far countries, meeting and observing people of different backgrounds and various religions. He ministered to sailors, passengers, and many others in distant lands. With some, he formed long-lasting friendships.

Brooks saw action during the English Civil War as chaplain to Colonel Thomas Rainsborough, whom he came to admire. Colonel Rainsborough was murdered by

English fleet at sea in the 1600s

Colonel Rainsborough

an act of treachery at Doncaster on October 29, 1648.

On short notice, Brooks was asked to preach at his November 14 funeral. Due to the late request and other pressing demands, Brooks had only a few hours to prepare. Although most of his sermon focused on the glorious resurrection of the saints, Brooks spoke briefly near the end about Rainsborough. He referred to the Colonel as an "honored champion," who "enjoyed God." He spoke of being with him a long time "both at sea and on land." Having known the Colonel so

well and being sure of his faith comforted Brooks. He said it gave him "abundance of sweetness and satisfaction in my own spirit, which to me exceedingly sweetens so great a loss."

Preacher and Author

By the time Brooks preached at Colonel Rainsborough's funeral, he was the minister at St. Thomas Apostle Church in London. That sermon was his first published work, even though he had not intended for the hastily written oration to be printed. He dedicated the publication to the "Right Honorable Thomas, Lord Fairfax, Lord General of all the Parliament's Forces in England," who apparently was a close friend.

About a month after Rainsborough's funeral, Brooks preached before the House of Commons for the first time. He was asked to deliver another sermon there on October 8, 1650, in a ceremony celebrating Oliver Cromwell's victory over Scottish forces at Dunbar.

Despite such honors and influential friends, Brooks remained a humble man, staying busy as a pastor and author. Like most other Puritan writers, he never listed an academic degree on the title pages of his books. He referred to himself simply as "Preacher of the Gospel" or "Preacher of the Word."

Soon after Brooks became the minister at St. Margaret's Church on New Fish Street Hill, he ran into trouble when he refused to administer the sacraments to those whose lives did not demonstrate a true conversion to God. Many members of the church tried to have Brooks removed, but they did not succeed. He wrote an extensive document addressing their accusations, which was later published as "Cases Considered and Resolved." This document shows his concern for the souls of those under his care. He signed it: "Your real friend and soul's servant." The large St. Margaret's congregation was a heavy burden, but he continued as its pastor for ten years.

During this decade, his sermons and other writings were regularly printed. *Precious Remedies against Satan's Devices* appeared in 1652, and *Heaven on Earth*, a classic on assurance of faith, was printed in 1654. Publications in 1657 included *Unsearchable Riches*, *Apples of Gold*, and *String of Pearls*. *Mute Christian under the Rod* and *The Believer's Last Day, His Best Day* were published in 1660.

It was probably during his time at St. Margaret's that he married a woman named Martha Burgess.

London Adversities

In 1662, Brooks was one of two thousand nonconforming ministers who were removed from their churches. His farewell sermon to the members of St. Margaret's contains no words of bitterness or ill will. Remaining in London, he preached unofficially at a building in Moorfields and continued writing, publishing *Ark for All God's Noahs* and *The Crown and Glory of Christianity* in 1662. Somehow Brooks was able to evade persecution, but he couldn't avoid London's Great Plague or its Great Fire.

The Plague took thousands of lives in 1665. Ministers deserted their posts and fled the city. But not Brooks. He stayed to provide spiritual care to his suffering congregation and many other people. He wrote *The Key of Heaven* and *A Heavenly Cordial for the Plague* in 1665.

The next year, a terrible fire destroyed much of London. St. Margaret's was the first of nearly ninety church buildings to burn. St. Thomas Church was also destroyed. After the fire, Brooks dared to preach more openly. Many copies of the books he'd written had been lost in the fire, but he wrote more books. *Cabinet of Jewels* was published in 1669.

A
GOLDEN KEY
TO OPEN
Hidden Treasures,
OR

Several great Points, that refer to the Saints prefent blefſednefs, and their future happineſs, with the refolution of feveral important queſtions.

Here you have alſo

The Active and Paſſive Obedience of Chriſt vindicated and improved, againſt men of corrupt minds, &c. Who boldly, in Pulpit and Preſs, contend againſt thofe glorious Truths of the Gofpel.

You have farther

Eleven ferious fingular Pleas, that all fincere Chriſtians may fafely and groundedly make, to thofe ten Scriptures in the Old and New Teſtament, that fpeak of the general Judgment, and of that particular Judgment, that muſt certainly pafs upon them all immediately after death,

The Godhead and Manhood of Chriſt, is here largely proved, and improved againſt all Gainfayers, by what names and titles foever they are diſtinguifhed and known among us. Several things concerning Hell, and hellifh torments, opened, cleared and improved againſt all Atheiſts, and all others that boldly affert, that there is no Hell, but what is in us. Some other points of importance are here cleared and opened, which other Authors* (fo far as the Author hath read) have paſſed over them in great filence, all tending to the confirmation of the ſtrong, and fupport, peace, comfort, fettlement and fatisfaction of poor, weak, doubting, trembling, ſtaggering Chriſtians.

By *Tho. Brooks* late Preacher of the Gofpel, at *Margarets-New-Fiſh-ſtreet.*

LONDON,
Printed for *Dorman Newman*, at the King's-Arms in the *Poultrey*; and at the Ship and Anchor, at the Bridg-foot, on *Southwark* fide, 1675.

Cover page to an early publication of Brooks's classic
A Golden Key

The Great Fire of London
CREDIT: MUSEUM OF LONDON

His reflections about the Great Fire appeared in *London's Lamentations*, which was published in 1670.

Later Years

Although Brooks was growing old, he continued to preach and write. The dedications he wrote for his books or those of other ministers indicated his close relationships with prominent people. He wrote that he had "troops of friends."

When Brooks was sixty-four years old, he received a license to preach under the Declaration of Indulgence. But his license was revoked only four years later in 1676. Two more of his books, *A Golden Key* and *Paradise Opened*, were printed the same year.

That was also the year he lost his wife, Martha. He thought highly of her and published an account of her Christian experiences. He wrote, "She was always best when she was most with God in a corner. She has many a whole day been pouring out her soul before God for the nation, for Zion, and the great concerns of her own soul."

A year or two later, he married a young woman named Patience Cartwright. He apparently didn't have any children or other relatives, but God fulfilled his desire for a family by providing him with this second wife. In his will, he called her his "dear and honored wife whom God has made all relations to meet in one."

Brooks died on September 27, 1680, at the age of seventy-two. He was buried in Bunhill Fields, a cemetery in London where many other nonconformist ministers were laid to rest. In the funeral sermon, John Reeve spoke about Brooks's personal traits: sweet nature, great gravity, large charity, wonderful patience, and strong faith. Reeve also talked about his experience, hard work, success, and delight in his ministerial work. He concluded, "And now he is at rest. And though he is gone, he is not lost. He is yet useful to the Church of God, and being dead he yet speaks by his example and writings, which were very profitable and spiritual."

The books written by Brooks, containing winsome figures of speech and vivid comparisons, remain popular today. They reveal how well he knew the Bible and how much he cared for people. A fellow minister once said about Brooks, "He had a body of divinity in his head and the power of it in his heart."

Thomas Brooks enjoyed rich experiences and influential friends, but he considered himself only as a servant called by God to care for souls.

~ 13 ~

Anne Bradstreet

1612–1672

Pilgrim Poet

A thundering noise woke Anne Bradstreet. Dreadful shrieks echoed through the house: "Fire! Fire!"

She jumped from bed, her heart thumping. An orange glow confirmed her worst fear—the house was burning. She cried, "Oh, God! Help me!"

Anne raced to the cradle to snatch up her granddaughter. She grasped her ill daughter-in-law's arm, and they ran through the noise and heat to stumble out the door. In the clearing, a safe distance from the inferno, they stopped and gasped deep breaths of cold air. Then Anne turned to watch the horrible destruction.

Fierce flames leaped high into the night sky, roaring as they devoured the sawn log timbers. Anne shivered in her thin nightgown. Tears ran down her face.

She and her husband had worked hard to make the wooden structure into a home. They had spent years gathering things to help them survive the harsh wilderness and make their lives more comfortable. Now her precious papers and books, the clothing she'd sewn, and the furniture her husband had made—all disappeared as quickly as the red sparks shooting up and fading away in the darkness.

This was the home where Anne had lived for nearly twenty years, the longest of any house during her lifetime. The home where three of her children and two of her grandchildren had been born. Where her oldest son and his wife had been married. Where friends had feasted, conversations had flowed, and dreams had become reality.

Anne's spirit darkened like the black smoke billowing over the New England village of North Andover. She couldn't bear to watch any longer.

Covering her face she turned away, but she whispered into her hands: "The Lord giveth, the Lord taketh away. Blessed be the name of the Lord."

―――――◆◆◆―――――

Anne's parents, Thomas and Dorothy Dudley, prized Puritan ideals and taught their children to apply Scripture to all of life. Even as a little girl, Anne felt troubled when she told a lie or disobeyed her parents. She found comfort

Anne Bradstreet

in confessing to God and reading the Bible. The better she understood God's Word, the more peace she felt.

Like many other women, Anne's mother instructed her from a young age on how to be godly and care for a home. But Anne's father was different from the men of his day. He taught his daughter how to read and—what was even more rare—how to write.

He encouraged Anne to study history, languages, literature, and poetry. During the years when her father managed an earl's estate, she read many books in the manor's well-stocked library. She was an intelligent girl who received an unusually good education.

When she was ten years old, her father hired Simon Bradstreet to assist him. Because he was nine years older than Anne, he probably first considered her only as one of the children playing on the grounds or eating in the servants' hall. But as she matured, he came to appreciate her quick mind and godly character. Anne liked kind and cheerful Simon from the start, but when she was fifteen, she experienced new feelings for him.

Then Anne became ill with smallpox. People often died from this dreadful disease, and those who survived usually had scars on their faces. Anne begged the Lord for healing and asked Him to forgive her sins. She slowly began to recover.

Simon had been praying for God to heal Anne too. Before she completely recovered, he asked her father's permission to marry her. Anne and Simon were married when she was sixteen years old.

The Bradstreets were happy together. As the months grew into years, only one thing spoiled Anne's joy. She and

Simon Bradstreet

Simon did not have any children. She pleaded with the Lord to grant her this desire.

Then another concern arose. The king put pressure on Puritans, even throwing some in prison. Anne's father and Simon began meeting with other men to discuss establishing a Puritan settlement in the New World. Anne's heart trembled at the thought of leaving her beloved home and country.

The organizers of the Massachusetts Bay Colony sent an advance party to clear land, build houses, and plant crops.

The Bradstreets and Dudleys would join the next group to sail. Anne soon found herself boarding the ship *Arbella*, part of the Winthrop fleet carrying seven hundred colonists to America.

The *Arbella* had barely reached the open seas when the lookout shouted: "Sails, ahoy! No markings!"

Fear rose in every heart. Did the ships carry pirates? Everyone rushed into action. Sailors loaded the cannons. Colonists strapped on swords and loaded muskets. Some of the sailors hurried through the hold, grabbing everything that might catch fire, disastrous on a wooden ship. They climbed the ladders and ran onto the deck to toss warm blankets and fine linens over the railing. Women had no time to watch their precious things sink lazily into the deep. They gathered up the children and descended below, where they huddled in prayer. Above their heads, footsteps pounded and men shouted. Then the flurry on the deck quieted.

In the dark and stuffy hold, Anne and the other women wondered what was happening. Were the pirates sailing closer, preparing to board? They prayed more fervently for God to rescue them.

Shouts rang out, but the women couldn't understand the words. Finally, a sailor called down the hatch. "All clear! The ships are friendly."

Tears of relief sprang into the women's eyes. They clutched their children in joy and thanked the Lord.

Although those ships proved to be no threat, the sailors and colonists remained alert for danger. Pirates or bad weather could descend any time, and it was common for people to die during the voyage and be buried at sea.

Burial at Sea
CREDIT: COPYRIGHT ©2015 BY P. J. LYNCH.
REPRODUCED BY PERMISSION OF THE PUBLISHER, CANDLEWICK PRESS, SOMERVILLE, MA.

After nearly three months, the ship dropped anchor. But the settlement was not at all what the travelers expected. Most of the advance party had died from illness or starvation during the harsh winter. Only a few crude huts had been constructed, and food was scarce. Anne and some other women discovered wild strawberries growing in the forest, but they also discovered fierce insects they'd never seen before—mosquitoes!

The leaders decided to settle downriver in the established village of Charlestown. Yet this was little more than a group of huts with dirt floors. The Bradstreets and six members of the Dudley family crowded together into one small house. Food was in short supply, and deaths occurred nearly every day.

To unite the people and boost their spirits, the leaders wrote a statement for the colonists to sign, showing their commitment to God and each other. Anne fought a silent battle within herself. She longed for the familiar ways of England and her old church home. How could she commit to this harsh new world and a new manner of worship?

As she always had, Anne laid her concerns before the Lord. She became convinced that this new life was God's will, and she joined the church.

During the first cruel winter, more than two hundred of the group returned to England. Another two hundred died. The Dudley and Bradstreet families moved inland and were settled in new homes by the second winter. Anne probably exhausted herself trying to prepare her household for the severe weather. In January, she became ill with fever and coughing. She felt sure she was dying, and she later wrote a poem reflecting those thoughts:

> My race is run, my thread spun,
> Lo, here is fatal death.
> All men must die, and so must I;
> This cannot be revoked.

But her poem went on to confess her hope in a glorious future beyond compare to this life:

> Yet live I shall, this life's but small,
> In place of highest bliss,
> Where I shall have all I can crave,
> No life is like to this.

Anne's poem showed how God had used her illness to bring her closer to Him. In those difficult days of forging a home in an unfamiliar world, Anne began to put her mind as well as her hands to work. She wrote poetry that demonstrated her knowledge of Latin, literature, and history. She wrote about current events in England and the relationship between that country and the colonists, sometimes praising her heroine, Queen Elizabeth. Her poems described her feelings and faith in poignant lines:

> I have a shelter from the storm,
> A shadow from the fainting heat,
> I have access unto His throne,
> Who is a God so wondrous great.
>
> Oh hast Thou made my pilgrimage
> Thus pleasant, fair, and good,
> Blessed me in youth and elder age,
> My Baca made a springing flood.

O studious am what I should do
To show my duty with delight;
All I can give is but Thine own
And at the most a simple mite.

The word "Baca" refers to Psalm 84:6 and means "a wilderness that God has made fertile." Anne surely saw such transformation every year the colonists grew larger gardens and better crops. These stanzas show how she trusted and adored God, and how she humbly delighted in serving Him to the best of her ability.

Five long years after Anne and Simon were married, God finally blessed them with a baby boy. He was the first of eight children, four boys and four girls. All would live to become adults, which was extremely rare in that place and time. Much later in Anne's life, she wrote a letter to her children, describing her desires for them:

> It pleased God to keep me a long time without a child, which was a great grief to me, and cost me many prayers and tears before I obtained one, and after him gave me many more, of whom I now take the care, that as I have brought you into the world, and with great pains, weakness, cares, and fears brought you to this, I now travail in birth again of you till Christ be formed in you.

Anne wanted her children to know that, while she suffered much in waiting for them to be born and in rearing them through many dangers, she now longed for each of them to love and serve Jesus Christ.

The Dudley and Bradstreet families moved several times to unsettled areas. After each difficult move, Anne

Anne Bradstreet and her husband, Simon, going to church

started over with setting up the home and caring for her growing family. Simon became a leader in the colony and frequently traveled to other areas to deal with important matters. Because he was sometimes away for weeks or months at a time, Anne learned how to manage business affairs as well as the home.

She didn't mind all the extra work, but she missed him when he was away. She wrote beautiful poems celebrating their love. One began with her declaration of their great affection for each other:

> If ever two were one, then surely we.
> If ever man were loved by wife, then thee.
> If ever wife was happy in a man,
> Compare with me, ye women, if you can.

THE TENTH MUSE *John Brand 1795.*
Lately sprung up in AMERICA.
OR
Severall Poems, compiled
with great variety of VVit
and Learning, full of delight.
Wherein especially is contained a com-
pleat discourse and description of
The Four {Elements,
Constitutions,
Ages of Man,
Seasons of the Year.
Together with an Exact Epitomie of
the Four Monarchies, viz.
The {Assyrian,
Persian,
Grecian,
Roman.
Also a Dialogue between Old England and
New, concerning the late troubles.
With divers other pleasant and serious Poems.
By a Gentlewoman in those parts.
Printed at London for Stephen Bowtell at the signe of the
Bible in Popes Head-Alley. 1650.

1650 printing of Anne Bradstreet's book of poems

I prize thy love more than whole mines of gold,
Or all the riches that the East doth hold.

Despite his frequent absences, Anne was sure no other woman could be as happy in her marriage as she was with Simon. In another beautiful poem, Anne described him as her sun and expressed her longing for his return:

If two be one, as surely thou and I,
How stayest thou there, whilst I at Ipswich lie?
So many steps, head from the heart to sever
If but a neck, soon should we be together:
I, like the earth this season, mourn in black,
My Sun is gone so far in's zodiac….
Flesh of thy flesh, bone of thy bone,
I here, thou there, yet both but one.

During Simon's absences, Anne found comfort in caring for her children. When they were older, she wrote a poem describing them as "eight birds hatched in one nest." She expressed her concern for them as they ventured into the world and the hope that they would convey the things she had taught them to their own children. The poem ends:

Farewell, my birds, farewell, adieu,
I happy am, if well with you.

Anne showed her poetry to her friends and family, but never sought publication. When her brother-in-law needed to travel to England, however, he took many of her poems with him. Unknown to Anne, he arranged for a book of her poems to be published.

Anne's surprise at receiving the book was only marred by her dismay in seeing all the mistakes in it. She set about making revisions and continued to write new poems, likely committing each poem to memory before writing it down. Anne didn't have a computer to cut and paste text, or even a notebook with many sheets for starting over. Paper was so costly and rare that Anne had to know exactly what she was going to write before putting pen to parchment.

Anne's most heartfelt poetry mourns her losses. Three grandchildren died at a very young age. She lost a fourth grandchild only a few days after birth, when both her daughter-in-law and the baby passed away.

After fire destroyed Anne's longtime home, she undoubtedly was overwhelmed at the thought of starting housekeeping again with nothing. But she lost more than furniture and bedding. It seems her revisions and some new poetry burned as well. She wrote:

> When by the ruins oft I past
> My sorrowing eyes aside did cast,
> And here and there the places spy
> Where oft I sat and long did lie:
> Here stood that trunk, and there that chest,
> There lay that store I counted best.

What had she stored in the chest that she counted best? Very likely her poetry, written with careful thought and planning during her few free hours in the night, while her family slept.

Anne's poem acknowledges that everything she had belonged to God:

> It was His own; it was not mine.
> Far be it that I should repine;
> He might of all justly bereft
> But yet sufficient for us left.

The Bradstreet's North Andover, Massachusetts home

While Anne grieved the losses, she trusted God to provide what her family needed. She ended the poem by reminding herself of her mansion in glory:

> Thou hast a house on high erect
> Framed by that mighty Architect,
> With glory richly furnished,
> Stands permanent though this be fled.
> It's purchased and paid for too
> By Him who hath enough to do.
> A price so vast as is unknown
> Yet by His gift is made thine own;
> There's wealth enough, I need no more,
> Farewell, my pelf [material goods],
>   farewell my store.
> The world no longer let me love,
> My hope and treasure lies above.

Does your hope and treasure lie above? Do you, like Anne, look forward to your heavenly home? The older she became and the more she struggled with ill health, the more eagerly she anticipated her eternal rest. One of her last poems reflects her longing:

> Oh, how I long to be at rest
>   And soar on high among the blest.
> This body shall in silence sleep,
>   Mine eyes no more shall ever weep,
> No fainting fits shall me assail,
>   Nor grinding pains my body frail,
> With cares and fears ne'er cumb'red be
>   Nor losses know, nor sorrows see.
> What though my flesh shall there consume,
>   It is the bed Christ did perfume,
> And when a few years shall be gone,
>   This mortal shall be clothed upon.
> A corrupt carcass down it lays,
>   A glorious body it shall rise.
> In weakness and dishonor sown,
>   In power 'tis raised by Christ alone.
> Then soul and body shall unite
>   And of their Maker have the sight.
> Such lasting joys shall there behold
>   As ear ne'er heard nor tongue e'er told.
> Lord, make me ready for that day,
>   Then come, dear Bridegroom, come away.

Anne expresses her desire to be free from the pain and sorrow of this world, but especially her hope for the resurrection. She didn't fear the grave, thinking of it as a bed Christ had perfumed by His own death and resurrection. She knew her body would be reunited with her soul when Christ returned in all His glory. Like Job, she was confident that one day she would see her Redeemer (Job 19:25–27).

Anne Bradstreet may have been a reluctant pilgrim to the New World, but she became America's first poet and the first woman whose poetry was published in England. Her popularity is all the more remarkable because she composed poems during a time when women were not considered capable of literary efforts. And she wrote poetry while raising eight children and making a home in the New England wilderness. But the most important thing about Anne Bradstreet was how she strove to serve God with a submissive spirit and humble heart. She realized her whole life was a pilgrimage toward her true home.

Richard Baxter

1615–1691

God's Pen

Snow fell on Richard Baxter's shoulders and muffled his horse's hoofbeats. Bridle rings jingled, and the horse's breath blew misty puffs in the icy air.

Baxter reflected aloud about the court life he'd left behind: "A stage play instead of a sermon on the Lord's Day! And what little preaching I heard was all against the Puritans."

The horse, his only audience, responded by shaking snowflakes from its mane.

Baxter patted the animal's neck. "My mother's illness grieves me, but I confess it is a great relief to leave London in order to go to her."

Creaking noises reached Baxter's ears, and huge shapes loomed ahead of him in the falling snow. A team of strong horses strained against the harness as they pulled a load closer every second. The rumbling wagon took up the entire road, blocking Baxter's way. He glanced at the hills rising on both sides. One looked less steep. He quickly kicked his heels against the horse and urged it up the bank. The girth, binding the saddle around the horse's belly, broke. The saddle suddenly slid down the horse's side, throwing Baxter through the air. He plummeted onto the frozen snow directly in front of the wagon's crunching wheel. He closed his eyes.

Everything became quiet, and Baxter opened his eyes. The motionless wheel stood nearly touching his body. There had been no time for the wagon driver to pull the reins or shout commands, but the horses had stopped.

Baxter whispered, "I thank thee, Lord God, for preserving my life."

His Writing

After the saddle was repaired, Baxter was able to ride on through the storm to his home. The groans of his ill mother greeted him at the door. He had always been sickly himself, but he spent many hours caring for her. From December until April, snow continued to fall. The long winter gave him plenty of time to think about how God had spared his life. He decided to use his talents to serve others and the Lord. The best gift God had given him was the ability to write.

Baxter had received a rather poor education, but he now began teaching himself and engaged in writing. After his mother's death, he focused even more on his studies. When he was twenty-three, a bishop ordained him to become a schoolmaster. He often preached to local people and soon became an assistant minister.

His Ministry

When he was twenty-five, Baxter was asked to preach in the town of Kidderminster. Civil war disrupted his quiet life of preaching and writing. He advocated moderate Puritan views, but so many people in the city favored the Royalist cause that his life was in danger. He went away for a month. Things were even worse on his return, however, and he left again.

On October 23, 1642, he was preaching for a friend in Alcester when the sound of cannon fire interrupted his sermon. The noise grew louder all day, until soldiers fleeing through town at sunset shouted about the Parliament army being defeated. At four the next morning, a messenger reported that the King's army had been routed. Eager to know which side was actually winning, Baxter set out for the site of the battle.

He came upon the Parliamentary army and later described the scene. "I found the Earl of Essex, with the remaining part of his army, keeping the ground, and the King's army facing them upon the hill about a mile off. There were about a thousand dead bodies in the field between them; and many I suppose were buried before."

This was not the last he would see of war. The Governor of the city of Coventry asked Baxter to stay at his home and preach to soldiers. Baxter enjoyed a quiet life for a couple of years, but then he felt led by God to serve as a chaplain with Parliament's New Model Army under Oliver Cromwell. The soldiers held many different theological convictions, and

Richard Baxter

Baxter's house in Bridgnorth

Baxter was distressed to see Cromwell promoting men with unbiblical beliefs. Baxter also grieved the loss of life he witnessed during this time. He later wrote, "O the sad and heart-piercing spectacles that mine eyes have seen in four years space! I went scarce a month, scarce a week without the sight and noise of blood."

Baxter's poor health couldn't bear the strain of military life, and he eventually collapsed. Some friends took him into their home and cared for him. While he lay ill, certain he was dying, he did the only thing he was able to do. He picked up his pen. He wrote the first part of *The Saints' Everlasting Rest*, which reflects in moving language on the glories of heaven. The book was reprinted dozens of times over the years and remains popular today.

When Baxter had recovered sufficiently, he returned to Kidderminster. He and an assistant visited fourteen families each week. So many people came to hear him preach that five balconies needed to be installed in the building. The character of the entire town changed. When he first came to the area, only about one family per street worshipped God. By the time he left, every family on some streets attended services. Hundreds were converted, which changed their behavior. He wrote, "On the Lord's day there was no disorder to be seen in the streets; but you might have heard a hundred families singing psalms and repeating sermons, as you passed through them."

Baxter distributed most of his earnings to poor people. If they didn't have a Bible, he gave them one. With the aid of wealthier friends, he sent promising students to the university.

Pain and weakness kept Baxter from being as productive as he would have liked. Yet he managed to write an extraordinary number of books and letters. A sense of death's nearness gave him an urgency to make use of every minute he was able to work. In a poem, he once wrote:

I preached, as never sure to preach again
And as a dying man to dying men.

During his fourteen years at Kidderminster, he published an abundance of written works. His well-known *The Reformed Pastor* encouraged ministers to be humble and sincere, applying their sermons to their own hearts. He urged them to spend many

Gildas Salvianus;

THE REFORMED PASTOR.

Shewing the nature of the Pastoral work; Especially in Private Instruction and Catechizing.

With an open CONFESSION of our too open SINS.

Prepared for a day of Humiliation kept at *Worcester*, Decemb. 4. 1655. by the Ministers of that County, who subscribed the Agreement for Catechizing and Personal Instruction, at their entrance upon that work.

By their unworthy fellow-servant

Richard Baxter.

Teacher of the Church at *Kederminster*.

The second Edition, with an Appendix, in answer to some Objections.

Luke 12. 47. [Ἐκεῖνος ὃ ὁ δῦλ⊖ ὁ γνὺς τὸ θέλημα τῶ κυρίε ἑαυτῦ, ⧵ μὴ ἑτοιμάσας, μηδὲ πιήσας πρὸς τὸ θέλημα αὐτῦ, δαρήσεϳ πολλάς.]

London, Printed by *Robert white*, for *Nevil Simmons*, Book-seller at *Kederminster*, and are to be sold by *Joseph Nevill*, at the Plough in *Pauls* Church-Yard. 1657.

Title page of The Reformed Pastor

hours studying God's Word and praying, because people "will likely feel when you have been much with God." He wrote, "In preaching, there is intended a communion of souls, and a communication of somewhat from ours unto theirs."

After the restoration of the monarchy, when Charles II became king in England, things changed for Baxter. He respected the new government and worked hard to unite Protestants of opposing political views, but all his efforts seemed to have no effect. Worse yet, he was prohibited from preaching and removed from his position in Kidderminster. He went to London. Two members of his congregation, a young woman and her mother, followed him there.

His Marriage

Margaret Charlton was twenty-one years younger than Baxter, but she had her heart set on him. And she was a godly woman of good character. After the two were married in 1662, they moved many times to try to find a place where he could preach in peace. Once they settled in Acton, Baxter picked up his pen and wrote more than ever.

He also preached in private homes. While he was administering the Lord's Supper one day, a loud shot shattered the somber mood. A bullet flew through the window and past Baxter. His sister-in-law screamed and fell to the floor. Everyone crowded around her. The shot had narrowly missed her head. She was shaken, but not hurt.

Even though it was dangerous and illegal, Baxter continued preaching, especially in his own home. The door to his house faced the door of the church. Many people gathered to hear him preach, and then they all walked over to the church service together. After the service, they returned to Baxter's house. The local parson became jealous and soon caused trouble for Baxter.

He was arrested, and Margaret went with him to jail. She brought along many housekeeping items and made their stay quite comfortable,

Margaret asking Baxter to marry her

although he suffered from the summer heat and often woke at night from the noise of prisoners on the floor below.

After his release, the Baxters moved to Totteridge, where they rented a place for the winter. But they were miserable. The chimney didn't work properly and allowed smoke to drift into the cold, drafty rooms. Such unhealthy conditions aggravated Baxter's medical problems, and he suffered severe pain. The following summer they moved to a different house.

After a new law permitted Puritans to preach again, Margaret encouraged Baxter to return to London. He first lectured in a hall, then in a meetinghouse, and then in a home Margaret had rented with her own money.

All too soon, Puritan preaching became illegal again. For the next eight years, the Baxters tried to avoid arrest by moving frequently. Margaret put her mind and money to work, finding places for her husband to preach.

She rented rooms over a newly constructed market house, but that proved nearly disastrous. While Baxter was preaching, Margaret heard a crack. She immediately left the service and found a carpenter, who propped up the main support beam for the heavy roof. Although the people were distracted by all the commotion, Baxter kept them calm and continued preaching.

Margaret arranged for other meeting places to be built, but Baxter could never preach for long. A member of Parliament spoke against Baxter twice and arranged for drums to be beaten under the windows during his preaching. Baxter once was forced to pay a heavy fine. Another time, Margaret hid or gave away his valuable books to avoid them being taken and destroyed. Soldiers came to arrest Baxter one

Sunday, but he had fled to the country. There he preached for ten weeks.

When he returned to London, he was watched every moment and stopped preaching. Margaret wasn't ready to give up yet. She rented a meetinghouse in Swallow Street, where Baxter preached undisturbed for a time. When law enforcement began guarding the door of the chapel every Sunday, Baxter again ceased preaching.

Margaret funded the building of meeting places for other ministers and searched for a place her husband could preach in safety. For the next several months, Baxter traveled some distance each Lord's Day to preach in Southwark.

But Margaret's wonderful assistance came to an end. After a lengthy illness, she died at the age of forty. In a book honoring her godly character, Baxter wrote, "She was the meetest helper that I could have had in the world." Despite their great age difference, she had been the best possible woman to assist him in his work.

His Last Years

Baxter was not allowed to mourn in peace. When he was nearly sixty-seven years old, ill on his bed, constables rushed into his home and served him six warrants. They took his books and household goods—even the bed on which he lay—and sold them to pay the fines.

He borrowed bedding and was laid up for most of the next two years, during which he continued to be watched and harassed. Carried to court repeatedly, he at first received only warnings to stop writing, but then he was put in jail and went to trial.

The judge treated Baxter disrespectfully, calling him an "old rogue," an "old blockhead," and an "unthankful villain."

Baxter and his supporters were not permitted to speak in his defense. He was convicted and sent to prison.

In God's providence, he was allowed at some point to live under a jailer's supervision in a nearby house, where his own servants cared for him. When he was seventy-one, he was released and lived in London. Laws had changed again, and he preached every Sunday when he was well enough. But he wrote that he was "scarce able to creep once a day to our assembly."

During these years of failing health, Baxter leaned more and more on the Lord. He wrote in a prayer to the Holy Spirit:

Let not the nights be so long, and my days so short, nor sin eclipse those beams which have often illuminated my soul. Without these, books are senseless scrawls, studies are dreams, learning is a glow-worm, and wit is but wantonness, impertinence, and folly. Transcribe those sacred precepts on my heart, which by Thy dictates and aspirations are recorded in Thy holy word. I refuse not Thy help for tears and groans; but oh, shed abroad that love upon my heart, which may keep it in a continual life of love….

Strengthen me in sufferings; and conquer the terrors of death and hell. Make me the more heavenly, by how much faster I am hastening to heaven; and let my last thoughts, words, and works on earth, be most like to those which shall be my first in the state of glorious immortality; where the kingdom is delivered up to the Father, and God will for ever be all and in all; of whom,

Statue of Richard Baxter at St. Mary's, Kidderminster

and through whom, and to whom, are all things, to whom be glory for ever. Amen.

His Death

When Baxter could no longer walk to church, he opened his home for worship. Then he preached from his room, and later from his bed. Finally, he was not able to preach.

Friends came to visit the dying preacher. As a fellow minister sat by his bedside, Baxter woke and said, "I shall rest from my labor."

The friend said, "And your works will follow you."

"No works," Baxter responded. "I will leave out works, if God will grant me the other." By "the other" he meant salvation by grace alone which results in eternal rest in Christ. His words demonstrate his belief that works do not earn salvation.

Another friend once remarked on how many people had been blessed by his preaching and writings. Baxter shook his head: "I was but a pen in God's hands; and what praise is due to a pen?"

Baxter suffered a horrible attack of pain one day and died the next, December 8, 1691.

His Legacy

Many times in his life, Baxter had been prohibited from preaching, but he thanked God that "when I might not speak by voice to any single congregation, He enabled me to speak by writings to many." Even during his lifetime, some of his books were translated into different languages and published in other countries.

Baxter isn't a hero because he was a perfect man with perfect theology. He made mistakes and, like every person on earth, he sinned every day. His work to unify the church was admirable, but his views on some theological issues were not Reformed—particularly those on justification.

He isn't even a hero for his devotional and pastoral writings, which are biblical and beneficial. Baxter is a Puritan hero because he used the God-given gift of writing for the good of others and the glory of God.

What gifts has God given you? Are you a good student? Do you excel at sports? Maybe schoolwork is difficult for you and you don't enjoy sports, but you have the gift of being kind to other people. Perhaps you struggle with health problems, but you can still read the Bible and pray. Whatever gifts God has given you, decide—like Richard Baxter—to use them to become God's instrument.

~ 15 ~

John Owen

1616–1683

God's Navigator

Fatigue seeped into John Owen's bones. He lifted his gaze from the toes of his boots, scuffing along the cobblestones, to the church tower ahead, jutting high into the blue sky. Relief briefly replaced his gloomy mood. Only a little longer, then he and his cousin could rest on a wooden pew while they listened to a good sermon.

Philip turned and motioned, "Why are you so slow this morning, John? Don't you want to hear Dr. Calamy?"

"Yes, of course, I'm eager to hear such a famous preacher." Owen panted as he picked up his pace. "I'm just tired today."

Philip shook his head. "You're always tired these days. When you were a student, you had no end of energy—throwing javelin, playing flute, ringing bells, and studying most of the night."

"It's true," Owen nodded. "I usually slept only four hours, but how I regret it now. It seems to have harmed my health."

"Maybe it did." Philip stopped to gaze at him. "At least you're well enough to venture out this morning. Last time I visited, you barely spoke, and what you said made little sense." He clapped his hand on Owen's shoulder. "Come along. You'll feel better after you hear a stirring sermon." He hurried ahead.

Black thoughts swirled in Owen's mind as he forced his weary legs to follow his cousin. Had other people noticed his confusion? Perhaps. But only he knew the depth of darkness in his spirit. So many of his plans had been blown off course, it was natural to feel discouraged. But why had this cloud of depression settled over his soul these last few years? Why did he feel sad and anxious all the time? He believed what his Puritan father had taught him about the Bible, but was he truly saved? Did God really love him?

As he entered the church, he removed his cocked hat. He saw Philip and slipped into the pew beside him.

"Finally," Philip whispered out of the corner of his mouth.

Owen didn't reply, because instead of the service beginning, people started talking aloud. He stared in amazement as some of them walked out. He touched the arm of a man passing by: "Why are you leaving?"

"Edmund Calamy was not able to come and will not be preaching today. I'm going to another church."

Philip stood. "Come on, John. Let's walk over to St. Michael's, where Arthur Jackson preaches."

"No." Owen shook his head. "I'm too tired to take another step."

"You'll like Jackson. He's an intelligent scholar and a famous speaker."

"Perhaps I would, but I'm staying here." Owen leaned back.

Philip spoke to a couple of men, and then turned to tap Owen's shoulder. "It's not certain if anyone will preach today. We may as well go somewhere else."

"If no one rises to speak soon, I'll just go home."

"All right." Philip sat and crossed his arms. "I hope someone shows up."

Before long, an unfamiliar minister climbed the steps into the pulpit. Owen turned to his cousin, "Who is this man?"

Philip shrugged. "I don't know."

A gentleman behind them leaned forward. "He's some country preacher. No one seems to know his name."

The minister prayed a simple but earnest prayer. Then he opened the Bible. "Our text this morning is Matthew 8:26, 'Why are ye fearful, O ye of little faith?'"

Immediately, Owen felt the Holy Spirit prick his heart. Jesus had spoken those words to His disciples, after they woke Him from a deep sleep in a boat being tossed about by a storm. But Owen felt as if Christ spoke directly to him.

Just as Jesus stilled the wind and waves, His Spirit calmed the storm within John Owen. The sermon was applied powerfully and personally to his heart. For the first

John Owen

time in his life, Owen was certain God loved him. Wherever the Great Pilot took him on life's journey, he would sail forward with joyful assurance.

———✦✦✦———

The voyage of Owen's life carried him through rough waters in England and the church. Much like a navigator guides sailors along the captain's chosen course, Owen showed many people—from kings and officers to students and families—the right way to live for Christ, the Captain of their souls.

Political winds often carried Owen in unexpected directions. An excellent student, he began university studies at only twelve years of age. He earned a master's degree and intended to obtain an advanced divinity degree, but he left the university rather than agree to new rules and practices contrary to his Puritan beliefs. He worked as a chaplain and tutor for one family and then another. He enjoyed this family's well-stocked library and their intellectual conversations. But the threatening civil war caused him to give up that job because his employer was for the king, while Owen favored Parliament.

When his wealthy uncle—who had paid for his education and promised to leave his estate to him—heard that his nephew had sided with Parliament, he withdrew his financial support and disinherited him. Owen moved to London, where he lived by himself in a poor section of the city.

Hearing that country preacher's sermon changed Owen's outlook and energized his body and mind. Assured of his security in Christ, he cared nothing about fame or fortune. And being filled with the Spirit's joy, he eagerly put his God-given talents to good use. In response to the errors of Arminianism being spread throughout Europe, he wrote a book that explained biblical teachings regarding salvation. *The Display of Arminianism* was widely read and was the first of more than eighty works he would write.

Owen was a pastor at heart, and he was excited to become the minister of a congregation in the country village of Fordham. Here he met and married Mary Rooke. He described her as excellent and beautiful, saying they deeply loved each other. His Fordham ministry lasted only three years, but during that time he was happy and busy. He visited families in his congregation and wrote catechisms to help explain the Bible's teachings. His clearly written books and sermons touched many hearts, and his writing became popular throughout England.

He was even invited to preach before Parliament. Owen spoke about the importance of bringing the good news of salvation to far areas of the kingdom. He also urged Christians to solve their differences by working together. These differences were a primary reason that civil war raged between the forces of King Charles I and Parliament. But Owen believed fighting was not the solution for disagreement between Christians. He said, "Cutting off men's heads is no proper remedy for it."

A short time later, Owen began serving a large congregation in Coggeshall, a town in Essex. People came from miles around to hear him speak, and he often preached to as many as two thousand. The war drew close when Parliament's army besieged a nearby city. Owen was asked to preach to the soldiers, and he became friends with Sir Thomas Fairfax, commander of the Parliamentary army.

All this time, Owen continued to write many books teaching important truths from the Bible. His *Death of Death*

Fifteenth-century church in Coggeshall, where Owen preached

in the Death of Christ, published in 1647, thoroughly explained the redemption of Christ and showed that it was a work of the triune God.

Owen believed prayer and Scripture reading were crucial for remaining steadfast in the truth. He wrote, "When we have communion with God in the doctrine we contend for—then shall we be garrisoned by the grace of God against all the assaults of men."

The battle imagery of garrisons and assaults most likely came from Owen's life. War swirled around him as the situation grew worse. People on both sides of the conflict were shocked when King Charles I was tried, convicted, and beheaded. Many thought it was wrong to execute the king God had ordained to rule over them.

The very next day, Owen was commanded to preach before Parliament. He didn't mention the sad event or speak in favor of either political side. Instead, he urged the country's leaders to allow all groups of Protestant Christians to worship in freedom.

Only a short time later, he again was invited to preach before Parliament. This time he begged the country's leaders to make Christ their personal king:

> Give the Lord Jesus a throne in your hearts, or it will not be to your advantage that he hath a throne and a kingdom in the world.
>
> Oh, that it were the will of God to put an end to all that pretended holiness, hypocritical humiliation, self-interested religion, that have been among us, whereby we have flattered God with our lips, whilst our hearts have been far from Him! Oh, that it might be the glory of this assembly, above all the assemblies of the world, that every ruler in it might be a sincere subject in the kingdom of the Lord Jesus!

Owen visited Commander Fairfax on the following day, and the two men strolled in the garden. Oliver Cromwell, the famous Parliamentary leader, strode up and put his hand on Owen's shoulder. "Sir, you are a person I must be acquainted with."

Owen replied, "That will be much more to my advantage than to yours."

Cromwell smiled. "We shall soon see." He pressured Owen to accompany him on a military campaign to Ireland. He needed a chaplain who could preach in a way to unify the religious differences among the soldiers. He also wanted someone to check out Trinity College in Dublin. He was convinced Owen was the man for the job. And he wouldn't take "no" for an answer.

Owen sailed with Cromwell's army across the Irish Sea to Ireland. He was on the island for six months, spending most of his time in Dublin due to ill health. He visited Trinity College and reported its sad state of affairs. Many buildings required repair, and few teachers and students lived there. Owen also preached to thousands of people, hungry for gospel food. He saw much suffering and some battles, although he did not witness the worst action of Cromwell's army, when hundreds of civilians were killed. After Owen returned to England, he went before the House of Commons to plead with the members to show Christ's love to the Irish:

> How is it that Jesus Christ is in Ireland only as a lion staining all his garments with the blood of his enemies; and none to hold him out as a Lamb sprinkled with his own blood to his friends?… Is this to deal fairly with the Lord Jesus?—to call him out to do battle and then keep away his crown? God hath been faithful in doing great things for you; be faithful in this one—do your utmost for the preaching of the gospel in Ireland.

Before long, Cromwell took Owen away from home again. During a six-month period, he traveled north to Scotland with two military expeditions.

Soon after these journeys, Owen was asked to serve as dean for Christ Church College at Oxford. He was reluctant to accept the appointment because he did not feel qualified to teach theology. He hadn't completed his divinity education, and his experience was only as a country preacher and

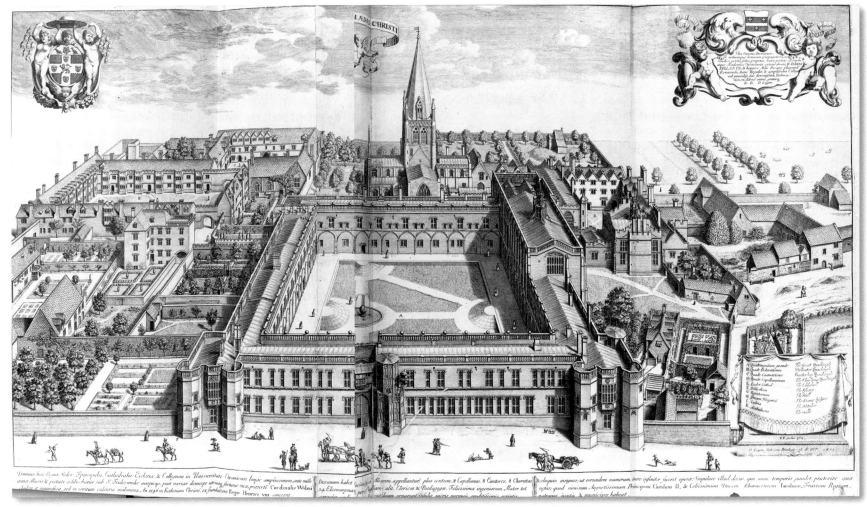

1675 layout of Christ Church College, Oxford

military chaplain. Yet, Owen obeyed the orders of his Captain, Jesus Christ, and went to Oxford.

The university was in sorry shape. The Royalist army had used it as headquarters during the war, and everything—from structures to staff—needed attention. Owen set to work and was soon promoted to Vice Chancellor over the entire university. This position enabled him to set a good direction for the school and install godly men as

Interior of Christ Church Chapel

instructors. He wanted students to receive an excellent academic education, but he especially wanted them to live for the Lord.

Instead of wearing drab clothes and a powdered wig like most professors, Owen dressed similarly to the students. He sported bright colors, high Spanish boots with cuffed tops, and a cocked hat. The young men admired him. They enjoyed talking to him on the grounds and listened intently to his sermons.

One of Owen's best-known books, *The Mortification of Sin in Believers*, was based on his sermons to students. The "mortification" of sin means dying to it and living more for Christ. This book has influenced many people for good, and still appeals to young people willing to invest time and mental energy into reading it. The preface to the book reveals Owen's heart:

> I hope I may own in sincerity that my heart's desire unto God, and the chief design of my life…are, that mortification and universal holiness may be promoted in my own and in the hearts and ways of others, to the glory of God, so that the gospel of our Lord and Savior Jesus Christ may be adorned in all things.

Owen wanted to increase holiness in his heart as well as in the hearts of others, not for his own fame but for God's glory. His goal was to help other people sail with him under the flag of King Jesus.

The student body grew, as did Owen's many responsibilities at the university and in the country. Still, he continued to write an astounding number of books, publishing more than twenty while teaching at Oxford.

Cromwell receives a deputation of Swiss Protestants seeking for aid

His *Communion with God the Father, Son, and Holy Ghost*, written in 1657, expanded on what he'd previously written about the Trinity. He explained that while God is One, each of the three Persons has unique roles. Christians become closer to God by praying to and praising each of the three Persons for their particular work. He called this having "distinct communion" with them, which increases the Christian's fellowship with God and assurance of faith.

During Owen's years at Oxford, Cromwell ruled England as its Lord Protector. He often asked Owen's advice on matters relating to the church and country. It was as if God had placed Owen on the deck of the ship of state.

But his good relationship with Cromwell didn't last. Some men proposed that Cromwell assume the kingship, which he seriously considered. Owen was one of many who disagreed with the proposal, and he helped write a document against it.

Cromwell declined to become king, but his relationship with Owen was never close after this incident. Following Cromwell's death in 1658, the political situation quickly deteriorated. In 1660, Charles II, the son of King Charles I, was made king. Many Puritans and Scottish Presbyterians had supported him due to his promises of religious tolerance.

Unfortunately, the king and Parliament worked together against Puritans. A storm of persecution threatened to destroy the biblical truths of the Reformation.

Owen lost his financial security and his position. He moved to a nearby village, where he began a church in his home. But new laws forced him to leave the congregation behind. He returned to London, where he lived in many places, gathering congregations and departing when necessary. When he had to leave these church families, he planned for their care and wrote letters of encouragement to them. He also wrote to pastors, suggesting how to minister to their flocks during these difficult times:

> I beseech you to hear a word of advice in case the persecution increases, which it is like to do for a season. Because you have no ruling elders, and your teachers cannot walk about publicly with safety, [I wish] you would appoint some [men to] go up and down from house to house and apply themselves peculiarly to the weak, the tempted, the fearful, those who are ready to despond, or to halt, and to encourage them in the Lord. Choose out those… endued with a spirit of courage and fortitude…. And I desire the persons may be…faithful men… by this means you will know what is the frame of

the members of the church, which will be a great direction to you, even in your prayers.

Many Puritan pastors, including Owen, ministered to suffering people in London during the Plague of 1665 and after the destructive fire in 1666.

At different periods of his life, Owen received invitations to work in other countries, where he could have preached freely. He was asked to head up a federation of churches, and later a university, in America. He also had offers to oversee universities in the Netherlands. Each time, he chose to remain in England and guide his countrymen along the correct course.

Owen sometimes used seafaring imagery in his books. When writing about Christ, he described how people can be "tossed up and down with conflicting thoughts," but when they are justified by faith, they have peace with God: "All is quiet and serene, not only that the storm is over, but they are in the haven where they would be."

Those words recall the life-changing sermon Owen heard. He likely had that experience in mind when he wrote about how the Spirit reassures believers:

> When the Lord Jesus at one word stilled the raging of the sea and wind, all that were with him knew that there was divine power at hand…. And when the Holy [Spirit] by one word stills the tumults and the storms that are raised in the soul, giving it an immediate calm and security, the soul knows his divine power, and rejoices in his presence.

Perhaps because Owen was well known and respected, he was never arrested. Many of his friends were, however, including John Bunyan, who spent twelve years in prison. Before he became a preacher, Bunyan had worked as a tinker, traveling from town to town to mend metal pots.

As the political situation began to improve in England, Owen used his influence to obtain Bunyan's freedom. Then Owen often went to hear Bunyan preach.

Bunyan had used his time in prison wisely, writing many works, including *The Pilgrim's Progress*, which Owen convinced his own publisher to print. That book became one of the most popular books in history.

Owen had written a letter of thanks to King Charles II for changing the law, and that opened communication between the two men. The king appreciated Owen's intelligence and learning, sometimes summoning him to the palace for discussions. He assured Owen of his good intentions toward Puritans. He once went so far as to give Owen money to help some ministers who had suffered the most.

One day as the king and Owen were talking, the king asked, "Why do you even bother going to hear an uneducated tinker like Bunyan preach?"

Owen responded, "Could I possess the tinker's abilities for preaching, please your majesty, I would gladly relinquish all my learning."

That considerable learning helped Owen explain biblical truth with great wisdom throughout his life. He began one of his most influential works, *Pneumatologia*, in 1674, when he was in his late fifties. This was a study of the person and work of the Holy Spirit, and no one had ever attempted anything quite like it before.

Much of his writing echoed God-centered themes of communion with the Trinity, holiness, and assurance. He

Illustration of John Owen by a contemporary

believed no one could enjoy continually perfect assurance in this life:

Our minds in this world are not capable of such a degree of assurance in spiritual things as to free us from assaults to the contrary, and impressions of fear sometimes from those assaults; but there is such a degree attainable as is always victorious; which will give the soul peace at all times, and sometimes fill it with joy.

While Christians may suffer with doubts or fears, we can know our final victory is sure, and that will fill our souls with peace and joy.

In 1676, Owen's beloved wife, Mary, died. This must have been a grievous blow, especially considering how he and Mary had lost all of their eleven children, most of them at a young age. Only one daughter reached adulthood and married, but it was an unhappy union. She moved back into her father's home, where she died a short time later.

By the time Mary passed away, Owen was sixty, an old age in those days. He struggled almost constantly with his health, and felt the need for someone to help him. Some months later, he married a godly woman, Dorothy D'Oyley.

During his difficult final years, Owen once prayed: "Let not the nights be so long, and my days so short, nor sin eclipse those beams which have often illuminated my soul. Amen."

Despite his illnesses, Owen continued writing. As he lay dying, his printer was editing *Meditations and Discourses on the Glory of Christ*. John Owen died on August 24, 1683, at the age of sixty-seven. A large procession of mourners followed his body to the cemetery on September 4.

In the later years of Owen's ministry, a man named David Clarkson had assisted him with pastoral work. In Clarkson's funeral sermon for Owen, he said:

> A great light is fallen; one of eminency for holiness, learning, parts and abilities; a pastor, a scholar, a divine of the first magnitude; holiness gave a divine luster to his other accomplishments, it shined in his whole course, and was diffused through his whole conversation.

Owen's voyage was finished. He had at last reached his home port. Shortly before his death, he wrote in a letter to a friend, "I am leaving the ship of the church in a storm, but while the great Pilot is in it the loss of a poor under-rower will be inconsiderable [not worth considering]."

Like a navigator, John Owen had shown the way to salvation for many people, both important leaders and lowly believers. He had been blessed with a great mind, deep spiritual insight, and writing talent, yet he remained humble. He didn't think of himself as the captain of his own ship or as the first mate or even as a navigator. He considered his influence small and thought of himself as only a lowly sailor, plying an oar in the belly of a boat for his great Pilot, Jesus Christ.

~ 16 ~

Christopher Love

1618–1651

Presbyterian Martyr

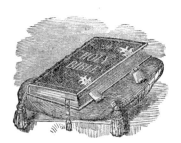

The door slammed, and a key clicked in the lock. Christopher Love stared in dismay as his father's voice carried through the thick wood: "You shall stay here!"

Christopher grasped the knob and shook the door, but it remained shut. He turned and surveyed the storage chamber at the top of the house. How could he get out? Light gleamed from a window. He pushed crates away, opened the pane, and leaned over the sill. He sighed. He'd probably break a leg if he dropped from this height. He paced the room, searching for some means of escape. Nothing. He kicked a box tied with a thick cord. His eyes lit up, and he quickly untied it. He fastened one end securely to a post, grasped the thin rope in his hands, and eased himself out the open window. Glancing down, he gulped. The ground was far below.

He took a deep breath. Then he slid down the side of the house, checking his speed so the friction didn't burn his hands. When he neared the first floor, he let go. As soon as his feet touched ground, he took off running.

Hours later, he returned home to face his furious father. His father shouted angrily, "What do you mean by disobeying me? I told you not to go to church!"

His Life

Why would a father forbid his son to attend a worship service? Mr. Love allowed his son great freedom to indulge in entertainments such as gambling. When Christopher was young, he was known as a gamester who often won at cards or dice, even against older men. Sadly, Christopher Love's father was not a Christian.

Only a few days before his father locked him in the chamber, something had happened to Christopher. Out of idle curiosity, he went to hear a man preach. It was the first sermon he'd heard in all his fifteen years. But God's Spirit convicted him of his sin, and he returned home a changed young man.

His father, noticing the difference, concluded his son was depressed. He suggested Christopher amuse himself with friends or play cards at a nearby

Christopher Love

gentleman's house. Instead, Christopher asked permission to hear the minister preach again.

To prevent him from going to church, his father locked him up. Christopher realized he had a choice. He could obey his earthly father or his heavenly Father. With determination that would characterize his brief life, he chose to obey God.

The preaching of God's Word led Christopher to change his ways. Instead of gambling with older men, he prayed with other students. They met late at night to avoid neglecting their studies or offending their parents.

But Christopher's father still disapproved of his son's newfound faith. When the young man chose to pursue an education at Oxford, where many ministers were trained, his father did nothing to support him except provide the horse on which Christopher rode from home.

While still a college student, Love became the first man to be expelled for refusing to conform to church requirements he believed were unbiblical. He later returned and received his Master of Arts degree.

For several years, he served as a chaplain in a sheriff's household. There he met Mary Stone, who lived with the family. She was a godly young woman, and the two were married on April 9, 1645.

A congregation in London asked him to be their lecturer, but the bishop prohibited the appointment because Love had declined ordination in the Church of England. He traveled to Scotland, hoping to be ordained there. Unfortunately, that presbytery ordained only men who agreed to minister in Scotland, and Love felt called to pastor people in England.

After Love's return, city leaders in Newcastle invited him to preach. He spoke about errors in the *Book of Common Prayer* and criticized superstitious ceremonies of the Church of England. He was immediately arrested. In jail with thieves and murderers, he slept on a bed of dirty straw. He often preached through the barred window to crowds gathered outside to hear him. Eventually he was tried and found not guilty.

When civil war broke out in England, he preached about just reasons for war. He was accused of treason and rebellion, but was again cleared of the charges.

Love became a chaplain for the royal regiment at Windsor Castle. When a plague broke out, he visited the sick and dying, comforting them from God's Word.

In 1644, following the establishment of Presbyterian government in England, Love was finally ordained. He preached for three years in one church and then at another nearby.

The Loves were blessed with a baby girl named Mary, but she died after a few days. About a year later, their second daughter was born. Also named Mary,

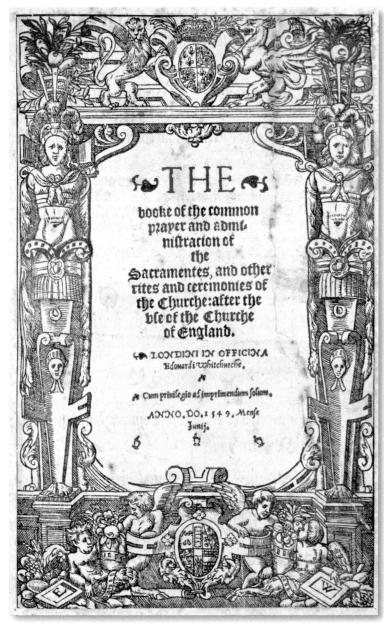

Book of Common Prayer, 1549

Windsor Castle

she, too, lived only a short time. Near the end of the next year, a son named Christopher was born. A fourth baby was born, although records reveal no details about that child.

Christopher loved his children and enjoyed teaching them about God. He told Mary, "If I had not been a preacher, I would have been content to teach children my whole life."

She smiled. "You have made our home a nursery for God."

He said, "Whatever others do, yet I and my house will serve the Lord."

"Like Joshua?"

He nodded. "Yes, Joshua 24:15, 'Choose you this day whom ye will serve; whether the gods which your fathers served that were on the other side of the flood, or the gods of the Amorites, in whose land ye dwell: but as for me and my house, we will serve the Lord.'"

Although Love rejoiced in his family, he was not happy with events in England. Parliament executed King Charles I, and Protestants argued about it. Love was one of many who believed that God appointed rulers and man should not dethrone them.

The Scottish people agreed. They crowned the king's son, Charles II, who had subscribed to the Solemn League and Covenant, and planned to expand his kingship over all the British Isles.

Love and many others liked this idea, even though it was against English law to support Charles II. Some sent money to fund the effort or communicated with Scottish leaders about it. Meetings were held in several English homes, including a few in Love's house, at which letters from Scotland expressing support for Charles II were read.

In the dark before dawn on May 2, 1651, pounding woke the Love family. The door broke open, and soldiers stormed in. Two pulled Love from his bed. Others jerked open drawers and cabinet doors, scattering papers and overturning furniture, as they looked for evidence.

Love swayed between the soldiers grasping his arms. "May I please get dressed?"

One soldier tightened his grip. "No. You are under arrest for high treason."

Mary held their wailing baby, while little Christopher clutched her and cried.

"Sir," Love begged, "may I please pray with my family?"

The soldier pulled him toward the door. "No, you are a traitor."

"Could I be permitted to pray in private?"

The soldier dragged him outside. "No! You are coming with us."

Mary and the children stood in the doorway, tears streaming down their cheeks.

Love turned his head and called back, "Do not be troubled. This is no strange thing to me."

The soldiers hauled him to the Tower of London, where he remained confined for many weeks. His trial began on the last day of June.

The clerk stated, "Christopher Love, you stand charged…of high treason and other high crimes and offenses against the Parliament and people of England; this high court therefore requires you to give a positive and direct answer whether you are guilty or not guilty of the crimes and treasons laid to your charge."

Love did not want to submit a plea until he had been permitted to speak, but the court did not want him to speak until he had entered a plea. Although Love attempted to speak, he was interrupted repeatedly. He cited legal standards in his favor, but the court demanded that he plead guilty or not guilty. Love questioned if the trial was legal since the charges did not specify Scotland.

The Attorney General asked, "Are you admitting that you received or sent letters to Scotland?"

Sending or receiving letters was illegal, but Love had only listened to letters being read. He responded, "I have so much of a Christian in me that I will deny nothing that is proved to be true, and so much of an Englishman that I will admit nothing that is seemingly criminal."

The court refused to grant his request for an attorney until he entered a plea. He said, "If I were to plead, it would be the same as admitting to the legality of the trial."

The Lord President of the Court threatened, "Plead now or you shall have judgment."

Reluctantly, Love said, "Not guilty." Immediately the court called witnesses against him. Love objected to each witness, saying they had been either paid to lie or threatened with death if they didn't testify.

"Your behavior bespeaks your guilt," accused a member of the court. "An innocent man would not carry on in such a manner."

"Sir, I am fighting for my very life!"

On the third day of the trial, Love spoke for two hours in his own defense. He pointed out how witnesses had contradicted themselves. None of them had shown that he had written any letters contrary to the law. He had only been present when some letters were read, and that was not a crime.

Love requested and received a famous lawyer, but even his attorney couldn't persuade the court. After five days, Love was found guilty. On the sixth day, July 5, 1651, he was sentenced to "suffer the pains of death by having his head severed from his body."

After a moment, Love said, "My Lord, I would speak a word."

The Lord President replied, "You cannot be heard now, Mr. Love."

"But a word, my Lord, and 'tis this, in the words of the Apostle, 'I have received the sentence of death in myself, that I should not trust in myself, but in God which raiseth the dead.' And my Lord, though you have condemned me, yet this I can say, that neither God nor my own conscience doth condemn me."

The Lieutenant of the Tower then took Love back into custody. Throughout July and August, Love and his wife sent petitions to the court. Mary, who was eight months pregnant at the time, even offered to give up her life in exchange for her husband's.

Some historians record that Cromwell sent a letter of reprieve, pardoning Love on promise of good behavior. But former Royalist soldiers stopped the courier and discovered the pardon. Angry about Love's sermons, they tore it up.

While waiting to hear from Cromwell, Parliament granted a one-month reprieve. The members listened to one of Love's petitions and an account of the matter. Then they voted against his petition, twenty-seven to sixteen.

Love's execution was set for August 22, 1651.

His Death

As Love faced death, he and Mary encouraged each other. During their last conversation, he assured her that the God of the widow and fatherless would never forsake her and would provide for her and the children. He said, "Though men take thy husband from thee; they cannot take thy God from thee." He added, "As soon as my head is severed from my body, it shall be united with Christ my Head in heaven, and I am persuaded that I shall tomorrow go up Tower Hill as cheerfully to be everlastingly martyred unto my Redeemer as I went to Giles' church to be married to thee."

Mary's last letter urged him to lay his head on the block with joy, thinking how he would wake to find it circled with a crown of glory. She ended, "O let me hear how God bears up thy heart, and let me taste of those comforts that support thee, that they may be as pillars of marble to bear up my sinking spirit. I can write no more. Farewell, farewell, my dear, till we meet there where we shall never bid farewell more."

Love was a popular preacher, and his case had captured the attention of the nation. When he was brought from

The Tower of London today

the Tower gates to the scaffold the next day, thousands of people wept aloud. Many pressed forward to touch him one last time.

He climbed the steps. The Sheriff showed him the warrant for his death, saying, "I take no pleasure in it, but it is a duty laid upon me."

Love replied, "I believe it, sir."

"I have done my duty for you."

"The Lord bless you."

The Lieutenant of the Tower said, "The Lord strengthen you in this hour of your temptation."

"Sir, I bless God, my heart is in heaven. I am well."

Love asked permission to address the crowd. He began, "I am made this day a spectacle unto God, angels, and men: and among men I am made a grief to the godly, a laughing stock to the wicked, and a gazing stock to all, yet, blessed be my God, not a terror to myself. Although there is but little between me and death, yet this bears up my heart: there is but little between me and heaven."

Following our Lord's example, Love said, "As concerning my accusers, I shall not say much. I do forgive them with all my heart, and I pray God forgive them also.

"And now I am to commend my soul to God and to receive my fatal blow. I am comforted in this: Though men kill me, they cannot damn me; and though they thrust me out of the world, yet they cannot shut me out of heaven. I am going to my long home and you are going to your short homes; but…I shall be at my Father's house before you will be at your own houses. I am now going to the heavenly Jerusalem, to the innumerable company of angels, to Jesus the Mediator of the New Covenant, to the spirits of just men made perfect, and to God the judge of all, 'in whose presence there is fullness of joy and at whose right hand are pleasures forevermore.'" He concluded, "The Lord bless you all."

Then he asked permission to pray.

"Most glorious and eternal Majesty, Thou art righteous and holy in all Thou doest…though Thou has suffered men to condemn Thy servant, Thy servant will not condemn Thee…blessing Thy glorious name, that though he be taken away from the land of the living, yet he is not blotted out of the Book of the Living. This Thy poor creature…hath desired to glorify Thee on earth; glorify Thou now him in heaven. He hath desired to bring the souls of other men to heaven; let his soul be brought to heaven.

"We entreat Thee, O Lord, think upon Thy poor churches…. Lord, heal the breaches of these nations; make England and Scotland as one staff in the Lord's hand…. O that men of the Protestant religion, engaged in the same cause and covenant, might not delight to spill each other's blood, but might engage against the common adversaries of our religion and liberty! God, show mercy to all that fear Thee.

"Lord Jesus, receive my spirit and…stand by me, Thy dying servant who hath endeavored in his lifetime to stand for Thee. Lord, hear…wash away his iniquity by the blood of Christ…and receive him pure and spotless and blameless before Thee in love. And all this we beg for the sake of Jesus Christ. Amen and Amen."

Having thanked the sheriff, he told the friends near him, "The Lord be with you all." He knelt to pray silently for a little while, then rose and said, "I am full of joy and peace in believing. I lie down with a world of comfort as if I were to lie down in my bed." His last words were: "Blessed be God for Jesus Christ."

An execution on Tower Hill

Dutch account of Christopher Love's execution, 1651
WELCOME COLLECTION

He pulled a red scarf from his pocket and had it placed on the block. Then he knelt, rested his head on the scarf, and stretched out his hands. The executioner swung the ax and severed Love's head from his body with one blow. The attending doctor quickly placed the head against the neck, and the body was put in a black-draped coffin.

Shortly after this, the clear blue sky filled with black clouds. Lightning flashed, and thunder rumbled. The storm raged throughout the entire night. Some saw it as a sign of God's anger at Love's death, while others believed it an expression of God's judgment against Love.

Love was thirty-three years old when he died, leaving behind two young children and his pregnant wife. The child, James, was born thirteen days after his father's death and died at seven months.

Other ministers had been arrested the same time as Love, but all were released after agreeing to submit to government requirements. As when he was fifteen, Love chose to obey God rather than men. His last speech included these words: "If I had renounced my covenant and debauched my conscience and ventured my soul, there might have been hopes of saving my life so that I should not have come to this place. But blessed be my God, I have made the best choice. I have chosen affliction rather than sin and, therefore, welcome scaffold and welcome axe and welcome block and welcome death and welcome all, because it will send me to my Father's house."

Despite an earthly father who didn't believe in God, Christopher Love came to believe in a tender heavenly Father. From then on, he chose to love and obey Him.

What choices do you make in your life? By grace, do you choose God and His will above all?

~ 17 ~

John Bunyan

1628–1688

Traveler and Prisoner

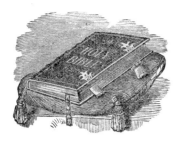

In the dark before dawn, John Bunyan bolted upright on his army blanket, his heart pounding. Vivid images of gleeful demons feeding hell fires danced in his mind. He forced himself to take slow, deep breaths. It was only a dream. An old nightmare from childhood. He shook his head to try to clear it. Perhaps dreadful scenes from recent battles had triggered it. Here he was, a soldier in Cromwell's army, trembling like a birch leaf in a stiff breeze. Not from facing sharp swords or seeing blood gush, but from a mere dream.

He leaped up and stretched. It was nearly time to rise anyway. And today he'd be off with other soldiers to lay siege to the nearby Royalist garrison. He carefully walked around his sleeping companions. Always surrounded by other men. What he wouldn't give for some time by himself—time to think. Why should those old sermons about hell still bother him? Some soldiers claimed that God didn't exist. Could it be true? Others said God was love, but why would a loving God let Mother and Margaret die? Why did He let Englishmen, who called themselves Christians, keep killing each other?

The sun soon rose, and many soldiers scurried around, preparing for the day's march. One hurried toward him. "Bunyan, you off to the siege then?"

"Aye, it's sentry detail for me. A long march and little sleep tonight, I fear."

"I'd be happy for a chance to see some action. I'll go in your place."

Bunyan studied the eager face of the young soldier. "Standing sentry is a cold and boring job. You spend the whole time longing to wrap yourself back in your blanket."

"At least something might happen. I'll take it any day over kicking my heels here in camp."

"All right." Bunyan shrugged. "You're welcome to it."

The eager musketeer dashed off to join the men forming ranks under the commander. Bunyan shook his head. He doubted the redheaded lad was even as old as he was. And he, although still in his teens, was considered a seasoned soldier.

As Bunyan went about his work, performing monotonous duties, thoughts about God faded from his mind. And no dreams disturbed his sleep that night. He woke glad for a full rest, unbroken by sentry duty.

When the soldiers returned, their mood was somber. Bunyan searched their ranks for the young man who'd taken his place.

A weary soldier sank to the ground and rested his back against a tree. "No use looking for him."

"The sandy-haired lad who took my place?"

"Aye. He's gone."

"Gone? You don't mean he's dead?"

"Dead and gone. Killed on sentry duty when a musket bullet pierced his head."

Bunyan trembled. That might have been him. It should have been him.

The other soldier peered up. "All I can say is God must have plans for you, Bunyan. Although I have no idea why He'd want to use such a foul-mouthed rascal."

———— ❖ ————

In his youth, John Bunyan led other rebellious boys in all kinds of mischief, swearing more than any of them. His mother died while he was in his early teens, and his sister, Margaret, only a month later. He joined the Parliamentary army when he was sixteen, and his military experience did nothing to improve his speech.

Bunyan returned home to join his father in working as a tinker. He walked around the countryside, stopping at homes and farms to repair pots and other metal items. The heavy bundle he carried on his back included an anvil weighing sixty pounds.

When he was twenty-one, he married a poor young woman whose dowry consisted only of two Puritan books she'd inherited from her father: Arthur Dent's *The Plain Man's Pathway to Heaven* and Lewis Bayly's *The Practice of*

John Bunyan

Bunyan's birthplace, County of Bedford

The Church and Village Green, Elstow, Bedfordshire

Piety. Primarily to please his wife, Bunyan read the books. He began to attend church but his heart didn't change. He continued swearing and still enjoyed playing sports on the Lord's Day.

One morning, he thought the minister's sermon on keeping the day holy was addressed directly to him. But as usual that afternoon, he played sports with his friends. Suddenly he seemed to hear a voice from heaven say, "Wilt thou leave thy sins and go to heaven, or have thy sins and go to hell?" He felt as if Christ frowned at him.

"It's too late," Bunyan muttered. "He'll never forgive me now." Filled with despair, he decided he might as well keep on sinning.

But the Holy Spirit was softening his heart. Sometime later, he was walking past a woman who had a terrible reputation. She heard him swearing and shouted at him, "When will you stop that terrible cursing? You're going to corrupt every young person in the entire town!"

He was furious that such a woman would criticize him, but he realized that he needed to change his ways. He finally stopped swearing, much to his own surprise. He also gave up dancing, ringing bells, and playing sports on Sunday. He began reading the Bible and started to think of himself as quite an expert on it. Other people even told him what a godly man he was becoming. He thought he must be, or they wouldn't say so. But he didn't really know and love Jesus Christ.

One day, he saw some poorly dressed old women sitting on a doorstep, talking joyfully with each other. When he overheard them mention the Bible, he joined the conversation. But they talked about Jesus in a way he'd never heard before.

They spoke about Him as if He were a close friend. And they praised God for His Spirit's work in their hearts to make them born again. Bunyan recognized that his religion based on works was empty. He needed more than changed behavior—he needed a changed heart.

He and his family attended the women's church. The pastor taught Bunyan much about the grace of God. And he learned even more when he read Martin Luther's commentary on the book of Galatians. The Holy Spirit transformed John Bunyan's heart. He devoured every word of the Bible, and he couldn't help sharing the good news of salvation in Jesus Christ with others.

People appreciated Bunyan's messages. He explained the Bible in ways they could easily understand and that touched their hearts. His vivid language and personal experience made the Word come alive for listeners. Amazement at God's grace in saving such a great sinner created within him what he called a "fire in mine own conscience."

He wrote, "I preached what I felt, what I smartingly did feel, even that under which my poor soul did groan and tremble to astonishment."

For quite a while after his conversion, Bunyan struggled with assurance. Sometimes he would feel peace, trusting that Christ had removed all his guilt. But he was often tormented by anxiety, fearing he would fall away from Christ. Whenever he felt anxious, he turned to God's Word. Over and over, it comforted and sustained him. Still he fought what seemed a losing battle regarding his own spiritual state. He had learned not to trust in his own righteousness. At times he felt like he was behaving rightly, but he frequently felt a heavy burden about his remaining sin.

Zoar Street Meetinghouse where Bunyan preached

Walking through a field one day, Bunyan suddenly was impressed by the sentence: "Thy righteousness is in heaven." With the eyes of his soul, he saw Jesus Christ at God's right hand. He realized that his righteousness didn't depend on himself, but on Christ. He wrote:

I saw that it was not my good frame of heart that made my righteousness better, nor yet my bad frame that made my righteousness worse; for my righteousness was Jesus Christ…the same yesterday, today, and forever. Now did my chains fall off my legs indeed, I was loosed from my afflictions and irons; my temptation also fled away… now I went home rejoicing, for the grace and love of God.

The glory of Christ's complete redemption filled him with joy. His mind and heart sang with a refrain of praise:

I lived for some time, very sweetly at peace with God through Christ. Oh! methought, Christ! Christ!

there was nothing but Christ that was before my eyes…. It was glorious to me to see His exaltation…now I could look from myself to Him, and would reckon that all those graces of God that now were green in me, were yet but like those cracked [coins] that rich men carry in their purses, when their gold is in their trunk at home! Oh, I saw that my gold was in my trunk at home! In Christ my Lord and Savior! Now Christ was all.

Bunyan now knew that he didn't have to worry about his salvation. Jesus had done it all for him. His future home in heaven was more secure in Christ than the treasure of a rich man locked in a trunk.

When Bunyan's first wife died, he had four children under the age of ten. The oldest, Mary, had been born blind. A few years later, he married a young woman, Elizabeth, who helped care for his children. The family was happy together, and his new wife soon became pregnant.

Even though Bunyan wasn't trained as a minister, his pastor and congregation encouraged him to use his speaking gifts for the Lord. He spoke to large crowds in many towns until he was no longer permitted by law to preach openly. Then he proclaimed God's Word at secret meetings in barns or houses. He often disguised himself to avoid arrest.

As the threats against unlicensed preachers became more intense, Bunyan wondered if he would be able to endure prison or face death. Two Bible texts helped him face his uncertain future. Colossians 1:11 assured him that he would be "strengthened with all might," according to God's glorious power, to "all patience and longsuffering with joyfulness." He realized he could bear a long prison sentence with joy by God's grace. He viewed death differently after reading 2 Corinthians 1:9, "But we had the sentence of death in ourselves, that we should not trust in ourselves, but in God which raiseth the dead." He wrote: "By this scripture I was made to see, that if ever I would suffer rightly, I must first pass a sentence of death on everything that can properly be called a thing of this life, even to reckon myself, my wife, my children, my health, my enjoyments, and all, as dead to me, and myself as dead to them."

From then on, Bunyan was able to give his concerns to the Lord and trust Him for whatever the future held.

One night he arrived at a barn and was told that a warrant had been issued for his arrest. But he didn't run away. He told the assembled people that the gospel was worth suffering for. A constable arrived and arrested him. As he was taken away, he urged the people to take courage and trust in the Lord.

Bunyan's imprisonment was difficult for his family. Elizabeth lost the baby she was carrying. While Bunyan grieved over the suffering she and the children endured, he trusted God to comfort and provide for them.

He could have been set free, if only he'd promise not to preach. But he said, "If I was out of prison today, I would preach the gospel again tomorrow, with the help of God."

Several months after Bunyan's arrest, Elizabeth pleaded with the court for his release. The judges mocked him and her. They told her he would be freed only if he no longer preached.

"He dares not stop preaching, as long as he can speak," she said. "As long as my husband has a voice, he will preach the gospel of Christ to the glory of our God and Father."

Elizabeth Bunyan interceding for her husband

This made the judges angry. One shouted, "He preaches the teachings of the devil!"

Remaining calm, Elizabeth replied, "My Lord, when the righteous Judge shall appear, it will be known that my husband's doctrine is not the doctrine of the devil."

Her courageous effort had no effect. Bunyan remained in prison for the next twelve years. He was able to earn a little money to send home by weaving twine into long shoe laces. Still, his family's welfare weighed on his heart during those long years.

Occasionally, a kind jailer allowed him to leave for a few hours. He'd visit his home and sometimes preach to a crowd gathered in secret at midnight.

Despite occasional discouragement during his imprisonment, Bunyan used that time to write books and preach to fellow inmates.

Bunyan's jail on Bedford Bridge

Bunyan in Bedford Jail

One Sunday he was particularly depressed and didn't know how he could give a sermon to the other prisoners. Paging through his Bible, he stopped at the description of the heavenly Jerusalem in the book of Revelation. Bunyan preached about how the hope of glory strengthens Christians to the end of their days. He wrote: "For when men do come to see the things of another world, what a God, what a Christ, what a heaven, and what an eternal glory there is to be enjoyed; also, when they see that it is possible for them to have a share in it, I tell you it will make them run through thick and thin to enjoy it."

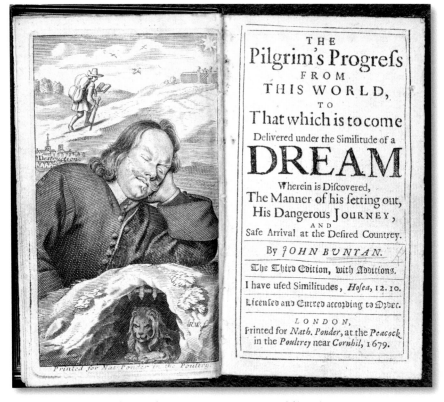

Pilgrim's Progress, *1679 publication*

Bunyan preached with great power that day. He wanted to help people have hope in their suffering by focusing on God and His glory. He longed to communicate this truth from Scripture with many other people, and he wrote much more about it in books.

Whenever Bunyan was given the option of release if he'd agree to stop preaching, he refused. He said, "I have determined, the Almighty God being my help and shield, yet to suffer, if frail life might continue so long, even till the moss shall grow on mine eyebrows, rather than thus violate my faith and principles." He knew he had to obey God rather than men.

When the law changed in 1672, Bunyan was finally let out of prison and permitted to preach. But only four years later, the government restricted religious freedoms again. He was put in jail for another year and a half. As before, he used his time to preach and write.

Out of the sixty books Bunyan wrote during his life, his most famous was a story called *The Pilgrim's Progress*. This imaginative tale about a traveler named Christian depicts the way of conversion in the believer's life, and the hope of heaven. Christian struggles through many different situations and meets unforgettable characters on his journey to the Celestial City.

The well-known theologian John Owen used his influence to get Bunyan out of jail. Then Owen convinced his own publisher to print *Pilgrim's Progress*. While the Bible was the most popular book in the English language, *Pilgrim's Progress* became the second most popular.

Bunyan's grave in Bunhill Fields, London

For the next few years, Bunyan preached in local villages, larger towns, and the city of London. He spoke to huge crowds, often to more than a thousand people and once to three thousand people. But persecution against Puritans flared up again, and Bunyan sometimes narrowly avoided arrest.

Because he was known as a man who could help people overcome their differences, a family begged him to come and mend the broken relationship between a father and son. He visited the men and helped them forgive each other. After leaving the house, he rode through a terrible storm in cold weather, getting completely soaked. He grew ill with a high fever. It became apparent he was dying.

Friends gathered around him, and he spoke: "Weep not for me, but for yourselves. I go to the Father of our Lord Jesus Christ, who will, no doubt, through the mediation of his blessed Son, receive me, though a sinner; where I hope we before long shall meet, to sing the new song, and remain everlastingly happy, world without end."

As his spirit failed, he said, "My greatest desire is to be with Christ." He lifted his hands toward heaven, crying, "Take me, for I come to Thee!" Then he died.

John Bunyan was a tinker turned preacher who traveled a long and difficult path on his Christian walk. He wrote *Pilgrim's Progress* because he wanted other believers to realize that life was full of temptations, afflictions, and concerns, but that the Lord would lead them through their life's journey and bring them safely to their heavenly home.

~ 18 ~

John Flavel

1628–1691

Providence's Servant

Hoofbeats pounded the turf and drew near. John Flavel glanced over his shoulder at the dim outlines of the pursuing soldiers. They would soon catch him. Sea water glimmered in the moonlight ahead. Without hesitation, he urged his horse into the cove's cold depth. The water soon rose above the animal's fetlocks, then its belly. It began swimming, blowing misty breaths into the night air.

Again Flavel glanced back. The soldiers had halted their mounts on the shore. A sharp whinny carried through the chilly air, but no horse plunged into the inky brink.

Water surged around Flavel's legs. He slipped off and swam beside his horse, one hand grasping the saddle. Eventually his feet touched ground and he led the horse onto the rocky bank. He thanked God for rescuing him from the soldiers who had broken up a secret worship service. Once again, Providence had protected His servant.

———— >•◆•< ————

Flavel was a loving pastor and powerful preacher. He showed Christ's love to people suffering in their bodies, but he cared even more about their souls. He knew the life-changing work of the Holy Spirit from personal experience.

His father was a Puritan pastor who often prayed and wept for his children. But for many years, young John cared only for his physical health and ignored his spiritual welfare. He later wrote:

> My body which is but the garment of my soul, I kept and nourished with excessive care, but my soul was long forgotten, and had been lost for ever, as others daily are, had not God roused it, by the convictions of his Spirit, out of that deep oblivion and deadly slumber. When the God that formed it, out of free grace to the work of his own hands, had thus recovered it to a sense of its own worth and danger, my next work was to get it united with Christ, and thereby secured from the wrath to come.

Flavel's attitude changed. He worked hard at his studies and became a minister in 1650. A year or so later, he married Joan Randall. Sadly, she and their infant son died during childbirth. He later wrote: "The Almighty visited my tabernacle with the rod, and in one year cut off from it the root, and the branch, the tender mother, and the only son."

After a few years passed, Flavel married Elizabeth Stapell. The two were happy and were blessed with a son they named John. Flavel preached to his congregation in the seaside town of Dartmouth and reached out to sailors and poor people with the good news of salvation.

One day, Flavel hurried along a dusty street. A bitter wind blew dirt in his eyes. He pulled the lapels of his coat together and pressed his hat down on his head. He rushed into a lodging house, where the owner met him. "Hurry! Up the stairs. The door is open." As Flavel dashed past, the man shook his head. "I fear he is not long for this world."

In the room, a young man lay, twisting in pain and blood from self-inflicted knife wounds to his throat and stomach. Flavel bent over him. "My son, do you trust God?"

Fading fast, the young man managed to gasp out, "Yes."

But Flavel responded, "Are you sure? Do you believe in Jesus Christ as the only hope for salvation?"

"Oh, I'm such a sinner!" The man wept. "God, forgive me. I beg you, forgive my many sins."

Flavel prayed with him and comforted him as much as he could before he left.

The next day, he returned to the lodging house, expecting to hear that the young man had died during the night. To Flavel's surprise, the injured man was still alive. After several surgeries, he recovered.

John Flavel

Flavel later wrote about the experience, "So it was that both the deep wound in his throat and in his stomach healed, and the more dangerous wound sin had made upon his soul was, I trust, effectually healed also."

Flavel's father, Richard, was prohibited from preaching in churches, so he preached wherever he could. A few years later, Flavel himself was one of nearly two thousand

Newgate Prison

ministers expelled from the state church. Because he was a well-educated man and knew eight languages, Flavel began a school. But then he was banished from teaching or preaching within five miles of his beloved Dartmouth. He moved to Slapton, where members of his previous congregation often traveled to hear him preach.

Officials arrested his parents for holding an unauthorized worship service in Covent Garden. His father and mother were locked up in Newgate prison, where they contracted the Plague. They both died from the disease soon after their release.

During these years of persecution, Flavel preached in strange locations at unusual times, leading secret meetings at night or deep in the woods. The strangest meeting place was a stony peninsula. People could walk across to it at low tide, but it was covered by the sea at high tide. Worshipers sometimes found his sermons so moving that they climbed into boats so they could remain listening while the tide rose.

One night, Flavel was preaching in a forest when men began shouting and women screaming. Soldiers rushed among the crowd, brandishing swords and arresting people. Someone jerked Flavel from the rock on which he stood and pulled him into the darkness. Glancing around, he found himself surrounded by friends. They dashed around trees, deeper into the woods, until the shouts faded. Finally, they stopped to catch their breath. More people trickled into the clearing. Flavel looked at their frightened faces in the moonlight. He stood on a log and exclaimed, "My friends, God comforts us from His Word!" He then continued preaching the same sermon the soldiers had interrupted.

Flavel was not above employing creative means to avoid arrest. A Puritan couple in another town asked him to

Seventeenth-century Dartmouth buildings still standing today

baptize their baby. Because he would certainly be arrested if soldiers recognized him on the way, Flavel disguised himself as a woman and rode behind another man on horseback.

When Flavel was in his early forties, he was permitted to return to preaching in Dartmouth. But the law changed after only one year, and he again resorted to preaching in secret. During this period, his wife Elizabeth died. Flavel then met and married Ann Downs. They were married for eleven years and had two sons. Sometime after her death, Flavel married his fourth wife, Dorothy, who would outlive him.

Persecution eventually became so strong in Dartmouth that Flavel sailed to London. Although a terrible storm nearly wrecked the ship, God brought him safely to the city. But London also was not safe for Puritans. One day soldiers broke into a secret meeting, and Flavel barely managed to escape. His coworker, William Jenkyn, was arrested and died in prison a year later.

By that time, Flavel had returned to Dartmouth, where he wrote and preached from his home. Although his congregation loved him, some people in the city didn't like him or his teachings. They marched through the streets, carrying an effigy of him, which they then burned. In spite of this, he loved all of Dartmouth's people and wrote: "O that there were not a prayerless family in this town!"

The law changed a couple of years later, and Flavel could preach in public again. When religious freedom seemed secure, Flavel's congregation built a large church, where he preached with great benefit to many.

Without Flavel even being aware of it, he blessed other people years later in far places. Luke Short, a young man of fifteen, heard Flavel preach a sermon that deeply moved most of the audience—but not him. Soon afterward, Short sailed to America. He lived a long life in good health. At one hundred years of age, he still worked his farm and was able to think clearly. One day, he sat in his field and reflected on his past. His mind drifted back to that long-ago sermon preached by John Flavel, and he remembered significant parts of it. He realized he had lived all his life in rebellion toward God. Convicted of his sin, he repented. He lived another sixteen years, showing by his changed life that his repentance was genuine.

Flavel not only wanted people to repent, but also wanted Christians to unite around the truth of Scripture. Unlike many ministers of his day, he worked to unify different factions in the church. Because Flavel didn't stir up controversy, he served effectively as a moderator among those with disagreements. Ordained as a Presbyterian and later licensed as a Congregationalist, he tried to bring those two groups together, continuing in these efforts to the end of his life.

The struggles and sorrows of Flavel's life took a severe toll on his body, and he began to weaken. He wrote about himself and other Puritan ministers, "We have long borne the burden and heat of the day; we are veteran soldiers almost worn out." While in another town to preach, he died from a massive stroke on June 6, 1691. His last words were, "I know that it will be well with me."

His Writings

John Flavel used vivid word pictures and convicting comparisons to make his writing come alive. His work could touch even the most unlikely person. One day a man walked into a bookshop to purchase some plays. The owner had none on hand, but recommended Flavel's book, *Keeping the Heart*. The man made fun of the book, threatening to burn it. But the shopkeeper persisted, and the man reluctantly bought it and promised to read it. He returned a month later as a changed man. "Sir, I most heartily thank you for putting this book in my hand; I bless God that moved you to do it, it saved my soul; blessed be God that ever I came into your shop." He purchased one hundred copies to give to poor people.

God used this book of Flavel to convert many other people. To this day, *Keeping the Heart* remains one of Flavel's most popular works. In it, he urges readers to keep their hearts humble and wholly devoted to God. He recommends ways to walk with the Lord and resist sin, loving God with reverence and joy.

The most popular of all Flavel's works is *The Mystery of Providence*. In it, he encourages readers to reflect on God's provision in all the good and bad events of life. He wrote numerous books about the providence of the Father, the love of Christ, and the equipping of the Spirit. His own experiences enabled him to write powerfully about suffering and the importance of a soul united with Christ.

He encouraged readers to resist temptation and to work for the Lord in every occupation. But he had a special affection for sailors and wrote several books for these wanderers of the sea.

In Flavel, God richly combined a pastor's heart and a theologian's mind. His works have remained so popular that they have been printed continuously since he died.

His Own Words

If John Flavel could step out of the pages of this book and speak to you now, he'd probably ask if you have the hope of eternal life. If you gave a quick answer you've learned in church or Christian school, he might peer into your eyes

Title page of The Mystery of Providence

and ask again—as he asked that horribly wounded young man so long ago—if you truly believe in Jesus Christ as your only hope for salvation. Think about it.

He might ask you if your parents have raised you in the Lord. If you assured him they had, he would say, "What a mercy was it to us to have parents that prayed for us before they had us, as well as in our infancy when we could not pray for ourselves!"

Then he'd likely urge you to make sure you someday teach your own children to walk with the Lord: "If you neglect to instruct children in the way of holiness, will the devil neglect to instruct them in the way of wickedness? No; if you will not teach them to pray, he will to curse, swear, and lie; if ground be uncultivated, weeds will spring."

If your parents aren't believers and you told him that your family is going through a difficult time, he might say: "Consider how all the troubles in this world would be sweetened, and all your burdens lightened, if once your souls were in Christ, and in covenant with God. O what heart's ease would faith give you! What sweet relief would you find in prayer! These things would suddenly cool, relieve, and ease your spirits; could you but go to God as a Father, and pour out your hearts before Him, and cast all your cares and burdens, wants and sorrows upon Him; you would find a speedy outlet to your troubles, and an inlet to all peace, all comforts, and all refreshments."

He would direct you to the Bible, saying, "The Scriptures teach us the best way of living, the noblest way of suffering, and the most comfortable way of dying."

Flavel would tell you about the love of Jesus and how God chose believers from before the foundation of the earth.

Perhaps you would hang your head and confess that you don't feel as if Jesus can love someone like you. Flavel would gently say, "As God did not first choose you because you were high, He will not now forsake you because you are low." He would ask, "Did Christ finish His work for us? Then there can be no doubt but He will also finish His work in us." If you sigh and say you just feel so overwhelmed sometimes, Flavel would say, "Jesus, our head, is already in heaven; and if the head be above water, the body cannot drown."

Maybe he would encourage you by saying, "They that know God will be humble. They that know themselves cannot be proud."

Before Flavel stepped back into the pages of this book, he might grasp your shoulder and say, "The care of God, engaged for you, is your convoy to accompany and secure you until it sees you safe into your harbor of eternal rest."

Although Flavel probably never imagined the far-reaching influence of his work, his hope was that every reader and every hearer would understand God's sovereign care and providence in their lives, even over their struggles. He saw himself as a servant, called to glorify God and love others, whose soul was held securely in God's hand.

In *The Mystery of Providence*, he wrote: "My hearty prayer is that providence will direct this treatise to such hands in such seasons, and so bless and prosper its design, that God may have glory, thou mayest have benefit, and myself comfort in the success thereof, who am, Thine and the church's servant, In the hand of Providence, John Flavel."

John Howe

1630–1705

Living Temple

What was all the shouting about? Little John Howe stretched on his tiptoes until he could peer over the stone ledge of the narrow window.

The Irish mob covered the green hillside like a busy army of black ants. They had been there for weeks, sometimes swooping down to attack the fortress like a flock of pecking crows.

But something was different today. A horseman rode up the hill, pulling behind him a man tied with a long rope. The rider kicked the horse into a run. The man fell, but the horse went faster, dragging the poor man between laughing and shouting people.

"John, come away from there." His father pulled John's cold fingers free from the ledge and drew him into a warm embrace. "I do not want you to see their savageries."

"Who is that man, Father?"

"He is one of us, a Protestant." His father's voice trembled. "They caught him trying to escape."

"Why are they hurting him, Father?"

"Here in Ireland, the Roman Catholics have suffered much at the hands of the English for many years." His father's arms tightened around him. "Now their land is being taken from them and given to Protestants. Is it any wonder they hate us?"

The boy pulled away to look into his father's face. "But we're safe as long as we stay inside, aren't we?"

"Oh, John." Father pulled him close again. "I am so sorry I brought you with me from England. I thought I was fleeing to safety, but now both our lives are in danger. I should have left you at home with your mother."

The boy brushed away his tears and straightened his back. "I'm five years old, Father. Big enough to travel with you."

"And I didn't want to be parted from you." Father smiled and grasped John's hands. "Let's pray together, my son."

As soon as he'd said the words, he bowed his head. "Oh, most gracious God, Thou art sovereign over all things, even the angry Papists on yonder hill. We beg Thee to release Thy captured servant from his suffering. We

John Howe

know Thou hast ordained all our days, and we trust Thou wilt bring us home to live with Thee in Thy perfect time. We pray for wisdom and guidance and protection. In Thy Son's name, Amen."

Father took a deep breath. "No matter what happens, John, God is always with us."

"Yes, Father." John smiled. "I remember what the Bible says. God's people are His temple."

His father's lips curved into a gentle smile. "You are right, my son. And even if these earthly temples are destroyed, believers' souls will go to heaven. And some day, Christ will come back and raise these temples from the dust."

The shouting outside stopped. Father and son sat like statues, listening to the silence. Suddenly the air was split with a loud wail that sailed over the green hills and faded into the distant purple mountains.

His father clutched John and said in a solemn voice, "Tonight, John. Tonight, you must do everything exactly as I say."

"Yes, Father."

The two sat together in the tower, while the sun dipped lower and shadows grew.

"I'm hungry, Father."

"I know, John, but there's nothing left to eat."

When the sun set, the mob grew louder, starting bonfires and carrying flickering torches back and forth on the hillside. All the Protestants in the fortress crowded into the tower. They gathered in front of the windows, sometimes pushing each other aside to look out and report what they saw to those huddled in fear.

A woman at the window screamed, "Oh, no! They're carrying down a battering ram!"

The man behind her shoved her away to look for himself. Then he turned to face the others. "It won't be long now."

Soon loud thuds echoed from the gate in the wall.

Father leaned close and took John's hand. "Come. But move slowly and quietly."

The two walked down the stairs to the lowest level. No one was around. Father opened a door and they slipped out. It was dark now.

Bang. Bang. Bang. The blows from the battering ram were much louder out here. Bang. Bang. It hit the gate again and again.

"Father—"

Father's finger touched John's lips. "Not one sound," he whispered in his ear.

He led John behind a cart. They crouched down, looking and listening. Then they dashed across an open space and squeezed behind some wooden crates along the wall. Father carefully and slowly pushed the crates closer to the small rear gate. Finally, he stopped and leaned back. The stones of the wall were cold and damp. One poked John's back, and he wiggled. His father touched his arm and shook his head. They waited and waited. John's muscles got stiff, and his eyelids grew heavy.

Crash! The front gate shattered, and shouts rang out. Through a crack between the boxes, John saw men run into the courtyard and thrust torches into the splintered remains of the gate. At the same time, horses thundered on the other side of the wall behind them. A fierce blow struck the rear gate, ripping off its bar and throwing the doors open. One slammed against the boxes in front of John. He cried out, but his father's hand quickly covered his mouth. The two cowered in the shadows as men poured through the gate,

shouting and brandishing swords. Eyes wide with fear, John saw the attackers rush to the front of the fortress to help the other men beat on its door.

Father grasped John in his arms and crept through the open gate. He dropped into the long grass, shadowed by the wall. The two crawled toward some nearby trees. When they reached the forest, Father picked up John and slung him onto his back. Then he ran.

He dashed from tree to tree, John bouncing on his back like a sack of potatoes. Shrieks pierced the cold air, and John glanced back. Flames rose into the dark sky.

Father's grip tightened. "Don't look back, John."

———❖◆❖———

John Howe and his father eventually made it to safety and sailed back to England, where the Howe family settled in Lancaster. After John received his Master's degree, he became a minister for a church in Great Torrington, Devon. He was a dedicated and hard-working pastor. On special fast days, he led worship from nine in the morning to four in the afternoon, taking only a fifteen-minute break around noon.

He became close friends with a fellow minister named George Hughes. Even though Hughes was much older than Howe, the two men shared common interests. They both enjoyed languages and wrote each other weekly letters in Latin.

On a visit to Hughes, Howe met his daughter, Catherine. He married her a year later.

One day Howe received a letter from his father-in-law that ended with this prayer (written in Latin): "Let the dew of heaven fall on your dwelling." Hughes had never before written anything like it, and it seemed an odd way to end a letter.

That very day, fire broke out in the Howe home. Constructed of dry timbers, the house was soon engulfed in flames. There were no firetrucks to speed to the rescue or nearby hydrants to spout water. All of Howe's notes and sermons, all the family's clothing and furniture appeared lost.

Suddenly, a torrential rain began falling. The downpour kept the raging fire from spreading. Finally the flames sputtered and went out. After the fire was quenched, the rain stopped. It seemed that strange prayer in the Latin letter had shown how God would save the Howe house.

On a visit to London when Howe was twenty-six, he met Oliver Cromwell. The forceful leader asked Howe to preach at a service, giving him the text to preach on while the congregation sang the psalm before the sermon. Taking the short notice in stride, Howe preached for an hour. Then he turned the hourglass and went on for another hour. He was turning the glass again, when Cromwell stopped him and asked him to be his family's chaplain.

Howe wasn't interested in political plots. He cared more about Christians learning to get along with each other. But he was Cromwell's chaplain during an assassination attempt that almost succeeded.

On January 8, 1657, a man known to dislike Cromwell was seen hanging around the chapel. At 11:30 that night, a guard discovered a lit fuse in a hole in the wooden wall. It was put out before it reached the explosives on the other side, which were said to be enough to "burn through stones."

Almost two years later, Cromwell died after a short illness. His son, Richard, was declared Lord Protector of England, and Howe became good friends with him. Although

Cromwell and Howe

Richard calmed threatening situations, some groups continued to cause conflict, and he resigned only eight months after becoming England's leader. Richard Cromwell did not have the strong leadership skills that his father had. Howe went back to his congregation at Torrington, where he preached and wrote.

Within the year, Charles II was crowned as King of England. Under his rule, laws against Puritans were put into effect. Howe wandered from place to place, preaching in private homes or in secret. An Irish lord offered Howe a position as his household chaplain. In a journey that may have reminded Howe of his childhood, he sailed for Ireland with his son, George.

Along the way, the travelers were delayed in Wales due to the weather. On Sunday, Howe preached to fellow passengers and a congregation at a nearby church. News of his preaching quickly spread through the countryside, and the little building was crowded for the afternoon service. The weather all the next week prohibited sailing, so a large crowd gathered the following Sunday, expecting to hear Howe again.

But Howe was lying in bed at the inn, ill with a fever. Messengers arrived and asked him to come and preach. He rose from his sickbed and cooled himself as quickly as possible, trusting God would equip him to speak. He felt that sermon was particularly blessed by the Holy Spirit and later said, "If my ministry was ever of any use I think it must be then."

In Ireland, he settled in comfortably at the lord's castle on the shore of a large lake. Here he wrote the first part of his most famous book, *The Living Temple*. That book describes how a Christian man is the temple of God. The first part shows that God exists and man can have a relationship with Him. The second part explains how that relationship is possible only through "Immanuel, an incarnate God among men…a most perfect Temple, the original one."

While in Ireland, Howe preached in many different churches and worked toward Christian unity. Enjoying this time of peace and security, Howe wrote another book called *Delighting in God*.

Only a few years later, Howe was persuaded to come back to London to preach to a church on Silver Street. The congregation loved him. He was also popular in the community and country, befriending people on both sides of political and religious issues. But he never compromised God's truth.

Persecution against dissenters increased until it was dangerous for Howe to walk openly in the city. When James II was crowned, Howe secretly left England with a lord who planned to spend a year in Europe.

But things were even worse a year later. Howe settled in the Netherlands, where he opened his home to other refugees and preached at the English church. He also became friends with the Dutch ruler, Prince William of Orange, who was married to the daughter of James II.

William of Orange

When James II appeared willing to accept dissenting pastors, Howe's former congregation begged him to come back. Prince William warned Howe that the King was trying to promote the Roman Catholic Church and urged him not to return to England.

Howe went back and discovered it was just as William had said. Many English leaders, tired of deceitful politics, united and asked William to become King of England. When William landed on November 5, 1688, Howe led the supporters meeting him. They prayed for God to bless William and the Protestant cause "throughout the Christian world." Even though the Puritans were still denied some freedoms, such as holding public office, at least their worship was tolerated again.

Despite failing health, Howe threw himself into the work of unifying the various Protestant Christians. He wrote about theological issues like predestination and the Trinity, trying to help people with differing views find a biblical balance.

Daniel Defoe, famous for his novel *Robinson Crusoe*, wrote against men who practiced "occasional conformity," by taking Holy Communion in the Church of England, to qualify for public office. Howe believed most men did it as a way to show unity among Protestants. In Howe's response to Defoe's criticisms, he wrote: "Though we cannot avoid

Richard Cromwell

William of Orange lands in England during the Glorious Revolution

thinking we are in the right in those particular things in which we differ, yet at the same time we know ourselves to be excelled by them in much greater and more important things." He believed people should focus on godly living rather than argue with each other unnecessarily.

Things again looked bleak for the Puritans when Queen Anne came to the throne in 1702. Howe still preached and cared for his flock, but he was over seventy and becoming frail. The people listening to him preach during his last communion service thought he might die in the pulpit.

In his final book, he wrote: "Long illness and the slow decay of the physical powers is not a curse but a blessing. It occasions such as endure it to live long upon the borders of eternity."

Finally, Howe was confined to his bed. Among those who came to visit was his old friend Richard Cromwell, who had long resided in another country but now lived quietly in England under an assumed name. Both men shed tears of joy and sorrow as they spoke together for the last time.

Howe died on April 2, 1705. In his last will and testament, he wrote: "I, John Howe, minister of the Gospel of Christ…cheerfully wait…for a…dissolution of this my earthly tabernacle, and translation of the inhabiting spirit into the merciful hands of the great God."

From the time he was a little boy, Howe realized that he was a living temple of the Holy Spirit. As he came to understand the Bible better, he wrote about Christ as the perfect Temple who purifies His human temples. When Howe grew old and weak, he looked forward to putting off his earthly temple. He knew that Christ would return one day and make his old body into a glorious new temple like His own.

~ 20 ~

Joseph Alleine

❖◆❖

1634–1668

God's Arrow

Strange sounds woke Joseph Alleine. The boy dashed to the window and gasped. Cannons lined the road in front of his house, pointing at the gate of the castle across the meadow. Soldiers poured powder into the barrels and rammed in balls.

His feet pounded down the stairs. "Father, Father!"

"Yes, my son." Tobie Alleine's voice calmed Joseph's thumping heart. "Do not be afraid. God has promised never to leave us or forsake us, and He is with us, even now."

"But why are soldiers here? Didn't the Royalists at the castle defeat the Roundheads only two years ago?"

"Aye, that was a great victory for the king's men, but the Parliamentarians have gained ground with their New Model Army. They are sweeping through the land."

A shout drew Joseph to the window. A tall man in a leather jerkin strode back and forth, commanding the soldiers: "Prepare to fire!"

Joseph turned to his father. "Who is that captain?"

His father's eyes were solemn. "That, my son, is Oliver Cromwell."

"Fire!" Cromwell's shout was immediately drowned by thundering cannons. Joseph clapped his hands over his ears.

From the castle turrets, arrows whizzed toward the Alleine home. Some skipped over the green grass and nearly reached the porch.

"Come away from the window, Joseph!" His mother motioned through an open doorway. "Stay in the back of the house with us." His younger sister peeked around Mother's skirts, her eyes large and frightened.

"Father, may I stay with you? I am almost a man."

His father put his arm around him. "For a little while only. And you must go to your mother the instant I say the word."

"Yes, Father."

Standing out of sight by a window, the two watched as musketeers advanced toward the castle. Pikesmen marched beside each infantry man, protecting him with long, pointed poles.

Joseph Allein.

Soldiers in bright red uniforms poured from the castle, marching straight forward. A swift motion in the corner of Joseph's eye made him turn his head. Cromwell's cavalry rode toward the Royalists from the side. Over the green, the strains of the soldiers singing drifted to Joseph's ears: "Let God arise, let His enemies be scattered: let them also that hate Him flee before Him."

At the head of the mounted men, Cromwell rode fiercely, brandishing his sword.

The Royalist ranks fell into chaos as the horses galloped into their midst. Swords flashed in the bright sunlight. Bodies fell, spilling red blood onto the green grass.

His father's strong hands turned Joseph away from the window. "You must go now, my son. Join your mother and brothers and sisters. You are a precious arrow in my quiver, and I do not want to lose you."

Joseph's feet shuffled on the wooden floor.

"Go." His father pushed him gently. "I will let you know what happens."

Most of the Alleine family and their servants cowered in the dark at the back of the house, furniture piled against doors and windows. For two days and nights, musket shots and cannon fire shook the walls. The men of the household periodically brought news and food to the huddled group.

On the third day, all became quiet outside. The baby cried in Mother's arms. Finally, Joseph's father opened the door. "Sir Charles Lloyd and his garrison have surrendered. The Parlimentarians allowed them to ride away." He gravely surveyed his family. "The blue flag waves above the castle."

———>•◆•<———

Joseph Alleine grew up with civil war swirling around him. He was eleven years old when he witnessed Cromwell's victory over the Royal garrison near his home. He realized then how short life was, and he determined to spend his for the Lord.

Even as a boy, Joseph found relief from worldly strife by walking through the woods and countryside, communing with his Creator. Sometimes other boys made fun of him, calling him "the lad that will not play." But he was

Oliver Cromwell leading his cavalry into battle
THE CROMWELL MUSEUM

a good-natured child, who early desired to be about his Father's business.

Alleine entered college when he was fifteen years old and became an excellent scholar. He often rose at four in the morning and sometimes stayed up until one the next morning, studying or praying and reading the Bible. On most days, he gave away one of his meals to a less fortunate student. While he served for a year as the college's chaplain, he became eager to reach more people with the gospel and began visiting prisons.

Because jails teemed with disease, few people took such a risk. But Alleine preached to prisoners every other week, each time giving them enough bread for seven days.

Although some people offered Alleine important positions, he felt led by the Lord to serve as a pastor's assistant in Taunton, where Puritanism flourished. He passed his ministerial exam, but he delayed taking up his duties for a personal reason. He had always been so generous to the poor that he couldn't afford to provide a home for the woman he hoped to marry.

His distant cousin, Theodosia Alleine, was an intelligent and godly woman. The two loved and respected each other very much. In his letters to her, Joseph called her "my dear heart." He once wrote to her: "My dearest, I love thee in truth and tenderness; but my love signifies little, unless it serve thy eternal good." He and Theodosia often discussed their faith and plans together, but were so poor they decided to wait several years before marriage.

The pastor at Taunton, George Newton, offered a solution to the problem. Since his wife's death, he had lived alone. He urged Alleine to marry Theodosia and suggested the couple live in the vicarage with him.

After two years of residing with Reverend Newton, the Alleines moved into their own home in order to expand their Christian service. Theodosia began a school, teaching twenty or thirty children who lived with them, and another fifty or sixty students from the community. Although the couple had no children, they parented dozens of young people, caring for their physical and spiritual needs. Theodosia later wrote about this work and her husband's role in it, "The Lord was pleased to bless us exceedingly in our endeavors; so that many were converted in a few years that were before strangers to God. All our students called him father; and indeed he had far more care of them than most of their natural parents, and was most tenderly affectionate to them, but especially to their souls."

The care of souls was Alleine's primary concern. He longed to prick hearts with gospel truth. He wrote to the people of Taunton, "Ah! That I did but know what arguments to use with you; who shall choose my words for me that I may prevail with sinners not to reject their own mercy? How shall I get within them? Oh, that I did but know the words that would pierce them!"

Feeling keenly the shortness of life, Alleine rushed forward in serving God like an arrow loosed from the bow. He spent several hours each day teaching catechism to girls and boys, men and women, poor and rich, even to students in the local school. He visited every family in his congregation regularly, teaching them how to live the Christian life. He encouraged everyone to take time for private devotions, but also to put their faith into practice. He said, "Religion was not a thing that knew only how to kneel, but not to walk, or work."

St. Mary Magadalene Church in Taunton where Alleine probably preached, and was buried

Alleine took his own advice. He regularly spent the hours between four and eight in the morning alone with God. If he heard hammers of smiths or the sounds of other craftsmen at work before he began his devotions, he would tell Theodosia, "How this noise shames me! Doth not my Master deserve more than theirs?"

His lifetime practice of walking and praying in God's creation taught him much about the natural sciences. He even dissected small creatures to learn their anatomy.

As things became more difficult for Puritan preachers, he set other interests aside and focused on preaching. Some Puritan ministers were being put in prison. Others were banished, sometimes sold as slaves to people in far countries. He and Theodosia sold their possessions in case they should be imprisoned. They discussed going to China as missionaries if he were banished from England. Despite frequent threats, Alleine preached six to fourteen times a week.

Alleine was arrested on May 26, 1663, but allowed to go home overnight. During the night, he preached to hundreds of people for three hours, praying for them and for his enemies. The next morning, he walked to the jail, which was located in another town. People lined the roads for miles, weeping and calling out to him. His own eyes filling with tears, he prayed for God to strengthen him. He carried his summons to the jail and preached one more time before he entered.

He was put in a crowded attic. The sun turned it into a stifling oven during the summer, while freezing wind and snow blew through it in winter. Despite these harsh conditions, the imprisoned ministers preached once or twice each day through the bars to large groups of people that came from as far as ten miles.

Alleine worked day and night, sometimes sleeping for only a few hours. He kept up his private prayer time and ministered to other prisoners. He wrote many letters, including one per week to his congregation. His letters overflowed with love, encouragement, and concern. In one, he urged believers to greater love for Christ:

> Let love constrain you, let love put you upon doing, and prepare you for suffering: Forget not a love so memorable, undervalue not a love so invaluable. I would have you all the captives of love: May the cords of love draw you towards, and knit you

to, your Redeemer; may the divided streams be united in him. Alas, that our souls are so narrow, that the waters are so shallow with us! How little, how very little, would our love be, if he had it all! Infinitely less than the glowworm to the sun, or the atom to the universe. And have we any of this little to spare for him? Oh that we might love him with our little all! That all our little powers were engaged for him! Brethren, here is no excess. Oh love the Lord, ye his saints!

After spending nearly a year in prison, Alleine was released. Although persecution intensified against people as well as pastors, he preached from his home and in nearby villages.

Prison had sapped his strength, and he became so ill that everyone thought he would die. But he recovered enough to teach and preach again. Constantly threatened with arrest, he lived from house to house. Friends convinced him to travel to Devizes, where he could rest and drink mineral waters that might improve his health.

As he preached a farewell sermon to his congregation, loud pounding shattered the door. Armed men burst into the room, shouting and brandishing swords. They arrested Alleine, his wife, his elderly father, seven ministers, and forty other people.

In prison, Alleine again ministered to others, took turns preaching, and wrote letters. In one, he described the blessing he'd found, even in prison:

> I can tell you little good of myself; but this I can tell you, that the promises of God were never so sweet in this world to me, as in and since my imprisoned

state. Oh the bottomless riches of the covenant of grace! It shames me that I have let such a treasure lie by so long, and have made so little use of it. Never did my soul know the heaven of a believer's life, till I learned to live a life of praise, and by more frequent consideration to set home the unspeakable riches of the divine promises, to which I trust, through grace, I am made an heir.

He frequently encouraged his fellow Christians to glorify God whatever their circumstances: "It matters not whether we are in riches or poverty, in sickness or health, in honor or disgrace, so Christ may be by us magnified in the condition we are in. Welcome prison and poverty, welcome scorn and envy, welcome pains or contempt, if by these God's glory may be most promoted!"

Alleine often urged his loving congregation to think less about him and more about God:

It is the sense of the infinite love of God your Father that I would have to dwell upon you. Forget me, so you remember Him. Let me be very little, so He be very lovely in your eyes. Let Him be as the bucket that goes up, though I be as the bucket that goes down. Bury me, so that you do but set the Lord always before you. Let my name be written in the dust, so His name be written deep upon all your souls.

As soon as Alleine was set free the second time, he took up a collection to help victims of the London fire. He gave a large contribution publicly and even more privately. His generosity remained strong, but his body was weak.

He finally went to Devizes for his health in June of 1667. While there, he learned that his father had died. He wrote:

It hath pleased the Lord to add to my affliction since my coming by taking away my dear father—the day of whose glorious translation was the day after my arriving here. But I bless the Lord, I do believe and expect that return of the Redeemer with all His saints, and the most glorious resurrection of my own dead body with all believers; and this makes me to rest in hope, and fills me with unspeakably more joy than the death of myself or any other saint can with grief.

Although Alleine revived for a short while, he soon became ill again. That September, while he and Theodosia stayed in Dorchester, he suddenly lost the use of his arms and legs. He lay helpless through the fall and winter. Many people from Taunton visited him, and some carried him back in the spring. For months, he suffered pain and convulsions or lay still with paralyzed limbs.

In July, he was taken to Bath, where he again experienced a marvelous recovery. He was able to teach sixty or seventy children at his lodgings on Sundays. He even visited schools and houses for the poor, distributing catechisms. His recovery was short-lived, however, and he grew gravely ill only a few months later.

His physician stood by his bedside, watch in hand, and said, "Only a few minutes now."

Alleine said, "Weep not for me; my work is done."

But God's work for him was not quite finished. Alleine recovered sufficiently to travel five miles to discuss a proposal with a friend. They agreed to publish, at their own expense, six thousand copies of the catechism and send one hundred to dozens of ministers. While there, his strength failed, and Theodosia had him carried back to Bath.

He told her, "Well, now, my dear heart, my companion in all my tribulations and afflictions, I thank thee for all thy pains and labors for me, at home and abroad, in prison and liberty, in health and sickness."

Strong convulsions wracked his body every hour for two days and nights. Theodosia begged God, "Please allow him to speak something of his heart before Thou dost take him from me."

God answered her prayer. Alleine spoke clearly for sixteen hours, saying among other things: "I am the Lord's. Christ is mine, and I am His." He died on November 17, 1668. According to his expressed wish, his body was brought back to Taunton to be buried.

Like a loosed arrow, Alleine's life flew past and was quickly spent. He was only thirty-four years old when he died. His goal was the salvation of souls to God's glory. Although he worked hard, he knew he sometimes shot wide of the target. He once said, "Too often do I take wrong aim, and miss my mark."

Yet Joseph Alleine aimed to serve God wholeheartedly during his short life. You do not know how many years God will give you to live for Him. How are you spending your time? If you believe in Jesus alone for salvation, you are an arrow in the quiver of your heavenly Father. Aim for God's glory!

~ 21 ~

Matthew Henry

1662–1714

Bible Commentator

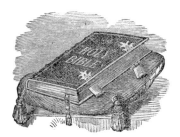

Matthew Henry and his sisters hurried downstairs. Even though they'd go to church later, their father still led family worship on Sunday mornings. It was actually a little longer and started earlier than the other days of the week.

Father smiled at them and said, "Christ is risen!"

"He is risen indeed," they responded, as earlier Christians had greeted each other on Easter morning. Father believed every Sunday reflected the first Resurrection Day.

"Let us pray."

Matthew closed his eyes and bowed his head.

Father asked the Holy Spirit to help them understand the Scripture. He prayed for people who were suffering, especially the families of the thousands of godly ministers who had been forced out of their positions and homes. Matthew couldn't help thinking how his family had been part of that huge group and had arrived at Broad Oak, his grandfather's farm, only two weeks before he was born. God had graciously provided a comfortable place for them to live, but few of the other ministers' families were so fortunate.

As usual, Father finished the prayer with the doxology from Ephesians 3:21, "Unto him be glory in the church by Christ Jesus throughout all ages, world without end. Amen."

Following prayer, the family sang a lively psalm. Father read a passage from the Bible, stopping at times to explain what he'd read or apply it to their lives. Then he asked the children questions about the reading. Their worship concluded with another prayer and with singing a psalm.

Although sermons preached by Church of England ministers often failed to convey biblical truth, the Henry family attended Whitewell Chapel whenever services were held there. Matthew and his four younger sisters—Sarah, Katharine, Eleanor, and Ann—brought along notebooks in which they recorded the sermon's points and things they learned from the text. From the time they were little children, they'd been taught to pay close attention to sermons and memorize as much as they could.

After the noon meal, the family sang a psalm. Father asked the children questions about the sermon and encouraged them to share what they remembered. Blessed with an excellent memory and armed with detailed notes, he was able to repeat the entire sermon. Then he closed in prayer. Later, the family attended the chapel's afternoon service.

That evening, a few neighbors slipped quietly into the Henry home. They joined the servants and farm workers gathering with the family. It was illegal for more than five adults to worship with the members of any household. The visitors and the family members could be fined, put in prison, or shipped out of England as slaves. But they were willing to take the risk to hear Philip Henry preach the truth from God's Word.

Matthew Henry

⸻ ◆ ⸻

Matthew Henry was a sickly but intelligent boy who could read a short section of the Bible and comment on it when he was only three years old. He loved pretending to be a preacher, but was never disrespectful in this play.

Four-year-old Matthew, his older brother John, and his younger sister Sarah became sick with the measles in 1667. John died on April 2. Everyone thought Matthew would die as well, but he and Sarah survived.

Philip Henry instructed his children in many subjects. Although most fathers didn't believe in girls receiving an education, he even taught Sarah the Hebrew language. Matthew sometimes had tutors, but when he was nine years old, he wrote an interesting letter without any assistance.

He addressed it to his "Honored Father," who was in London. Matthew assured his father that he had done his lessons in Latin and Greek every day since his departure and would continue to do so until his return. He wrote, "All my sisters (blessed be God) are in good health," and "my

Philip Henry

two little sisters desire you if you think good to buy each of them a Bible." Matthew politely asked his father to consider buying him a Bible with space for marginal notes, which he greatly desired, and letting one of the girls have his. He wrote, "Longing to see you, which will be very welcome to all the family and especially to him who is and will remain, your dutiful son and obedient servant," before signing his name. He added a few postscripts including, "Please pardon my scribbling."

This letter gives us a wonderful glimpse of a boy who loved his father and his family and God's Word. We even see how much he enjoyed taking notes about the Bible. When he was eleven, Matthew's heart was touched by his father's sermon on Psalm 51:17, "The sacrifices of God are a broken spirit: a broken and a contrite heart, O God, thou wilt not despise."

Matthew later wrote how that text had melted his heart. He discussed his faith with his father, who helped him assess its genuineness. The two often discussed spiritual matters. At thirteen, Matthew described that earlier experience and listed several blessings for which he thanked God, including the gift of salvation.

Philip Henry encouraged his children to have devotions together during the week and especially wanted them to prepare for the Sabbath. He put Matthew in charge of their devotional hour on Saturday afternoon. All the children enjoyed this time of reading the Bible and praying together. If a sister's prayer was too short, Matthew would gently say that "it was impossible, in so short a time" to pray for all the problems and people they could bring before God. The girls didn't seem to mind. When they were adults, they wrote that Matthew's example and comments had encouraged them in the faith.

Dissenting Academy and Law School

While most boys his age were going off to Cambridge or Oxford, Matthew remained at home. Nonconformists were no longer permitted to study theology at those schools or be ordained to the ministry. His parents supervised his instruction until he was eighteen. He then traveled to London to attend Reverend Thomas Doolittle's dissenting academy. Such schools were illegal, but many of them provided a better education than the national universities.

Only about a month after Henry arrived, he and his roommate were among a number of students who became very ill. His roommate died, but Henry recovered enough to return home. He suffered a relapse, but eventually recovered and continued his education under

Gray's Inn, interior
BY KIND PERMISSION OF THE MASTERS OF THE BENCH OF THE "HONOURABLE SOCIETY OF GRAY'S INN"

his father's instruction. He longed to become a minister of the Word, but that door seemed closed. A family friend, who was a dissenting minister, suggested Matthew study law. After much discussion and prayer, Matthew and his father decided that was his best option. He enrolled in law school at Gray's Inn in London when he was twenty-two. His keen mind and amazing memory made him an excellent student. The intense persecution occurring in France captivated his attention as he took private French lessons.

Persecution was strong in England during this time. His father was arrested and spent three weeks in prison at Chester Castle. Henry was careful in his actions and in what he wrote in his letters home. He probably heard nonconformist ministers preach in secret meetings, but he wrote only about Church of England sermons.

Henry concluded his legal studies and preached a farewell sermon to his fellow students. In it, he spoke about the glorious return of Christ and the resurrection of the dead, urging the students to be sure of their faith in Jesus Christ. Then they would be gathered with all believers from around the globe to be united as one church at Christ's return. With the current fierce persecution caused by divisions among Christians, his message must have made an impression on the young men.

Preaching and Ordination

The desire to become a minister was still strong within Henry. After his return home, he began preaching at houses in the neighborhood, developing a reputation for convicting sermons that touched people's hearts. On a trip to Chester, he preached to people in three different locations. When it seemed nonconformists might be allowed to worship more freely, the people of Chester asked him to be their minister.

He agreed to come, but only after he had visited London. Perhaps he wanted to determine if and how he should be ordained. In London, he found several dissenting congregations worshipping openly. The King's Declaration of Indulgence in April of 1687 paved the way for more freedom. Six Presbyterian ministers examined Henry, asking him questions about his beliefs and life. He did his own soul-searching as well. On May 9, 1687, the six pastors ordained Henry as a minister of the gospel of Jesus Christ. On June 2, he preached in Chester on 1 Corinthians 2:2, "I determined not to know any thing among you, save Jesus Christ, and him crucified."

Family Life—and Death

Six weeks after Henry arrived in Chester, he married Katharine Hardware. Less than two years later, Katharine became ill with smallpox and died in childbirth. She was only twenty-five. Henry named the baby Katharine, after her mother. Her grandfather, Philip Henry, baptized her. The congregation wept when Matthew spoke of his loss. He confessed that God had made "an everlasting covenant" with him and "this is all my salvation, and all my desire," and accordingly "I offer up this my child to the Great God, a plant out of dry ground, desiring she may be implanted into Christ."

Mrs. Hardware, Henry's mother-in-law, later advised him to marry again. She suggested a relative of hers, Mary Warburton. Matthew married Mary on July 8, 1690. God soon blessed the couple with a daughter, Elizabeth.

Little Elizabeth's parents rejoiced to see her grow and begin to walk and talk. But at only a year of age, she became feverish with whooping cough. Henry sat by her bedside one morning, having watched her suffer a great deal during the night. He wrote: "The will of the Lord be done. I have said, if the Lord will spare her, I will endeavor to bring her up for him. I am now sitting by her, thinking of the mischievous nature of original sin, by which death reigns over poor infants."

Three days later, Elizabeth died. Henry called Elizabeth's funeral "a sad day's work" and wrote, "There is now a pretty little garment laid up in the wardrobe of the grave to be worn again at the resurrection. Blessed be God for the hope of this."

Less than a year later, another daughter was born. The baby, named Mary, died at only three weeks. On the following Lord's Day, Henry said in his sermon, "If a sparrow does not fall without the will of God, then a child does not. Comfort yourselves at such a time in God's covenant with you and your seed. Fetch your comforts from the Lord Jesus who was dead, and is alive, and lives for evermore."

Mary gave birth to a third daughter, Esther, in 1694. No doubt her parents prayed often for God to bless her with good health. Henry's first daughter, Katharine, was five years old by this time.

On June 23, 1696, Philip Henry—the father Matthew loved and admired so much—experienced sudden and severe pain. Matthew and the doctor arrived late that evening. While his mother held Philip's hand, Matthew sat beside the head of the bed, supporting his father with a pillow behind his back.

Philip knew he was dying. He said, "Son, the Lord bless you and grant that you may do worthily in your generation, and be more serviceable to the church of God than I have been."

"Oh, Sir," Matthew said, "pray for me that I may but tread in your steps."

For a while, Philip prayed and quoted from the Bible. But with his final words, he was not able to finish one verse: "O death, where is thy—" A few moments later, the Lord took him home. He was sixty-five years old. This loss astonished and grieved Matthew, but he turned to Christ for comfort as he had after the deaths of his first wife and two of his daughters.

In 1697, another daughter was born to Matthew and Mary. The Henrys named her Ann, probably after Matthew's sister. He was still close to all four sisters, three of whom lived in Chester and attended his church with their families.

In the summer of the same year Ann was born, three of Henry's sisters became very sick. Katharine recovered, but Eleanor died at the beginning of August and Ann passed away early in September.

An outbreak of measles swept through Chester the following year. Both four-year-old Esther and one-year-old Ann caught the infection. Out of the many sick children in the area, only Ann died.

Still more sorrow visited the Henry family. Two of his brothers-in-law died unexpectedly in 1699: Katharine's husband, Dr. Tylston, and Eleanor's husband, Samuel Radford. Because Eleanor had died only two years earlier, the Radfords' three daughters and one son were left without parents. Matthew and Mary Henry legally adopted those four children. Suddenly the sounds of six children rang in their household.

And the family continued to grow. A son was born in May of 1700 and named after his grandfather, Philip Henry. Over the next ten years, four more daughters were born: Elizabeth, Sarah, Theodosia, and Mary.

As his father had done, Henry spent time in worship each morning with his family. He put together a book of Psalm selections for family worship. Every afternoon, he reviewed simple catechism questions and answers with the younger children. After they had gone to bed at night, he taught the older ones. Throughout the week, he reviewed the previous Sabbath's sermons with all the children.

Chester Ministry

During the years of joys and sorrows within his family, Henry worked tirelessly as a faithful minister for his congregation at Chester. When he first arrived, the church's forty-five members met in a converted stable. The congregation later moved to a more permanent building in White Friars. Within three years of Henry's arrival, the church included 250 people.

Henry's practice was to begin Lord's Day worship at nine in the morning with singing Psalm 100, followed by a short and meaningful prayer. He read a passage from the Old Testament, explaining it as he went through it. The congregation sang another psalm, followed by Henry praying for a half hour. Then he preached. After the sermon, he gave the blessing. He followed the same pattern for the afternoon service, except he used a New Testament passage instead. His sermons were based on texts that went through the books of the Bible. The Lord's Supper was administered on the first Sunday of the month. Nearly every month, ten to fifteen new members partook of Holy Communion.

On Saturday afternoons, Henry instructed the church's children. He alternated methods annually, teaching them catechism for a year and preaching simple sermons to them the next.

From the beginning of his time in Chester, Henry ministered to people beyond his own congregation. He regularly preached to prisoners in Chester Castle. He held monthly services at several neighboring villages and traveled every year to preach in locations farther away. He organized theological conferences at which participating

Chester Castle Chapel, where Matthew Henry reputedly preached to prisoners
PHOTO BY RICHARD NEVELL

Dissenter's Chapel, built 1699–1700

pastors spoke on a specific subject. Crowds of people gained immeasurable benefit from these meetings.

In 1699, the church purchased land and constructed a beautiful new building between Crook Lane and Trinity Street in Chester. Services began there in 1700. Six years later, another congregation joined Henry's and increased the membership to 350. A gallery was added for additional seating.

Commentary and Writing

A two-story summerhouse in Henry's backyard served as his study. Not only a popular preacher, but also a well-known author, he wrote and published many books; but he is best remembered for his famous *Bible Commentary*. Ever since he could read and write, he had kept detailed notes about Scripture texts. He wrote and collected observations over his years of careful study and preaching. When he was forty-two, he began writing commentaries on the books of the Bible.

Hackney Ministry and Death

Several London congregations asked Henry to be their minister over the years. He always turned them down, cherishing the strength that came to God's people when a long-visioned shepherd cared for their souls. In 1710, he agreed to serve the church at Hackney, but he said he could not come for some time. He struggled with his decision, and two more years passed before he finally preached his farewell sermon at Chester. He and many others were filled with sorrow at the parting.

He served the Hackney church as faithfully as he had in Chester, and he was every bit as busy. He preached three sermons each Lord's Day in his own church, and sometimes preached in other churches earlier in the morning and later in the evening. During the week, he often preached two or three times a day in the London area. On Saturdays, he taught catechism, bringing these truths alive for a new generation of youth and leading to a renewal of its instruction all over London. He visited charity schools and encouraged generous giving to the needy, which he reinforced by his own example. His commentary continued to take form as he finished the Old Testament books and began in the New Testament.

The Hackney church had suggested that Henry take a few weeks each year to return to Chester and preach in the area. He did so in 1713, and enjoyed seeing old friends and preaching in familiar places. In 1714, he made his second visit to Chester. He began the return journey on June 21, planning to preach that day at Nantwich, where his sister Sarah lived. On the way, his horse stumbled, and Henry was thrown off. His companions urged him to rest, but he insisted on continuing to Nantwich.

Sarah noticed that his preaching was not as lively as usual and he seemed very sleepy afterward. He was obviously not well enough to continue his journey and was taken to the nearby home of a fellow minister.

Henry asked his friends to pray for him, saying that "for now I cannot pray for myself." At five the next morning, he suffered a stroke. He died three hours later. It was Tuesday, June 22, 1714, and he was fifty-one years old.

The funeral procession included coaches and horses of many important people and ministers paying their last respects to a man admired by people of differing views. Several ministers preached funeral sermons in Hackney and Chester.

Memorial to Matthew Henry in Chester, England
PHOTO BY CHRIS KEMP

Henry was buried in Chester, next to his first wife, Katharine. His widow, Mary, was left to raise their five youngest children: Philip (14), Elizabeth (12), Sarah (10),

Theodosia (6), and Mary (3). By this time, Katharine was twenty-five, Esther was twenty, and the four adopted Radford children were probably in their twenties as well.

Although little is known about what happened to the daughters, Philip served as a Member of Parliament. He never married and owned a large estate. When Matthew and Mary named him after his grandfather, they may have hoped he would become a minister. They certainly prayed for him to live a godly life. But he didn't demonstrate the strong faith of his father and grandfather. In fact, he had the meeting house on his grandfather's farm torn down. And he cared so little for the Henry name that he took his mother's maiden name to become Philip Warburton.

His Enduring Legacy

Henry completed Genesis through Acts of his commentary. After his death, thirteen of his friends used his notes and writings to compile Romans through Revelation. *Matthew Henry's Bible Commentary* has been reprinted numerous times in different formats over the years. Most sets contain six volumes, but it can also be found in one book. The single volumes usually have been abridged, losing much of Henry's Reformed emphasis. While a few other commentaries may go into more detail regarding language and grammar, none supersede Henry's practical and personal application. This amazing work remains one of the most widely used commentaries of all time.

Henry would have been surprised at its popularity. Rather than focusing on fame and fortune, he desired only to live for God. One of his most repeated quotes is: "A life spent in the service of God, and communion with him, is the most comfortable life anyone can live in this world."

Jonathan Edwards

1703–1758

In the Hands of a Loving God

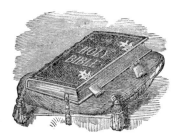

In a secret spot deep in the thick forest, a young boy sat alone in a wooden shack. He stared out intently, his hand resting on a scrap of paper on his knee. The breeze lifted the paper's edge. He smoothed it down and jotted a note. Then he gazed outside again.

The boy's name was Jonathan Edwards. And he wasn't pretending to be a spy or a soldier or a pirate. He was watching spiders.

He observed them spinning webs and long threads. He guessed they ejected a liquid, which became a sticky string in the air. The spiders laid so many eggs that he wondered why the world wasn't overrun with millions of the creatures. Then he saw the hatchlings weave delicate balloons and rise to catch the east breeze. He realized most would drift on air currents to the Atlantic Ocean, where they would be lost. He bent his head and carefully recorded what he was learning about spiders and their amazing gift for spinning.

"Multitudes of times I have beheld with wonderment and pleasure the spider marching in the air from one tree to another," he wrote, "their little shining webs and glistening strings of a great length and at such a height. One would think they were tacked to the sky by one end were it not that they were moving and floating."

He spent many hours in the shack, studying God's creation and praising Him for its beauty and variety. He and his friends—none older than ten—had built the crude booth by themselves. But the shed hadn't been built for play or for a secret boys' club. Its purpose was prayer.

Although only a boy, Jonathan longed to become closer to God. He was blessed with a sharp mind and a keen interest in nature. Later, as a teenager, he wrote his observations about spiders into an essay that demonstrated his amazing ability for scientific observation. Throughout his life, Jonathan marveled at God's beautiful world, but he loved God's beautiful Word even more.

Jonathan Edwards was born in East Windsor, Connecticut, on October 5, 1703. He lived at the end of the Puritan era and during times of spiritual revival in New England. In a generation of great thinkers, he became one of the greatest.

Many people still believe he was America's most important theologian.

His father and his grandfather were Puritan preachers, and there was never any question that Jonathan, the only son out of eleven children, would follow their footsteps into ministry.

While Jonathan loved to pray and think about religious things, he was often frustrated by the continuing sin in his life. But one day he was struck by the words of 1 Timothy 1:17, "Now unto the King eternal, immortal, invisible, the only wise God, be honour and glory for ever and ever. Amen."

He later wrote about this experience:

> As I read the words, there came into [and through] my soul…a sense of the glory of the Divine Being… quite different from any thing I ever experienced before. I thought…how excellent a being that was; and how happy I should be, if I might enjoy that God…and be as it were swallowed up in Him.

He repeated the words of the verse over and over to himself, almost singing them in his mind, and prayed for the ability to enjoy God. From that time on, he meditated on Christ as much as possible. When he walked alone in the forests or fields, talking with God, he felt a "sweet burning" in his heart and a great love for Jesus in his soul.

Jonathan's father ran a school in their home and earned a reputation as a good teacher. When Jonathan was only thirteen years old, he began attending the college that would later become known as Yale.

A dedicated student, Edwards enjoyed all his classes and especially the study of philosophy. Instead of adopting a worldly outlook, he applied what he was learning to the

Jonathan Edwards

Birthplace of Jonathan Edwards, East Windsor, Connecticut

truths he already knew from the Bible. When he was eighteen, he graduated as a student of theology and was asked to minister to a congregation in the growing city of New York.

He later wrote, "I went to New York to preach and my longings after God and holiness were much increased. I felt in me a burning desire to be in every thing a complete Christian; and conformed to the blessed image of Christ."

Sometimes Edwards would turn away from the busy streets to walk on the banks of the Hudson River and meditate about God. He often wrote down ways he was determined to improve his behavior or attitude.

Although he loved the congregation in New York, his father wanted him closer to home. He hoped Jonathan would someday take over for his grandfather, Solomon Stoddard, in Northampton, Massachusetts Bay Colony.

For a brief time, Edwards served a church in Bolton, which was only about seventy-five miles from Northampton. Then he agreed to teach at the college he had attended in New Haven. This allowed him to become better acquainted with Sarah Pierrepont, who had become his friend while he was a student. Although Sarah was quite a bit younger than Jonathan, she shared many of his interests. She loved the Lord and enjoyed walking alone in fields or groves, praying to God.

But Yale College was in a terrible state. With no regular director, the instructors had to run the school, teach classes, and try to maintain order among the unruly students. The stress soon made Edwards sick. He tried to travel to his parents' home, but became so ill he nearly died on the way.

After three months, he recovered enough to return to Yale. Although things had not improved, Edwards decided to view his struggles as opportunities to trust God more.

In 1727, his father's dream came true. The Northampton congregation asked Jonathan to assist his grandfather, Solomon Stoddard, with ministerial duties. The security of this position allowed Edwards to propose to Sarah, and the two were married a few months later. Their ceremony was unusual for that day because it included music, which he believed was the "most perfect way" for expressing "sweet" fellowship.

Edwards shared his grandfather's concern for people who seemed indifferent about their souls. Both men felt it was important and also kind to warn people about the real danger of hell. But during Edwards's initial months in Northampton, his preaching appeared to have little effect.

Solomon Stoddard, Edwards's grandfather

very ground rolled like a surging sea. It was an earthquake! Walls cracked and chimneys fell from rooftops. The strong quake shook all of New England, and aftershocks continued to strike for nine more days.

People were terrified. Convinced the earthquake was a sign of Christ's return and God's judgment, they flocked to churches for special days of prayer and fasting. Edwards preached at a community service, urging people to repent of their sins. While admitting earthquakes "may often have

Edwards's church in Northampton

Young people might attend church on the Lord's Day, but as soon as the sun set, they'd meet for rowdy parties that lasted all night and often included sinful behaviors. No sermon could shake them out of their stubbornness—until October 29, 1727.

That Sunday evening, many of the young people went off to party with their friends as usual. Suddenly dishes rattled and buildings creaked. Bushes and trees waved. The

natural causes," he emphasized God's control and how He could be using the earthquake to warn young people. They and many older people took it to heart, and revival spread through the town and countryside.

Soon God blessed Jonathan and Sarah with a baby. They would eventually have three sons and eight daughters, children whom they loved and raised well. They set aside time each evening for family devotions and lively conversation.

Edwards studied and prayed for about thirteen hours each day, but took a break in the afternoon for outdoor exercise like chopping wood or planting trees. He often rode his horse to a grove about three miles away, where he would pray and jot down his reflections. To keep track of these thoughts, he pinned them to different parts of his clothing. Sometimes Sarah had to "unpin" him when he came home.

After his grandfather's death, Edwards prayed for another spiritual revival. The Holy Spirit worked through Edwards's preaching to change the hearts of hundreds. The Northampton congregation grew even larger, and plans were made to construct a new building.

One Sabbath morning during a crowded worship service, the balcony of the old building fell—directly on more than seventy people! Miraculously, no one was killed. The high backs of the pews may have helped protect them, but certainly God's hand was their greatest protection.

This revival in Northampton lasted about a year and spread to many other towns. About five years later, an even bigger revival began and lasted nearly two years. It became known as the Great Awakening, and involved an English evangelist named George Whitefield.

Whitefield preached with dramatic speech and gestures, which Edwards didn't think necessary. But he invited Whitefield to come to Northampton to preach and to stay in his home. By grace, Whitefield's preaching was effectual in the hearts of the congregation, bringing many to tears. He traveled to other parts of New England, drawing crowds of thousands each time he preached.

Edwards didn't like too much emotion in worship, but he also knew the Holy Spirit could do anything. The Spirit worked powerfully on July 8, 1741, when Edwards preached his most famous sermon, "Sinners in the Hands of an Angry God."

In this sermon, Edwards used spider web imagery—no doubt based on his lifelong observation of the creature's fragile threads—to vividly describe the real danger of hell for the unrepentant sinner. "There is nothing between you and hell but the air; it is only the power and mere pleasure of God that holds you up," he said. "Your wickedness makes you as…heavy as lead…and if God should let you go, you would immediately…plunge into the bottomless gulf…and all your righteousness, would have no more influence to uphold you and keep you out of hell, than a spider's web would have to stop a falling rock." He added, "The God that holds you over the pit of hell, much as one holds a spider… over the fire…is dreadfully provoked."

People began to weep with grief over their sins. Edwards did not leave them hanging in hopelessness, but pointed them to the cross. "But here you are in the land of the living and in the house of God, and have an opportunity to obtain salvation." He ended, "Therefore, let every one that is out of Christ, now awake and fly from the wrath to come."

The preaching of George Whitefield
BOLTON LIBRARY & MUSEUM

God transformed many hearts through that powerful sermon. Edwards took no credit for himself, recognizing it as the work of the Spirit, who "alone can revive the church and awaken the world."

When conflict arose in the American churches after the Great Awakening, Edwards tried to bring balance to the discussion. He wrote about how conversion had to be genuine. He compared hypocrites to comets that flared brightly before burning up, while true believers were like stars glowing steadily in space. He wanted people to stop arguing about the Great Awakening and focus instead on living in ways that glorified God.

Edwards also wanted the people in his congregation to worship according to the Bible. His grandfather had been very popular in the church and throughout New England, but Edwards disagreed with two of his practices: allowing the partaking of the Lord's Supper by non-professing Christians, and allowing the baptism of their children. These non-professing Christians were church members who lacked personal assurance of salvation. They could not be admitted to the Lord's Supper, according to Edwards, because they could not give a credible testimony of personal conversion. Edwards believed that the church had to change these long-standing practices.

He taught that only true Christians who had professed their faith should come to the Lord's Table. Many in the congregation became upset with him for doing things differently than his grandfather had done. When Edwards preached against particular sins or tried to discipline church members, the people became angrier. They complained that he was being paid too much money, even though he needed a good income to care for his large family and to practice the hospitality that he and Sarah always extended to visitors.

On top of all these problems, grief visited the Edwards family. Daughter Jerusha was engaged to David Brainerd, a missionary to the Indians. When visiting the Edwards's house, he became ill and died. Jerusha, who had nursed him during his illness, died only four months later. Then Edwards lost an uncle who had been a great friend and strong supporter. With him gone, other relatives dared to criticize Edwards more openly.

People began to call for his dismissal. A Council of Churches was asked to decide the matter, and those men sided with the congregation rather than Edwards. On June 22, 1750, the church voted to dismiss him. In his farewell sermon, he set a calm tone and left the issue up to the Lord. He focused on the needs of the people rather than his own.

David Brainerd

The following months of uncertainty must have been difficult for the Edwards family, but they trusted God for their future. Edwards wrote to a friend, "We are in the hands of God, and I bless Him; I am not anxious concerning His disposal of us."

In August of 1751, Edwards became a missionary to the Housatonic Indians in Stockbridge, Massachusetts. Most of the white people lived on a hill at the edge of the village, but he and his family chose to live in the center of town, among the Indians. The younger Edwards children made new friends and learned a new language.

Once again, conflict made his work difficult. One family (related to Edwards) tried to control everything in the settlement. Some of the people supervising the mission cared more about making money from trade than they did about spreading the gospel. Despite these troubles and sickness in his family and himself, Edwards wrote prolifically during this time.

Edwards taught the Indian children not just to read English words, but to understand the things those words represented. He included singing with the lessons because he believed "music, especially sacred music, has a powerful effect to soften the heart into tenderness…and to give the mind a relish for objects of superior character." The native people liked and trusted him.

But other people broke promises to the natives that caused increasing problems. Several families left. Relations between the English and the Indians were deteriorating all over New England. The French, fighting against the English in other parts of the world, convinced Indians to help them attack the English. Disheartened by all that was happening to the mission and in the country, Edwards became quite ill.

On the first day of September in 1754, Edwards preached for the first time in several weeks. He was still extremely weak, and his knees shook. He made it through the service, but nothing could have prepared him for what happened after it.

A man rushed into town, shouting and weeping. He had seen a Canadian Indian taking a child from a home in the country. When he gave chase, the Indian killed the child and fled. The shocked man hurried back to the house, where he found the bodies of a servant and a baby. An Indian, standing over the terrified father and two other children, ran away when the Englishman entered.

The entire town of Stockbridge panicked. Some people fled without bothering to pack. Soon soldiers poured into town and built a fort around the Edwards home. Edwards had to make sure the soldiers and their horses had lodging and food. After things calmed down a bit, the soldiers left.

During this time of war, Edwards continued maintaining the school and mission as best he could. He and Sarah sent some of their children to live with relatives in safe locations, but they allowed ten-year-old Jonathan Jr. to travel with a missionary to another Indian settlement two hundred miles away. The boy's ability to speak the language pleased those natives and helped the missionary a great deal.

When the war reached that village, Jonathan Jr. and the missionary walked many miles through deep snow to a mansion that had been turned into a fort near Albany, New York. At the end of winter, the boy returned home safely.

The Edwards's daughter, Esther, had married Aaron Burr, a pastor in Newark and President of New Jersey College. In 1757, he visited Stockbridge and reported that a revival was taking place at the college. Edwards, of course,

rejoiced to hear it. But only a month later, Burr died. The trustees of the college, now named Princeton, asked Jonathan Edwards to become the next president.

Edwards wrote a long letter in response, stating all the reasons he didn't feel qualified for the position and describing the books he was busy writing. Despite these objections, the trustees still wanted him to come. They agreed to everything he asked. Edwards doubted the Stockbridge church would release him, but the council decided he should go to serve the college. When they made the announcement, Edwards—who rarely showed his emotions—wept.

Perhaps he hated to leave the people he loved so much. Maybe he felt overwhelmed by the task he faced. Whatever created his unusual reaction, he quickly controlled his tears and declared he would follow God's will in the matter.

In January of 1758, Edwards traveled to Princeton, although most of his family stayed behind to sell their property and follow him later. His daughter, Susannah, wrote that he bid them farewell "as affectionately, as if he should not come again." After leaving the house, he turned and said, "I commit you to God."

His daughter Lucy was already in Princeton, staying with her recently widowed sister Esther. He was warmly welcomed at the college, and immediately threw himself into his work. The future finally looked hopeful for this important theologian.

Lucy had been very ill with smallpox the previous summer, and Edwards—always interested in scientific advances—decided to take advantage of the relatively new inoculation against the dreaded disease. On February 23, he and other family members received the smallpox vaccination. Although he initially felt fine, Edwards became ill with

Early Princeton Seminary

smallpox a few days later. Sores in his throat prevented him from taking any medicine, and nothing could be done to heal the infection. For a month, Lucy nursed him as he suffered with no hope of cure.

One day he wrote:

Dear Lucy, it seems to me to be the will of God that I must shortly leave you; therefore give my kindest love to my dear wife, and tell her that the uncommon union, which has so long subsisted between us, has been of such a nature, as I trust is spiritual, and therefore will continue forever. And I hope she will be supported under so great a trial and submit cheerfully to the will of God.

As to my children, you are now like to be left fatherless, which I hope will be an inducement to you all, to seek a Father who will never fail you.

After writing this and other messages, Edwards glanced around and asked, "Now where is Jesus of Nazareth, my true and never-failing Friend?" Those gathered around him cried, but he said, "Trust in God, and you need not fear."

On March 22, 1758, Jonathan Edwards died at the age of fifty-four.

Edwards had a brilliant mind and a humble heart. He saw God's beauty in all creation and longed only to serve the Lord. It's hard to understand why God called him home at such a young age, when he was just beginning important work in Christ's kingdom as Princeton Seminary's president. But he would have been the first person to urge us not to question God's will in the matter. All his life, he'd been learning to accept the things that happened to him as part of God's plan. He knew that no matter what, he was safe in the hands of his loving heavenly Father.

~ 23 ~

Conclusion

What Can We Learn from the Puritans?

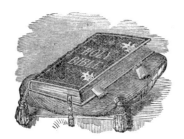

Over the course of this book, you have met many godly Christian people who were called "Puritans." We hope you have learned more about the history of God's works and have been encouraged to follow Jesus Christ. We want to end this book in a practical way. Puritan sermons and books often ended with "uses," or practical lessons we can apply to our lives. What are some lessons we can learn from the Puritans?

If the Puritans could speak to you today, the most important question they would ask is, "Are you born again?" Have you repented of your sins and trusted in Christ Jesus to save you from sin and bring you to God? Can you, by the Spirit's grace, see that God has given you a new heart so that you love God and try to keep His commandments? If not, then no other lesson can help you until you are saved by grace. By grace, you must first come to Christ by faith in His death and resurrection. If, however, you are a child of God, then there are many things you can learn from the Puritans. Here are some of them.

1. *Fill your mind with the Bible.* Read the Bible, listen to the Bible, memorize the Bible, speak the Bible, sing the Bible—do whatever you can to soak your life in God's Word. It was said of John Bunyan that you could cut him anywhere, and he would bleed Bible. Don't just read your favorite parts in the Bible. Read the whole book, and then read it again. The person blessed by God does not listen to bad people but loves God's Word and thinks about it often (Ps. 1:1–2).

2. *Believe that God is in control and people must make good choices.* Many people believe one or the other: either God is in control of all that happens and people do not have the freedom of choice, or people make real choices and God is not in control. The Puritans believed in both God's control and people's choices, for the Bible teaches both to encourage our faith and obedience. Take your stand upon the truth that God works everything according to the plan that He chose (Eph. 1:11), and the truth that Christ will judge us all for what we did in this life, whether good or bad (2 Cor. 5:10). Like Moses, choose by gracious faith "rather to suffer affliction with the people of God,

than to enjoy the pleasures of sin for a season; esteeming the reproach of Christ greater riches than the treasures in Egypt" (Heb. 11:25–26).

3. *Keep your eyes on Jesus Christ*. A Puritan named Isaac Ambrose wrote that the whole Christian life is a matter of "looking unto Jesus" (Heb. 12:2). Look to Christ for every spiritual blessing. We have no other righteousness before God than Christ's obedience and blood. Christ is our light, and without Him we are blind people stumbling about in the darkness. In Christ alone do we find the strength to overcome sin and Satan. Abide in Christ as a branch in the vine, and you will bear much fruit (John 15:5). On the last day, you will rise with Christ in glory.

4. *Love the true God*. The Puritans were God-centered people. They longed to be true worshipers of God and close friends with Him. John Owen taught us that you should get to know each person in the Trinity: the Father as your loving Father, the Son as your Savior, and the Holy Spirit as the One who makes you holy. As Thomas Goodwin said, we must not be satisfied until all three persons are near to us, pouring out God's love upon us. Pray for yourself and others that you would enjoy "the grace of the Lord Jesus Christ, and the love of God, and the communion of the Holy Ghost" (2 Cor. 13:14). The more you know God's love, the more you should love Him in return, until your whole soul is a flame of love.

5. *Keep following Christ through trials*. Don't be surprised when it gets hard to be a Christian. The Lord Jesus said that being His disciple is like carrying a cross—which means dying to yourself and this world (Luke 9:23). Remember that God is in control even of bad things, and He uses hard things to train His children to share in His holiness (Heb. 12:6, 10). Christian, your painful trials are the path to glory. Puritan John Trapp said that a man riding his horse to be crowned as king will not worry about a rainy day. We can bear our troubles if we remember that we are on the way to reign with Christ forever.

6. *Make your family a little church*. Don't put away your Bible after church until the next Lord's Day. Read your Bible with your family and pray together. Talk to each other about God's Word whatever you are doing (Deut. 6:7). If you are a child, pray for the Holy Spirit to work in your father and mother so that they can lead you well. Encourage them and thank them whenever they teach you God's Word and pray with you. Thomas Brooks compared a family without prayer to a house without a roof—it's open to all the storms of heaven.

7. *Pray daily, especially for the Holy Spirit*. Prayer should not be only for emergencies. Rather, give your life to praying and thanking God (Col. 4:2). Just as children ask their parents for food and believe they will get it, so Christians should ask our Father in heaven every day for the Holy Spirit and believe He will feed our souls (Luke 11:11–13). Remember, you are in a battle against the devil. Matthew Henry said that prayer buckles on all the Christian's armor. If you don't know how to pray, then follow Henry's advice: read the Bible and pray back to God what He says in His Word. If God's Word tells you who God is, then turn it into praises. If it gives you commands to obey, then confess to God how you have broken them. If it offers promises, then ask God to do what He said He will do.

8. *Seek good Christian friends.* Following Christ fully can be lonely, for many will stand against you, as Joshua and Caleb learned (Num. 14:6–10, 24). If you find someone who loves God and obeys His Word, then be a friend to him and receive his friendship. Don't be proud and foolish and pretend that you don't need anyone's help. "Two are better than one," and "a threefold cord is not quickly broken" (Eccles. 4:9, 12). The Puritans were glad to have spiritual brothers and sisters to help them follow Christ. Christians are members of Christ's body, and every member needs the other members (1 Cor. 12:20–21). As John Howe looked back over fifty years of sweet friendship with one man, he enjoyed warm memories of how they often prayed together and gave each other good advice.

9. *Pray for your church and be there with them.* Come with your family to all the regular meetings and services of the church (Heb. 10:25). Be there whenever the church gets together for teaching, fellowship, or prayer (Acts 2:42). The church is God's temple (1 Cor. 3:16), and God especially meets with us through preaching and praying together (Matt. 18:20). The Puritans often faced persecution, and sometimes had to worship in the woods to hide from the authorities. However, they still took the risk because they valued God's church so much. Be a committed part of the church, even if you are too young to join its membership yet. That should be shown in your prayers. Your prayers and requests should be "for all the saints" (Eph. 6:18), especially the Christians whom you know in your church.

10. *Be a serious, humble, and joyful Christian.* Never play at being a Christian while your heart is not in it. By God's grace, give Christ your whole heart and your whole life. Don't be afraid that people will make fun of you if you take God's Word seriously. Fear God and not man (Matt. 10:28). Remind yourself that life is short and heaven and hell are real. Think little of yourself and much of the greatness of God. Also do not think that faithfulness means being sour in your attitude and bitter in your words. "Serve the LORD with fear, and rejoice with trembling" (Ps. 2:11). If Christ died for your sins, He will come again to bring you to glory. Rejoice in the Lord. Have hope. If you are a true believer, one day you will stand with the Puritans and all Christians—past, present, and future—around the throne of God and the Lamb, singing the praises of the Savior. Be sure of this: whatever the cost, Christ is worth it.

Appendix A

Glossary

Act of Toleration. A law passed in 1689 that allowed freedom of worship for Puritans.

Acts of Uniformity. Laws requiring ministers to use only the *Book of Common Prayer* in worship or be punished. The Act of Uniformity of 1662 resulted in the Great Ejection, when 2,000 ministers were removed from their positions.

Archbishop of Canterbury. The title of the highest ranking official in the Church of England.

Bay Psalm Book. The first book published by the Massachusetts Bay settlers, who translated the Psalms from Hebrew to English and set the text to music for singing in worship.

Book of Common Prayer. The Church of England's authorized liturgy that caused problems of conscience for many Puritans. The Puritans particularly objected to four ceremonies that the liturgy in the prayer book insisted upon: (1) the use of the wedding ring in the marriage service, which to the Puritan mind was equivalent with supporting the Roman Catholic belief that marriage is a sacrament; (2) kneeling to receive the signs and seals at the Lord's Supper, which the Puritans regarded as encouraging the continuation of transubstantiation—that Christ is physically present in the elements so that we worship Him in the bread and wine; (3) the wearing of the ministerial surplice—a white outer garment, which to the Puritan mind, implied that the clergy were somehow closer to God by their special clothing, which reflected the Roman Catholic hierarchical system; and (4) marking the forehead of one being baptized with the sign of the cross, which the Puritans felt added something to the Scriptures and obscured the real nature of the sacrament.

Book of Sports. King James I published this book in 1617, approving Sunday participation in certain sports and games, which many Puritans believed failed to keep the day holy. His son, Charles I, required in 1633 that ministers read from the book at worship services. Some Puritan pastors obeyed but reminded the congregation that these were the words of a man, not God. Other Puritans refused to read from the book.

Congregationalists. People who believe in a form of church government (Congregationalism) in which each congregation is ruled only by its own leaders. (See "Independents.")

Conventicle Acts. Laws forbidding Puritans to meet in small or secret gatherings for worship.

Court of High Commission. The supreme church court in England that prosecuted many Puritans.

Declarations of Indulgence. Declarations permitting some forms of dissent or disagreement, which were issued occasionally from 1669 to 1687. Harsh treatment of Puritans flared up between these declarations.

Diocese. The territory ruled by a particular bishop within the Church of England.

Dissenters. People or groups who disagreed with some aspects of the established national churches in England and Scotland.

English Civil War. Between 1642 and 1651, three main conflicts occurred between royalist and parliamentary forces. Because battles took place in England, Scotland, and Ireland, these are sometimes called the Wars of the Three Kingdoms. Political and religious reasons fueled and complicated the Civil War. Although most Puritans favored Parliament's efforts toward more religious freedoms, other Puritans supported the king as God's ordained ruler. Nearly all Puritans were dismayed by the execution of Charles I in 1649. The Civil War ended when his son, Charles II, was exiled in 1651.

Five Mile Act. This law prohibited Puritan pastors from living or preaching within five miles of any town in which they had formerly ministered.

Glorious Revolution. The English Parliament invited Prince William of Orange from the Netherlands and his wife, Princess Mary Stuart, to rule the United Kingdom. As committed Protestants, they ended the suffering and persecution of Puritans.

Great Awakening. A Protestant religious revival that took place primarily in America. Often accompanied by powerful and passionate preaching, it stressed the need for true conversion and a personal relationship with Christ.

Great Ejection. More than 2,000 Puritan ministers were expelled from their churches and homes, and lost their incomes, because they refused to fully follow the *Book of Common Prayer* in public worship.

Great Plague. An outbreak of Bubonic Plague in London from 1665–1666 that took about 70,000 lives, although some historians think unrecorded deaths could make the number as high as 100,000 or even 200,000. Many Puritan pastors remained in the city to minister to the sick and grieving.

House of Commons. Lower house of the English Parliament with members elected from the common people.

House of Lords. Upper house of the English Parliament with members belonging to the aristocracy or to the hierarchy of the church.

Independents. People who believed congregations should govern themselves without the interference of synods or religious officials such as bishops. Churches within this movement later developed a congregational system of government.

King Philip's War. A Wampanoag chieftain called King Philip raised an army and began attacking European settlers in New England in 1675. Some Puritans, like John Eliot, tried to help peaceful Native Americans, especially those who had become Christians. But most colonists distrusted Native Americans, and many fought against the natives. Hundreds, perhaps even thousands, of Native American Christians were driven from their homes and most lost their lives.

Lecturer. A minister who preached on Scripture passages during the week. These lectures often focused on longer texts than Sunday sermons. Sometimes towns, trade associations, parishes, or wealthy individuals sponsored the lecturer.

Long Parliament. The session of the English Parliament that lasted from 1640 to 1660.

Lord Protector. The title Oliver Cromwell took for himself while he ruled the Commonwealth of England.

Massachusetts Bay Colony. A group of Puritans formed a company in England and then sailed to New England to found this settlement on the shore of Massachusetts Bay in 1630.

New Model Army. The Parliamentary army was organized and trained in a new way. Rather than officers being men only from the upper classes, anyone who was a capable leader could become an officer. Mounted men were outfitted with sturdy leather jerkins instead of heavy armor, so the cavalry could quickly break through enemy ranks. Instead of facing the enemy and advancing from the front, Oliver Cromwell used a new tactic of attacking the enemy's weaker flanks. He also trained the soldiers to stay with the main battle instead of chasing individuals. Most of the New Model Army were Puritans or became Puritans. They often sang Psalms when attacking.

Nonconformists. People who believed some Church of England's practices were unbiblical and could not participate in them.

Nonconformists were ridiculed as "Puritans" for trying to practice a more pure religion.

Parliamentarians. People who supported the rights of Parliament over against the Stuart kings who tried to exercise absolute power.

Pequot War. The Pequot had conquered other Native American tribes and controlled the Connecticut area. When they began attacking Europeans in 1637, the colonists and some friendly tribes fought against the Pequot and eventually defeated them.

Presbyterians. Those who hold that Christ placed His church under the government of presbyters (ministers and elders), which were to meet local, regional, and national assemblies. Nearly all Puritans adhered to Presbyterian polity; in fact, many Puritans found a way, at least for a time, to operate as Presbyterian churches within the bounds of the Church of England.

Restoration of the monarchy. The return of Charles II in 1660 brought back to England the reign of a king. For about eleven years before this, Parliament and a Lord Protector had ruled the country as a Commonwealth or Protectorate.

Roundheads. "A Puritan or member of the Parliamentary party who wore his hair cut short" (Webster).

Royalists (sometimes called Cavaliers). The troops and supporters of the king.

Savoy Declaration. A modification of the Westminster Confession so as to promote Congregational polity. Most Puritans viewed the Savoy Declaration as an abridged and spiritually diminished version of the Westminster Confession.

Separatists. People who separated from the Church of England and thought individuals and congregations should have nothing to do with it.

Solemn League and Covenant. A 1643 treaty between England and Scotland that included both political and religious elements. It resulted in the work of the Westminster Assembly.

Synod of Dort. An international church meeting held at Dordrecht, the Netherlands, to respond to the threat of Arminianism. The Synod approved final forms of the Belgic Confession and the Heidelberg Catechism and developed the Canons of Dort. These documents, known as the Three Forms of Unity, still guide many Reformed churches today.

Vicar. A minister serving a parish who is appointed by a wealthy or influential individual known as a patron.

Westminster Assembly. A large group of theologians who met at Westminster Abbey from July 1, 1643, to February 22, 1649, to try to bring unity to the churches in England, Scotland, and Ireland. In addition to other significant documents, they wrote catechisms and a confession known as the Westminster Standards that still guide Presbyterian churches today.

Appendix B

Timeline

Puritan Heroes

1542–1594	Richard Greenham
1558–1602	William Perkins
1576–1633	William Ames
1577–1635	Richard Sibbes
1584–1652	John Cotton
1586–1647	Thomas Hooker
1600–1646	Jeremiah Burroughs
1600–1679	Thomas Goodwin
1604–1690	John Eliot
1605–1649	Thomas Shepard
1608–1680	Thomas Brooks
1612–1672	Anne Bradstreet
1615–1691	Richard Baxter
1616–1683	John Owen
1618–1651	Christopher Love
1628–1688	John Bunyan
1628–1691	John Flavel
1630–1705	John Howe
1634–1668	Joseph Alleine
1662–1714	Matthew Henry
1703–1758	Jonathan Edwards

Rulers and Events

1547	Edward VI is crowned as King of England
1549	*Book of Common Prayer* first published
1549	First Act of Uniformity
1552	*Book of Common Prayer* revised
1552	Second Act of Uniformity
1553	"Bloody Mary" Tudor becomes Queen of England
1558	Elizabeth I is crowned Queen of England
1559	Act of Uniformity makes *Book of Common Prayer* a requirement for worship
1567	Ministers required to wear special vestments
1571	Parliament approves Thirty-Nine Articles of Religion
1603	James VI of Scotland becomes James I, King of England
1604	James I rejects Puritan requests for reform
1611	King James (or Authorized) Version of the Bible published
1618	James I promotes games on Sunday through his *Book of Sports*
1625	Charles I crowned King of England
1628	Oliver Cromwell becomes Member of Parliament
1633	William Laud appointed as Archbishop of Canterbury

1642	English Civil War breaks out between Parliament and King Charles I
1643	Westminster Assembly begins
1645	Archbishop Laud executed by action of Parliament
1645	Cromwell's Parliamentary army defeats Charles I
1649	Parliament orders beheading of Charles I and proclaims Commonwealth of England
1653	Cromwell becomes England's "Lord Protector"
1658	Cromwell dies
1660	Restoration of the monarchy, Charles II becomes King of England
1662	*Book of Common Prayer* republished
1662	Third Act of Uniformity causes the Great Ejection
1665	The Great Plague devastates London
1665	Five Mile Act drives nonconforming ministers from former parishes
1672	Declaration of Indulgence pardons some imprisoned Puritans
1685	James II becomes King of England, persecution grows
1688	Glorious Revolution, William and Mary become King and Queen of England
1689	Act of Toleration

Events in New England

1620	Pilgrims (Separatists) land in Plymouth
1630	Massachusetts Bay Colony (Puritans) land in Boston
1633	"Great Migration" of Puritans to New England
1636	Harvard College established
1636	Hartford, Connecticut founded
1637	Pequot War between Native Americans and colonists
1640	*Bay Psalm Book* published
1651	John Eliot establishes first of villages for "Praying Indians"
1675	King Philip's War
1735	Great Awakening begins

Appendix C
Study Questions

Chapter 1: Who Were the Puritans?

1. Why were the godly in England labeled *Puritans*?
2. The Puritans stood out in society because they worked to apply what earlier movement to all aspects of life?
3. The Puritans were different first and foremost because they believed in following the Bible more thoroughly than most in their day. In what ways was this true?
4. The Puritans taught that there is only one way God can be known savingly. What is that one way?
5. According to the Puritans, who needs to be converted to Christ? Why do they need to be converted?
6. The Puritans taught that conversion should affect how much of the individual? Which parts of the individual should be transformed by conversion?
7. Where does the path of spiritual growth ultimately lead?
8. How did the hope of heaven influence the Puritans when they endured suffering?
9. What are the means of grace that helped the Puritans so much?
10. Where should Christian love first appear?
11. The Puritans did not think that Christianity's influence should stop at church and home. What other parts of life should it impact?
12. In what ways did the Puritans show their passion for evangelism?
13. The Puritans thought that when it comes to God, the church, and how people should live, the old biblical and Reformation ways were the best ways. They based this on the fact that God never changes. How can God's changeless ideas about right and wrong help you in our own day, when people want to change public opinion about what is true and what is right?

Chapter 2: Richard Greenham

1. Who produced the Geneva Bible?
2. What did Richard Greenham mean when he said, "Where the Scripture hath not a mouth, we ought not to have ears"?
3. List four ways in which Greenham was a pioneer.
4. How did Greenham help people who had "afflicted consciences"?
5. How did Greenham help people's physical needs?
6. How did Greenham train pastors for the ministry?
7. What did Greenham teach about Sabbath-keeping?
8. According to Greenham, how many years of a person's life can be devoted solely to God without distraction? How did Greenham calculate this number? Whether or not he is perfectly accurate, how should this affect your life?

Chapter 3: William Perkins

1. What incident got the unconverted William Perkins thinking about his soul?
2. In what ways did Perkins's preaching differ from most of the Church of England's ministers?

3. In what ways did Perkins keep peace with the Church of England, even though he didn't agree with some of its practices?
4. What qualities mark Perkins's writing?
5. What are some directions Perkins gave to ministers on how to preach?
6. How did Perkins's influence reach all the way to America?
7. How does Perkins's busy, short life serve as an example for us about how we can use our gifts in fruitful ways for His glory? In what ways could you make better use of your time for God's glory and the good of others?

Chapter 4: William Ames

1. Why did William Ames flee England to live in The Netherlands?
2. What were some distinctive viewpoints of the Anglicans, Separatists, Presbyterians, and Congregationalists?
3. What important Synod did Ames contribute to in 1618–1619? What important role did he play at that Synod?
4. What false doctrine did Ames often refute in his writings?
5. Which of Ames's books became the standard theological textbook for seminarians all over the world?
6. What challenges did Ames face while teaching at the college at Franeker?
7. Though Ames longed to find a home in America, he died in Rotterdam before realizing his dream. On his deathbed, he testified of his hope in a heavenly home. When you face disappointments in life and hopes or dreams fail to come to pass, how can Ames's example encourage you?

Chapter 5: Richard Sibbes

1. Despite his desire to study, Richard Sibbes submitted to his father's insistence that he be a wheelwright. Allowing his talents to lie dormant was difficult for Richard. How did God providentially make a way for Sibbes to use his gifts? How can this encourage you, when you feel that your abilities aren't being fully used?
2. What did Sibbes mean when he said, "If cold dark bodies have light and heat in them, it is because the sun hath shined upon them first"? See 1 John 4:19.
3. Good actions may be done by a hypocrite, but, according to Sibbes, what is a primary difference between a hypocrite and a godly person?
4. If we find cold affections toward God in our hearts, what must we do to revive our love for Him?
5. Sibbes taught that daily meditation on Scripture helps love for God burn brightly in the soul. Are you regularly meditating on Scripture? If not, what can you do to begin? See Joshua 1:8 and Psalm 1:1–3.

Chapter 6: John Cotton

1. What situation in England led John Cotton to move to America?
2. Describe Cotton's first controversy in the church at Boston and how he handled it.
3. Describe the conflict over Roger Williams and how Cotton handled it.
4. Cotton's influence was greatest in his popularizing his preferred form of church government. What is this form called?
5. Cotton wrote an influential catechism that was used in America for two hundred years. What was it called? What other volume was it later published within?
6. Explain the following quote: "Could wound at argument without division, cut to the quick, and yet make no incision." What important scriptural principle does this exemplify? See Ephesians 4:3.

Chapter 7: Thomas Hooker

1. What situation led Thomas Hooker and Samuel Stone to leave Massachusetts and found a new colony?
2. Describe some of the challenges Hooker and his company faced in the first few years of their settling in Connecticut.
3. How did Hooker's "Fundamental Orders for Connecticut" differ from Massachusetts's style of government?
4. In what ways did Hooker reveal that he was (1) a capable leader and (2) a compassionate pastor? How can we learn to both use our gifts effectively and show compassion to others generously at the same time?
5. What were Hooker's practices and views on private prayer? How can his ideas about prayer help your spiritual life? See Matthew 24:12 and Psalm 51:10.

Chapter 8: Jeremiah Burroughs

1. Describe the efforts of Archbishop Laud and Bishop Wren against Jeremiah Burroughs.
2. How did Burroughs respond to being deposed?
3. How did Burroughs encourage Oliver Cromwell long before Cromwell became Lord Protector? See Psalm 56:11.
4. Burroughs was excited by the call to be a pastor in Rotterdam, but he wanted to be sure that it was God's will. How did he seek to discern God's will for his life? What can you learn from his example? See Proverbs 11:14 and Ephesians 5:17.
5. List several ways God used Burroughs's preaching ministry to bless people.
6. What were some of Burroughs's duties as a member of the Westminster Assembly?
7. Explain the motto above Burroughs's door: "Difference of belief and unity of believers are not incompatible." What can you learn from Burroughs's example, and in

what situations could you apply it? See Romans 14:1–9 and 16:17.

Chapter 9: Thomas Goodwin

1. Thomas Goodwin spent years examining himself looking for evidence that he was a genuine believer in Christ. What finally brought him assurance of salvation? See Galatians 6:14.
2. What important advice did Richard Sibbes once give Goodwin?
3. With whom did Goodwin serve? Both men were called "living and walking Bibles." How does a person become a walking Bible? See Psalm 119:11, 15, 18, 27.
4. What great loss did Goodwin suffer in the fire of London in 1666? How did he respond to this loss? How can you learn from his example? See James 1:3, 5:10–11.
5. Though Goodwin had little assurance of salvation earlier in his life, he died with great joy and love for Christ in his heart. Do you struggle with assurance of salvation? Has your conscience been calmed by looking to Christ's death on the cross and being able to discern the Spirit's work and fruits in your own soul and life? See Hebrews 10:1–4 and Romans 8:15–16.

Chapter 10: John Eliot

1. Why did early settlers of Massachusetts find little time to evangelize the Indians?
2. John Eliot is most remembered for what literary work?
3. Describe how the Indians' conversion influenced their culture.
4. How did King Philip's War harm the Algonquins and their Praying Towns?
5. It would be easy for a missionary to despair after setbacks such as Eliot experienced during King Philip's War. How

did Eliot respond to the setbacks? What can you learn from his response? See Acts 14:2–3.

Chapter 11: Thomas Shepard

1. List the many hardships Thomas Shepard endured.
2. When Thomas Shepard experienced hardship—which he did often—what was his typical response to it? How did he think about God and how did he think about himself? See Romans 5:2–4, 8:28; Luke 13:3.
3. Laud's persecution led Shepard to reject the church liturgy and become a Puritan. When Laud's persecution only grew worse, what did the Shepards finally do in response?
4. What important ministries did Shepard carry out in Massachusetts?
5. When he was near death, how did Shepard describe his preaching ministry to the pastor who visited him? How might his perspective be helpful to preachers today?

Chapter 12: Thomas Brooks

1. Consider Thomas Brooks's comment about Satan's tempting people according to their particular situations and tendencies. Does his comment help you see how Satan might tempt you personally?
2. What are some of the important books that Brooks wrote?
3. Brooks was removed from his pulpit in The Great Ejection of 1662. He was in London during the Plague outbreak in 1665. He also suffered great loss in the Fire of London in 1666. How did he respond to all this hardship? How might his example encourage you?
4. How did Brooks respond to growing older? How are his actions different from those common in our own times? How ought we to view the time given to us? See Ephesians 5:16.
5. What was Brooks's fellow minister talking about when

he said that Brooks "had a body of divinity in his head and the power of it in his heart"? See Psalm 1:1–3, 119:11; Colossians 3:16; 2 Corinthians 3:18.

Chapter 13: Anne Bradstreet

1. List the hardships Anne Bradstreet endured once she departed for the New World.
2. When she faced death during her second winter in America, what did Anne do to comfort herself? What were the thoughts that sustained her during those times?
3. List several scriptural truths Bradstreet wrote about in her poems.
4. What was Anne's greatest desire for her children?
5. Bradstreet concentrated on her heavenly hope in her poetry, probably due to the many hardships she endured in the New World. Do you share her perspective as a pilgrim, looking for the heavenly country? See Hebrews 11:16.

Chapter 14: Richard Baxter

1. Richard Baxter's poor health hindered him all his life, and yet he accomplished much for God. Do you also have a situation in life that hinders your opportunity to serve? How can you be encouraged by Baxter's example? See 2 Corinthians 12:9.
2. Richard Baxter's poor health caused him to feel how fragile life was. How did this affect his preaching ministry?
3. What did Baxter mean when he said he preached as a dying man to dying men?
4. What are some main principles that Baxter teaches ministers in his book, *The Reformed Pastor*?
5. List various ways Margaret Baxter helped her husband

Richard. What biblical principle does she exemplify? See Genesis 2:18.

6. What was Baxter's point when he said, "I was but a pen in God's hands; and what praise is due a pen?" See 1 Corinthians 10:31.

Chapter 15: John Owen

1. What sacrifices did John Owen make when he sided with parliament in the English Civil War?

2. What are some of the many books Owen wrote, and what are they about?

3. Owen had the opportunity to preach before Parliament on several occasions. What ideas did he promote during these sermons?

4. Owen, just like Baxter, had to move a lot during the years of persecution following the restoration of King Charles II to the throne. Sometimes Owen gathered a church together and then had to leave them because of persecution. How did he keep pastoring them, even after leaving them? What did he tell them?

5. How did Owen help John Bunyan, the author of *The Pilgrim's Progress*?

6. Why did Owen sometimes use sea-faring imagery in his books? List several ways he made use of this imagery. How can his use of it help you in your spiritual life?

Chapter 16: Christopher Love

1. From the moment he came to Christ, Christopher Love faced hardships. What were some of them?

2. Is it right to disobey human authority in order to obey a command of God? See Acts 5:29.

3. Christopher Love is notable for his decisive nature. From the moment of his conversion, he followed God wholeheartedly, no matter the consequences. How can

this encourage you? See Joshua 24:15 and 1 Kings 18:21. What situations can you foresee that might tempt you to put something else above God's will?

4. Love was against the beheading of Charles I, and he wanted to see Charles II crowned as England's rightful king. But these were considered treasonous ideas. What were the consequences?

5. After a dubious trial, Love was found guilty and sentenced to death by beheading. In the record of his last words, what thought reoccurs that encouraged him immensely as he faced the chopping block? See 2 Timothy 4:6–8.

Chapter 17: John Bunyan

1. List the various factors that led a young John Bunyan to realize that he needed to change his life.

2. What experience taught Bunyan that he needed a change of heart by the Spirit's power, not just a change of behavior?

3. What idea from God's Word finally brought assurance of salvation to Bunyan's troubled soul? See 1 Corinthians 1:30. Have you realized that your righteousness before God does not depend upon your frame of mind or the state of your feelings? What does it depend upon?

4. How did 2 Corinthians 1:9 help Bunyan to be prepared for suffering? How can Bunyan's thoughts about suffering help you?

5. How long was Bunyan's first term in prison? He could have been released if he had been willing to stop preaching, but he wasn't willing. Did he view his preaching ministry as a career, or as a holy and sacred calling from God? See Acts 4:18–20.

6. How successful has *The Pilgrim's Progress* become? If you haven't read this great spiritual classic, please do so, and if you have read it, read it again! Why do you think this book has been used so greatly in God's church?

Chapter 18: John Flavel

1. List the various ways John Flavel engaged in evangelism.
2. Flavel was ejected from his pulpit in 1662, along with approximately 2000 other ministers. What did Flavel do in response to his ejection? Consider the connection between Acts 14:2 and Acts 14:3. How can this challenge and encourage you?
3. Flavel's ministry became full of danger, and he was quite creative in his attempts to avoid capture. What things did he do to avoid capture and keep on ministering?
4. How was Luke Short influenced by Flavel? How might Luke's story encourage people who feel that few people are currently being savingly influenced by the Word? How can it encourage those who feel that God will never save them?
5. How has God used Flavel's writings? What are some of his best-known books?
6. Flavel used helpful comparisons in his writings. What are some of his sayings that convict or encourage you?

Chapter 19: John Howe

1. John Howe preached for two hours on a passage that Cromwell assigned to him without any advance notice. What biblical principle did Howe's preaching exemplify? See 2 Timothy 4:2.
2. When Howe was a child, he fled Ireland because of persecution, only to return as an adult, again escaping persecution. After returning, he enjoyed a time of peace and security. How did he use this blessed time? How ought Christians in our time use their freedoms and security? See Ephesians 5:16.
3. As many of the Puritans did, Howe traveled when persecution grew worse. How would you respond if someone accused them of cowardice? See Matthew 10:23.

4. How did the Glorious Revolution of 1688 benefit Puritans?
5. How did Howe respond to Daniel Defoe's criticisms? What biblical principle was Howe trying to apply?
6. How did the idea of God's temple crop up in the various stages of John Howe's life?

Chapter 20: Joseph Alleine

1. Joseph Alleine's father said to him, "You are a precious arrow in my quiver." What did he mean? See Psalm 127:4–5.
2. Witnessing the ravages of the English Civil War taught Alleine something about life. What was it?
3. What was Alleine's primary concern?
4. Keenly feeling the brevity of life, Alleine hastened to serve God. What did he do in service to God?
5. Describe Alleine's heroic efforts at preaching.
6. Alleine's letters from prison show his concern for the souls of his people. Summarize the selections from his letters in your own words.
7. It is a fact that none of us know how long we have to live. How should the uncertainty of life influence what we decide to do? See Psalm 39:4, 90:12.

Chapter 21: Matthew Henry

1. Describe the home life in which Matthew Henry grew up.
2. In what ways did Philip Henry, Matthew's father, encourage his children to be Bible-centered?
3. How early in life did Matthew display a penchant for commenting on the Bible? What other early signs of this tendency can you discern?
4. Matthew was educated in law but, after the King's declaration of indulgence in 1687, what did he pursue instead?

5. In what area of life did Matthew Henry experience much hardship?

6. After Henry lost a baby named Mary at only three weeks of age, he gave words of comfort to others who might experience a similar time of trial. What did he encourage them to take comfort in?

7. What method did Matthew Henry use in his preaching ministry, and how did his method fit together with his later commentary writing?

Chapter 22: Jonathan Edwards

1. Jonathan Edwards exemplified loving God with his heart as well as with his mind. How could his example of a robust intellectual life and warm piety correct problems with Christianity in the twenty-first century?

2. What surprising event shook worldly souls out of their apathy shortly after Edwards arrived in Northampton to begin his pastorate?

3. Edwards was unusually devoted to seeking God. Describe his devotional life, and how he balanced it with physical exercise and family life.

4. Edwards was a keen observer of the natural world. How did he use this knowledge to portray the precarious state of sinners in his sermon *Sinners in the Hands of an Angry God*?

5. How did Edwards use astronomy to compare and contrast hypocrites and true believers?

6. How did George Whitefield's preaching contrast with Edwards's approach to worship?

7. Though Edwards was a central figure in the Great Awakening, he took a humble and correct view of his role in it. What did he say about his role in the revival?

8. What did Edwards do that led to his dismissal from Northampton?

9. Describe the life of Edwards in Stockbridge.

10. What did Edwards write to his children before his death?

Chapter 23: Conclusion

1. What must a person experience before he or she can profit from the lessons the Puritans teach?

2. What can you do to fill your life with more of the Bible? See Psalm 1:1–3.

3. Do you accept both that God is completely sovereign and that you are fully responsible for your actions?

4. Are you seeking a saving relationship with Christ for your own soul? Are you seeking to love God as He has revealed Himself in the Trinity?

5. What did John Trapp mean when he said, "A man riding his horse to be crowned king will not worry about a rainy day"?

6. Is your family like a little church? What can you do to make it so? See Deuteronomy 6:7.

7. What did Matthew Henry tell people who didn't know how to pray?

8. How are you seeking out people who love Christ in order to have friendship with them?

9. Are you devoted to your church? Do you believe that God meets with us in a special way when we meet together for preaching and for prayer? Would you be willing to meet in hiding, if need be, in order to attend Christ's ordinances?

10. How do the Puritans as a whole teach us the importance of living intentionally and humbly to God's glory on a daily basis?

Bibliography

This selected bibliography begins with a sampling of books on Puritanism as a whole, and then follows the order of the chapters of this book. The bibliography includes books written for adults as well as for older children and teens, so that parents can pursue further studies with their children. Books of a highly academic nature are often not included.

English Puritanism

Barker, William. *Puritan Profiles: 54 Influential Puritans at the Time When the Westminster Confession of Faith was Written.* Fearn, Ross-shire: Mentor, 1999.

Beeke, Joel R. *Heirs with Christ: The Puritans on Adoption.* Grand Rapids: Reformation Heritage Books, 2008.

———. *Puritan Reformed Spirituality.* Grand Rapids: Reformation Heritage Books, 2004.

Beeke, Joel R. and Mark Jones. *A Puritan Theology: Doctrine for Life.* Grand Rapids: Reformation Heritage Books, 2012.

Beeke, Joel R. and Randall J. Pederson. *Meet the Puritans: With A Guide to Modern Reprints.* Grand Rapids: Reformation Heritage, 2006.

Beveridge, W. *A Short History of the Westminster Assembly.* Ed. J. Ligon Duncan III. Greenville, S.C.: Reformed Academic Press, 1993.

Bradshaw, William. *English Puritanisme and Other Works.* Westmead: Gregg Reprints, 1972.

Bremer, Francis, ed. *Puritanism: Transatlantic Perspectives on a Seventeenth-Century Anglo-American Faith.* Boston: Northeastern University Press, 1978.

Bronkema, Ralph. *The Essence of Puritanism.* Goes, Netherlands: Oosterbaan and LeCointre, 1929.

Brook, Benjamin. *The Lives of the Puritans.* 3 vols. London: J. Black, 1813; reprint, Pittsburgh: Soli Deo Gloria, 1994.

Broome, J. R. *Some Puritan Divines.* Hertfordshire, England: Gospel Standard Trust, 2013.

Brown, John. *The English Puritans.* London: Cambridge University Press, 1912.

Burrage, Champlin. *The Early English Dissenters in the Light of Recent Research (1550–1641).* 2 vols. New York: Russell & Russell, 1967.

Byington, Ezra Hoyt. *The Puritan in England and New England.* Boston: Little, Brown and Co., 1990.

Campbell, Douglas. *The Puritan in Holland, England, and America.* 4th ed. 2 vols. New York: Harper and Brothers, 1892.

Carden, Allen. *Puritan Christianity in America: Religion and Life in Seventeenth-Century Massachusetts.* Grand Rapids: Baker, 1990.

Carruthers, Samuel William. *The Everyday Work of the Westminster Assembly.* Philadelphia: Presbyterian Historical Society, 1943.

Collinson, Patrick. *The Elizabethan Puritan Movement.* Berkeley: University of California Press, 1967.

———. *English Puritanism.* London: Historical Association, 1987.

———. *Godly People: Essays on English Protestantism and Puritanism.* London: Hambledon Press, 1983.

Coolidge, John S. *The Pauline Renaissance in England: Puritanism and the Bible.* Oxford: Clarendon Press, 1970.

Cragg, C. R. *Puritanism in the Period of the Great Persecution, 1660–1688.* London: Cambridge University Press, 1957.

Emerson, Everett H. *English Puritanism from John Hooper to John Milton.* Durham, N.C.: Duke University Press, 1968.

———. *Puritanism in America.* Boston: Twayne Publishers, 1977.

Fincham, Kenneth, ed. *The Early Stuart Church, 1603–1642.* Hampshire, England: Macmillan, 1993.

Gardiner, Samuel Rawson. *History of England from the Accession of James I to the Outbreak of Civil War 1603–1642.* 10 vols. New York: Longmans, Green, and Co., 1896–1901.

Garrett, Christina H. *The Marian Exiles: A Study in the Origins of Elizabethan Puritanism.* Cambridge: Cambridge University Press, 1938.

George, Charles H. and Katherine George. *The Protestant Mind of the English Reformation, 1570–1640.* Princeton: Princeton University Press, 1961.

Haller, William. *Liberty and Reformation in the Puritan Revolution.* New York: Columbia University Press, 1955.

———. *The Rise of Puritanism.* New York: Columbia University Press, 1938.

Hetherington, William M. *History of the Westminster Assembly of Divines.* New York: Robert Carter & Brothers, 1859.

Hill, Christopher. *Puritanism and Revolution: Studies in Interpretation of the English Revolution of the 17th Century.* New York: Schocken Books, 1964.

Howard, Leon, ed. *Essays on Puritans and Puritanism.* Albuquerque: University of New Mexico Press, 1989.

Hulse, Erroll. *Who are the Puritans?* Darlington, England: Evangelical Press, 2000.

Kapic, Kelly M. and Randall C. Gleason, eds. *The Devoted Life: An Invitation to the Puritan Classics.* Downers Grove, Ill.: InterVarsity Press, 2004.

Kendall, Robert T. *Calvin and English Calvinism to 1649.* New York: Oxford University Press, 1979.

Kevan, Ernest. *The Grace of Law: A Study in Puritan Theology.* Morgan, Pa.: Soli Deo Gloria, 1993.

Knappen, M. M. *Tudor Puritanism: A Chapter in the History of Idealism.* Chicago: University of Chicago Press, 1939.

Lewis, Peter. *The Genius of Puritanism.* Haywards Heath, Sussex, England: Carey Publications, 1975.

Lloyd-Jones, D. M. *The Puritans: Their Origins and Successors. Addresses delivered at the Puritan and Westminster Conferences 1959–1978.* Edinburgh: Banner of Truth Trust, 1987.

Loane, Marcus L. *Makers of Puritan History.* Grand Rapids: Baker, 1980.

McNeill, John T. *The History and Character of Calvinism.* New York: Oxford University Press, 1973.

Macphail, Andrew. *Essays in Puritanism.* London: T. Fisher Unwin, 1905.

Marsden, J. P. *The History of the Early Puritans.* 2nd ed. London: Hamilton, Adams, & Co., 1853.

———. *The History of the Later Puritans.* 3rd ed. London: Hamilton, Adams, & Co., 1872.

Martin, Ralph P. *A Guide to the Puritans: A Topical and Textual Index to Writings of the Puritans and Some of their Successors Recently in Print.* Edinburgh: Banner of Truth Trust, 1997.

Morgan, Irvonwy. *The Godly Preachers of the Elizabethan Church.* London: Epworth Press, 1965.

Murray, Iain. *The Puritan Hope: A Study in Revival and The Interpretation of Prophecy.* Edinburgh: Banner of Truth Trust, 1971.

Oldridge, Darren. *Religion and Society in Early Stuart England.* Aldershot, England: Ashgate, 1998.

Packer, J. I. *A Quest for Godliness: The Puritan Vision of the Christian Life.* Wheaton, Ill.: Crossway Books, 1990.

———, ed. *Puritan Papers.* 5 vols. Philipsburg, N.J.: Presbyterian and Reformed, 2000–2005.

———. *Puritan Portraits.* Fearn, U.K.: Christian Focus, 2012.

Porter, H. C. *Puritanism in Tudor England.* New York: The MacMillan Co., 1970.

———. *Reformation and Reaction in Tudor Cambridge.* London: Cambridge University Press, 1958.

Reid, James. *Memoirs of the Lives and Writings of those Eminent Divines who convened in the famous Assembly at Westminster in the Seventeenth Century.* 2 vols. Paisley: Stephen and Andrew Young,

1811; reprint, 2 vols. in 1, Edinburgh: Banner of Truth Trust, 1982.

Ryken, Leland. *Worldly Saints: The Puritans as They Really Were*. Grand Rapids: Zondervan, 1986.

Simpson, Alan. *Puritanism in Old and New England*. Chicago: University of Chicago Press, 1955.

Smithen, Frederick J. *Continental Protestantism and the English Reformation*. London: J. Clarke & Co., 1927.

Toon, Peter. *Puritans and Calvinism*. Swengel, Pa.: Reiner, 1973.

Trinterud, Leonard J., ed. *Elizabethan Puritanism*. New York: Oxford University Press, 1971.

Warfield, Benjamin B. *The Westminster Assembly and Its Work*. Cherry Hill, N.J.: Mach Publishing, 1972.

Ziff, Larzer. *Puritanism in America: New Culture in a New World*. New York: Viking, 1973.

Richard Greenham

Greenham, Richard. *The Works of the Reverend and Faithful Servant of Jesus Christ M. Richard Greenham*. Boston: Da Capo, 1973.

Knappen, M. M. "Richard Greenham and the Practical Puritans under Elizabeth." PhD diss., Cornell University, 1927.

Parker, Kenneth L. and Eric J. Carlson. *'Practical Divinity': The Works and Life of Revd Richard Greenham*. St. Andrews Studies in Reformation History. Aldershot, U.K.: Ashgate, 1998.

Primus, John H. *Richard Greenham: The Portrait of an Elizabethan Pastor*. Macon, Ga.: Mercer University Press, 1998.

Short, Kenneth R. "The Educational Foundations of Elizabethan Puritanism: With Special Reference to Richard Greenham (1535?–1594)." Ed.D. diss., The University of Rochester, 1970.

William Perkins

Augustine, John H., ed. *A Commentary on Hebrews 11*. New York: Pilgrim Press, 1991.

Beeke, Joel R. "William Perkins on Predestination, Preaching, and Conversion." In *The Practical Calvinist: An Introduction to the Presbyterian & Reformed Heritage*. Ed. Peter A. Lillback. Fearn, U.K.: Chirst Focus, 183–213.

Beeke, Joel R. and J. Stephen Yuille. *William Perkins*. Darlington, England: Evangelical Press, 2015.

Breward, Ian. "The Life and Theology of William Perkins." PhD diss., University of Manchester, 1963.

———, ed. *The Work of William Perkins*, vol. 3 of The Courtenay Library of Reformation Classics. Abingdon, England: Sutton Courtenay Press, 1970.

Ferguson, Sinclair, ed. *The Art of Prophesying*. Edinburgh: Banner of Truth Trust, 1996.

Markham, C. C. "William Perkins' Understanding of the Function of Conscience." PhD diss., Vanderbilt University, 1967.

McKim, Donald Keith. *Ramism in William Perkins's Theology*. New York: Peter Lang, 1987.

Merrill, Thomas F., ed., *William Perkins, 1558–1602, English Puritanist— His Pioneer Works on Casuistry: "A Discourse of Conscience" and "the Whole Treatise of Cases of Conscience."* Nieuwkoop, The Netherlands: B. DeGraaf, 1966.

Munson, Charles R. "William Perkins, Theologian of Transition." PhD diss., Case Western Reserve, 1971.

Patterson, W. B. *William Perkins & the Making of a Protestant England*. Oxford: Oxford University Press, 2014.

Perkins, William. *The Art of Prophesying*. Edinburgh: Banner of Truth Trust, 1996.

———. *The Works of William Perkins*. 10 vols. Grand Rapids: Reformation Heritage Books, 2014–2018 (vols. 8–10 forthcoming).

Pipa, Joseph A., Jr., "William Perkins and the Development of Puritan Preaching." PhD diss., Westminster Theological Seminary, 1985.

Priebe, Victor L. "The Covenant Theology of William Perkins." PhD diss., Drew University, 1967.

Shaw, Mark R. "The Marrow of Practical Divinity: A Study in the Theology of William Perkins." PhD diss., Westminster Theological Seminary, 1981.

Sheppard, Gerald T., ed. *A Commentary on Galatians.* New York: Pilgrim Press, 1989.

Song, Young Jae Timothy. *Theology and Piety in the Reformed Federal Thought of William Perkins and John Preston.* Lewiston, New York: Edwin Mellin, 1998.

Tipson, Lynn Baird, Jr. "The Development of a Puritan Understanding of Conversion." PhD diss., Yale University, 1972.

Tufft, J. R. "William Perkins, 1558–1602." PhD diss., Edinburgh, 1952.

Yuille, J. Stephen. *Living Blessedly Forever: The Sermon on the Mount and the Puritan Piety of William Perkins.* Grand Rapids: Reformation Heritage Books, 2012.

William Ames

Ames, William. *An Analytical Exposition of Both the Epistles of the Apostle Peter.* London: E. G. for John Rothwell, 1641.

———. *Conscience, with the Power and Cases Thereof.* Norwood, N.J.: Walter J. Johnson, 1975.

———. *The Marrow of Theology.* Trans. and ed. John Dykstra Eusden. Grand Rapids: Baker, 1997.

———. *A Sketch of the Christian's Catechism.* Trans. Todd M. Rester. Grand Rapids: Reformation Heritage Books, 2008.

———. *Technometry.* Ed. Lee W. Gibbs. Philadelphia: University of Pennsylvania Press, 1979.

Beeke, Joel R. and Jan van Vliet, "*The Marrow of Theology* by William Ames." In *The Devoted Life: An Invitation to the Puritan Classics.* Ed. Kelly M. Kapic and Randall C. Gleason. Downers Grove, Ill.: InterVarsity Press, 2004.

Horton, Douglas. *Let Us Not Forget the Mighty William Ames.* Nashville, Tenn.: Abingdon Press, 1960.

Nethenus, Matthew, Hugo Visscher, and Karl Reuter. *William Ames.* Trans. Douglas Horton. Cambridge: Harvard Divinity School Library, 1965.

Sprunger, Keith L. *The Learned Doctor William Ames: Dutch Backgrounds of English and American Puritanism.* Urbana, Ill.: University of Illinois Press, 1972.

Van Vliet, Jan. *The Rise of Reformed System: The Intellectual Heritage of William Ames.* Bucks, England: Paternoster, 2013.

———. "William Ames: Marrow of the Theology and Piety of the Reformed Tradition." PhD diss., Westminster Theological Seminary, 2002.

Richard Sibbes

Affleck, Bert, Jr. "The Theology of Richard Sibbes, 1577–1635." PhD diss., Drew University, 1969.

Beeke, Joel and Mark Jones. "Richard Sibbes on Entertaining the Holy Spirit." In *A Puritan Theology: Doctrine for Life*, 573–86. Grand Rapids: Reformation Heritage, 2012.

Dever, Mark. *The Affectionate Theology of Richard Sibbes.* Sanford, Fla.: Reformation Trust, 2018.

———. *Richard Sibbes: Puritanism and Calvinism in Late Elizabethan and Early Stuart England.* Macon, Ga.: Mercer University Press, 2000.

Farrell, Frank E. "Richard Sibbes: A Study in Early Seventeenth Century English Puritanism." PhD diss., Edinburgh, 1955.

Shelly, Harold Patton. "Richard Sibbes: Early Stuart Preacher of Piety." PhD diss., Temple University, 1972.

Sibbes, Richard. *The Bruised Reed.* Edinburgh: Banner of Truth, 1998.

———. *Glorious Freedom.* Edinburgh: Banner of Truth, 2000.

———. *The Works of Richard Sibbes.* 7 volumes. Edinburgh: Banner of Truth, 2001.

Weisiger, Cary Nelson, III. "The Doctrine of the Holy Spirit in the Preaching of Richard Sibbes." PhD diss., Fuller Theological Seminary, 1984.

John Cotton

Come, Donald R. "John Cotton: Guide of the Chosen People." PhD diss., University of Illinois, 1956.

Cotton, John. *Christ the Fountain of Life.* Manchester, N.H.: Arno Press, 1972.

———. *The Correspondence of John Cotton*. Chapel Hill, N.C.: University of North Carolina Press, 2001.

———. *Ecclesiastes & Song of Solomon*. Stoke-on-Trent, England: Tentmaker Publications, 2005.

———. *An Exposition of First John*. Evansville, Ind.: Sovereign Grace Publishers, 1962.

———. *The Keys of the Kingdom of Heaven*. London: M. Simmons for Henry Overton, 1644.

———. *The New Covenant*. London: by M. S. for Francis Eglesfield and John Allen, 1654.

———. *The True Constitution of a Particular Visible Church*. London: for Samuel Satterthwaite, 1642.

———. *The Way of Life, Or, God's Way and Course, in Bringing the Soul Into, and Keeping It In, and Carrying It On, in the Ways of Life and Peace*. London: by M. F. for L. Fawne and S. Gellibrand, 1641.

Emerson, Everett H. *John Cotton*. New York: Twayne, 1965.

Rosenmeier, Jesper. *'Spirituall Concupiscence': John Cotton's English Years, 1584–1633*. Boston: Richard Kay Publications, 2012.

Welles, Judith B. "John Cotton, 1584–1652: Churchman and Theologian." PhD diss., Edinburgh University, 1948.

Ziff, Larzer. *The Career of John Cotton, Puritanism and the American Experience*. Princeton: Princeton University Press, 1962.

Thomas Hooker

Bush, Sargent. *The Writings of Thomas Hooker: Spiritual Adventure in Two Worlds*. Madison: University of Wisconsin Press, 1980.

Denholm, Andrew T. "Thomas Hooker: Puritan Preacher, 1586–1647." PhD diss., Hartford Seminary Foundation, 1961.

Hooker, Thomas. *The Application of Redemption, by the Effectual Work of the Word, and Spirit of Christ, for the Bringing Home of Lost Sinners to God, The First Eight Books*. New York: Arno Press, 1972.

———. *The Application of Redemption, by the Effectual Work of the Word, and Spirit of Christ, for the Bringing Home of Lost Sinners to God, The Ninth and Tenth Books*. New York: Arno Press, 2008.

———. *The Christian's Two Chief Lessons*. Ames, Ia.: International Outreach, 2002.

———. *The Poor Doubting Christian Drawn to Christ*. Morgan, Pa.: Soli Deo Gloria, 2001.

———. *The Soul's Humiliation*. Ames, Ia.: International Outreach, 2000.

———. *The Soul's Preparation for Christ*. Ames, Ia.: International Outreach, 1994.

Pellman, Hubert. "Thomas Hooker: A Study in Puritan Ideals." PhD diss., University of Pennsylvania, 1958.

Shuffleton, Frank. *Thomas Hooker, 1587–1647*. Princeton: Princeton University Press, 1977.

Tipson, Baird. *Hartford Puritanism: Thomas Hooker, Samuel Stone, and Their Terrifying God*. Oxford: Oxford University Press, 2015.

Jeremiah Burroughs

Burroughs, Jeremiah. *Contentment, Prosperity, and God's Glory*. Puritan Treasures for Today. Grand Rapids: Reformation Heritage Books, 2013.

———. *The Evil of Evils*. Morgan, Pa.: Soli Deo Gloria, 1992.

———. *Gospel Conversation*. Orlando, Fla.: Soli Deo Gloria, 1995.

———. *Gospel Fear*. Pittsburgh: Soli Deo Gloria, 1991.

———. *Gospel Worship*. Morgan, Pa.: Soli Deo Gloria, 1990.

———. *Moses' Self-Denial*. Grand Rapids: Soli Deo Gloria, 2010.

———. *The Rare Jewel of Christian Contentment*. Puritan Paperbacks. Edinburgh: Banner of Truth Trust, 2002.

Simpson, Phillip L. *A Life of Gospel Peace: A Biography of Jeremiah Burroughs*. Grand Rapids: Reformation Heritage Books, 2011.

Thomas Goodwin

Beeke, Joel R. and Mark Jones, eds. *A Habitual Sight of Him: The Christ-Centered Piety of Thomas Goodwin*. Profiles in Reformed Spirituality. Grand Rapids: Reformation Heritage Books, 2011.

——. "Thomas Goodwin's Christological Supralapsarianism" In *A Puritan Theology: Doctrine for Life*, 149–160. Grand Rapids: Reformation Heritage Books, 2012.

——. "Thomas Goodwin on Christ's Beautiful Heart." In *A Puritan Theology: Doctrine for Life*, 387–400. Grand Rapids: Reformation Heritage Books, 2012.

Brown, Paul Edward. "The Principle of the Covenant in the Theology of Thomas Goodwin." PhD diss., Drew University, 1950.

Carter, Rembert. "The Presbyterian-Independent Controversy with Special Reference to Dr. Thomas Goodwin and the Years 1640–1660." PhD diss., University of Edinburgh, 1961

Chang, Paul Ling-Ji. "Thomas Goodwin (1600–1680) on the Christian Life." PhD diss., Westminster Theological Seminary, Philadelphia, 2001.

Crompton, Gordon Douglas. "The Life and Theology of Thomas Goodwin." ThM thesis, Greenville Presbyterian Theological Seminary, 1997.

Fienberg, Stanley P. "Thomas Goodwin, Puritan Pastor and Independent Divine." PhD diss., University of Chicago, 1974.

Goodwin, Thomas. *Christ Set Forth and the Heart of Christ in Heaven Towards Sinners on Earth.* Fearn, Scotland: Christian Focus, 2011.

——. *The Works of Thomas Goodwin.* 12 vols. Grand Rapids: Reformation Heritage Books, 2006.

Horton, Michael S. "Thomas Goodwin and the Puritan Doctrine of Assurance: Continuity and

——. Discontinuity in the Reformed Tradition, 1600–1680." PhD diss., Wycliffe Hall,

——. Oxford, and Coventry University, 1995.

——. *Why Heaven Kissed Earth: The Christology of the Puritan Reformed Orthodox Theologian: Thomas Goodwin (1600–1680).* Göttingen: Vandenhoeck & Ruprecht, 2010.

McNally, Alexander. "Some Aspects of Thomas Goodwin's Doctrine of Assurance." ThM thesis, Westminster Theological Seminary, 1972.

John Eliot

Cogley, Richard W. *John Eliot's Mission to the Indians Before King Philip's War.* Cambridge, Mass.: Harvard University Press, 1999.

Eliot, John. *The Eliot Tracts: with Letters from John Eliot to Thomas Thorowgood and Richard Baxter.* Santa Barbara, Calif.: Greenwood, 2003.

——. *The Indian Grammar Begun: Or, an Essay to Bring the Indian Language into Rules, for Help of Such as Desire to Learn the Same, for the Furtherance of the Gospel among Them.* Boston: Applewood Books, 2001.

Gray, Kathryn N. *John Eliot and the Praying Indians of Massachusetts Bay: Communities and Connections in Puritan New England.* Lewisburg, Pa.: Bucknell University Press, 2013.

Kim, Do Hoon. "'By prophesying to the wind, the wind came and the dry bones lived': John Eliot's Puritan Ministry to New England Indians." PhD diss., University of Edinburgh, 2012.

Winslow, Ola. *John Eliot: Apostle to the Indians.* Boston: Houghton Mifflin, 1968.

Thomas Shepard

Hasler, R. A. "Thomas Shepard: Pastor-Evangelist (1605–1649): A Study in New England Ministry." PhD diss., Hartford Seminary Foundation, 1964.

McGiffert, Michael, ed. *God's Plot: Puritan Spirituality in Thomas Shepard's Cambridge.* Amherst: University of Massachusetts Press, 1994.

Shepard, Thomas. *The Parable of the Ten Virgins.* Morgan, Pa.: Soli Deo Gloria, 1994.

——. *The Sincere Convert and the Sound Believer.* Morgan, Pa.: Soli Deo Gloria, 1999.

——. *Theses Sabbaticae.* Morgan, Pa.: Soli Deo Gloria, 1992.

Whyte, Alexander. *Thomas Shepard, Pilgrim Father and Founder of Harvard: His Spiritual Experience and Experiential Preaching.* London: Oliphant, Anderson & Ferrier, 1909.

Thomas Brooks

Brooks, Thomas. *Heaven on Earth: A Treatise on Christian Assurance.* Edinburgh: Banner of Truth, 1996.

———. *The Mute Christian Under the Smarting Rod.* Choteau, Mont.: Gospel Mission, n.d.

———. *Precious Remedies Against Satan's Devices.* Edinburgh: Banner of Truth Trust, 2000.

———. *The Secret Key to Heaven: The Vital Importance of Private Prayer.* Edinburgh: Banner of Truth Trust, 2006.

———. *The Works of Thomas Brooks.* 6 vols. Edinburgh: Banner of Truth Trust, 2001.

Broome, J. R. "Thomas Brooks (1608–1680)." In *Some Puritan Divines,* 93–99. Hertfordshire, England: Gospel Standard Trust, 2013.

Spurgeon, C. H. *Smooth Stones Taken from Ancient Brooks: Selections from the Writings of Thomas Brooks.* Edinburgh: Banner of Truth, 2011.

Anne Bradstreet

Bradstreet, Anne. *The Complete Works of Anne Bradstreet.* Cambridge, Mass.: Belknap Press, 1981.

———. *To My Husband and Other Poems.* Mineola, N.Y.: Dover Publications, 2000.

Cook, Faith. *Anne Bradstreet: Pilgrim and Poet.* Darlington: Evangelical Press, 2010.

Gordon, Charlotte. *Mistress Bradstreet: The Untold Life of America's First Poet.* New York: Little, Brown and Co., 2005.

Kellogg, D. B. *Anne Bradstreet.* Nashville: Thomas Nelson, 2010.

Nichols, Heidi L. *Anne Bradstreet: A Guided Tour of the Life and Thought of a Puritan Poet.* Phillipsburg, N.J.: Presbyterian and Reformed, 2006.

Richard Baxter

Baxter, Richard. *A Call to the Unconverted.* Grand Rapids: Zondervan, 1953.

———. *Dying Thoughts.* Edinburgh: Banner of Truth, 2004.

———. *The Practical Works of Richard Baxter.* Morgan, Pa.: Soli Deo Gloria, 2000.

———. *The Reformed Pastor.* Edinburgh: Banner of Truth, 1999.

———. *The Saints' Everlasting Rest.* Fearn, Scotland: Christian Focus, 1999.

Beougher, Timothy K. *Richard Baxter and Conversion: A Study of the Puritan Concept of Becoming a Christian.* Fearn, Scotland: Christian Focus, 2007.

Boersma, Hans. *A Hot Pepper Corn: Richard Baxter's Doctrine of Justification in its Seventeenth-Century Context of Controversy.* Zoetermeer, The Netherlands: Boekencentrum, 1993.

Ladell, A. R. *Richard Baxter: Puritan and Mystic.* London: Society for Promoting Christian Knowledge, 1925.

Martin, Hugh. *Puritanism and Richard Baxter.* London: SCM Press, 1954.

Nuttall, Geoffrey F. *Richard Baxter.* London: Nelson, 1966.

Packer, J. I. *A Grief Sanctified: Through Sorrow to Eternal Hope, Including Richard Baxter's Timeless Memoir of His Wife's Life and Death.* Wheaton, Ill.: Crossway Books, 2002.

———. *The Redemption & Restoration of Man in the Thought of Richard Baxter.* Vancouver: Regent College Publishing, 2003.

Powicke, Frederick J. *A Life of the Reverend Richard Baxter, 1615–1691.* Boston: Houghton Mifflin Co., 1924.

Salisbury, Vance. *Good Mister Baxter: Sketches of Effective, Gospel-Centered Leadership from the Life of Richard Baxter.* Nevada City, Calif.: Piety Hill Press, 2007.

John Owen

Barrett, Matthew and Michael A. G. Haykin. *Owen on the Christian Life: Living for the Glory of God in Christ.* Wheaton, Ill.: Crossway, 2015.

Beeke, Joel and Mark Jones. "John Owen on Communion with the Triune God." In *A Puritan Theology: Doctrine for Life,* 101–116. Grand Rapids: Reformation Heritage Books, 2012.

Carr, Simonetta. *John Owen.* Christian Biographies for Young Readers. Grand Rapids: Reformation Heritage Books, 2010.

Daniels, Richard. *The Christology of John Owen.* Grand Rapids: Reformation Heritage Books, 2004.

Davis, J. C. W. "John Owen, D.D.: Puritan Preacher and Ecclesiastical Statesman." MA thesis, Liverpool University, 1962.

Ferguson, Sinclair. *John Owen on the Christian Life.* Edinburgh: Banner of Truth Trust, 1987.

———. *The Trinitarian Devotion of John Owen.* Orlando: Reformation Trust, 2014.

Gribben, Crawford. *John Owen and English Puritanism: Experiences of Defeat.* New York: Oxford University Press, 2016.

Griffiths, Steve. *Redeem the Time: Sin in the Writings of John Owen.* Fearn, Scotland: Christian Focus, 2001.

Kapic, Kelly M. *Communion with God: The Divine and the Human in the Theology of John Owen.* Grand Rapids: Baker Academic, 2007.

Kapic, Kelly M. and Justin Taylor, ed. *Overcoming Sin & Temptation: Three Classic Works by John Owen.* Wheaton, Ill.: Crossway Books, 2006.

Kapic, Kelly M. and Mark Jones. *The Ashgate Research Companion to John Owen's Theology.* Farnham, Surrey, England: Ashgate, 2012.

Oliver, Robert, ed. *John Owen: The Man and His Theology.* Edinburgh: Banner of Truth Trust, 2002.

Orme, William. *Life of the Rev. John Owen, D.D.* Reprint, Choteau, Mont.: Gospel Mission Press, 1981.

Owen, John. *Biblical Theology.* Morgan, Pa.: Soli Deo Gloria, 1994.

———. *The Correspondence of John Owen, 1616–1683.* Cambridge, England: James Clarke Press, 1970.

———. *An Exposition of the Epistle to the Hebrews.* Edinburgh: Banner of Truth, 1985.

———. *The Glory of Christ: His Office and Grace.* Fearn, Scotland: Christian Focus, 2004.

———. *Spiritual-Mindedness.* Edinburgh: Banner of Truth, 2009.

———. *The Works of John Owen.* 16 vols. Edinburgh: Banner of Truth, 1996.

Toon, Peter. *God's Statesman: The Life and Work of John Owen.* Exeter: Paternoster, 1971.

Trueman, Carl R. *John Owen: Reformed Catholic, Renaissance Man.* London: Routledge, 2016.

Vose, Godfrey Noel. "Profile of a Puritan: John Owen (1616–1683)." PhD diss., State University of Iowa, 1963.

Wallace, Dewey D., Jr. "The Life and Thought of John Owen to 1660: A Study of the Significance of Calvinist Theology in English Puritanism." PhD diss., Princeton University, 1965.

Christopher Love

Beeke, Joel and Mark Jones. "Christopher Love on the Glories of Heaven and Terrors of Hell." In *A Puritan Theology: Doctrine for Life,* 819–840. Grand Rapids: Reformation Heritage Books, 2012.

Kistler, Don. *A Spectacle unto God: The Life and Death of Christopher Love.* Morgan, Pa.: Soli Deo Gloria, 1994.

Love, Christopher. *The Dejected Soul's Cure.* Morgan, Pa.: Soli Deo Gloria, 2001.

———. *Grace: The Truth, Growth, and Different Degrees.* Morgan, Pa.: Soli Deo Gloria, 1997.

———. *Heaven's Glory, Hell's Terror.* London: for Peter Barker, 1671.

———. *The Mortified Christian: A Treatise on the Mortification of Sin.* Morgan, Pa.: Soli Deo Gloria, 1998.

———. *The Penitent Pardoned.* Morgan, Pa.: Soli Deo Gloria, 2002.

———. *Preacher of God's Word: Sermons by Christopher Love.* Morgan, Pa.: Soli Deo Gloria, 2000.

———. *A Treatise of Effectual Calling and Election.* Morgan, Pa.: Soli Deo Gloria, 1998.

———. *The Works of that Faithful Servant of Jesus Christ, Christopher Love.* 2 vols. Glasgow: W. Lang, 1806.

———. *The Zealous Christian.* Morgan, Pa.: Soli Deo Gloria, 2002.

John Bunyan

Beeke, Joel R., and Paul M. Smalley. *John Bunyan and the Grace of Fearing God*. Phillipsburg, N.J.: P&R, 2016.

Bunyan, John. *Come and Welcome to Jesus Christ*. Edinburgh: Banner of Truth, 2004.

———. *The Fear of God*. Morgan, Pa.: Soli Deo Gloria, 1999.

———. *Grace Abounding to the Chief of Sinners*. Ed. Roger Sharrock. Oxford: Clarendon Press, 1962.

———. *The Holy War*. Fearn, Scotland: Christian Focus, 2007.

———. *The Pilgrim's Progress*. Edinburgh: Banner of Truth, 2017.

———. *Prayer*. London: Banner of Truth, 1965.

———. *The Works of John Bunyan*. Ed. George Offor. 3 vols. Edinburgh: Banner of Truth, 1999.

Calhoun, David B. *Grace Abounding: The Life, Books & Influence of John Bunyan*. Fearn, Scotland: Christian Focus, 2005.

Crosby, Brian H. *John Bunyan: The Journey of a Pilgrim*. Fearn, Scotland: Christian Focus, 2009.

Dengler, Sandy. *John Bunyan: Writer of Pilgrim's Progress*. Chicago: Moody Press, 1986.

de Vries, Pieter. *John Bunyan and the Order of Salvation*. Trans. C. van Haaften. New York: Peter Lang, 1994.

Dunan-Page, Anne. *The Cambridge Companion to Bunyan*. Cambridge: Cambridge University Press, 2010.

Greaves, Richard. *John Bunyan*. Grand Rapids: Eerdmans, 1969.

Gunn, Judith. *Bunyan of Elstow*. London: Hodder and Stoughton, 1985.

Harrison, Frank Mott. *John Bunyan: A Story of His Life*. Edinburgh: Banner of Truth Trust, 1995.

Hill, Christopher. *A Tinker and a Poor Man: John Bunyan and His Church, 1628–1688*. New York: Alfred A. Knopf, 1989.

Wellman, Sam. *John Bunyan: Author of the Pilgrim's Progress*. Uhrichsville, Ohio: Barbour, 1996.

John Flavel

Cosby, Brian H. *John Flavel: Puritan Life and Thought in Stuart England*. Lanham, England: Lexington Books, 2014.

———. *Suffering & Sovereignty: John Flavel and the Puritans on Afflictive Providence*. Grand Rapids: Reformation Heritage Books, 2012.

Embry, Adam, ed. *An Honest, Well Experienced Heart: The Piety of John Flavel*. Profiles in Reformed Spirituality. Grand Rapids: Reformation Heritage Books, 2012.

———. *Keeper of the Great Seal of Heaven: Sealing of the Spirit in the Life and Thought of John Flavel*. Grand Rapids: Reformation Heritage Books, 2011.

Flavel, John. *Christ Knocking at the Door of the Heart*. Choteau, Mont.: Gospel Mission, 1978.

———. *Facing Grief: Counsel for Mourners*. Edinburgh: Banner of Truth, 2010.

———. *The Fountain of Life*. Choteau, Mont.: Gospel Mission, 1977.

———. *Keeping the Heart*. Grand Rapids: Soli Deo Gloria, 2012.

———. *The Method of Grace*. Choteau, Mont.: Gospel Mission, 1977.

———. *The Mystery of Providence*. Edinburgh: Banner of Truth, 2002.

———. *Triumphing over Sinful Fear*. Puritan Treasures for Today. Grand Rapids: Reformation Heritage Books, 2011.

———. *The Works of John Flavel*. 6 vols. Edinburgh: Banner of Truth, 1997.

Yuille, J. Stephen. *The Inner Sanctum of Puritan Piety: John Flavel's Doctrine of Mystical Union with Christ*. Grand Rapids: Reformation Heritage Books, 2007.

John Howe

Field, David P. *Rigid Calvinism in a Softer Dress: The Moderate Presbyterianism of John Howe, 1630–1705*. Rutherford Studies in Historical Theology. Edinburgh: Rutherford House, 2004.

Haig, C. A. *John Howe*. London: Independent Press, 1961.

Horton, Robert F. *John Howe*. London: Methuen & Co., 1895.

Howe, John. *The Redeemer's Tears Wept Over Lost Souls*. Grand Rapids: Baker, 1978.

———. *The Works of the Reverend John Howe (1630–1705)*. 3 vols. Ligonier, Pa.: Soli Deo Gloria, 1990.

Rogers, Henry. *The Life and Character of John Howe*. London: Religious Tract Society, 1863.

Joseph Alleine

Alleine, Joseph. *An Alarm to the Unconverted* (also titled as *A Sure Guide to Heaven*). Edinburgh: Banner of Truth, 1995.

———. *The Precious Promises of the Gospel*. Morgan, Pa.: Soli Deo Gloria, 2000.

Baxter, Richard and Thoedosia Alleine. *The Life & Letters of Joseph Alleine*. Grand Rapids: Reformation Heritage Books, 2003.

Samuel, David N. *Joseph Alleine: Author of* An Alarm to the Unconverted. Cambridge: The Harrison Trust, 2012.

Stanford, Charles. *Joseph Alleine: His Companions and Times*. London: Jackson, Walford, and Hodder, 1861.

Wallace, Dewey D. *Shapers of English Calvinism, 1660–1714: Variety, Persistence, and Transformation*. New York: Oxford University Press, 2011.

Matthew Henry

Beltz, Roy A. *Matthew Henry: Mighty in the Scriptures*. Des Moines: Boone Publishing, 1947.

Chapman, Charles. *Matthew Henry, His Life and Times*. London: Arthur Hall, Virtue & Co., 1859.

Eveson, Philip H. *Matthew Henry*. Darlington, England: Evangelical Press, 2012.

Harman, Allan. *Matthew Henry (1662–1714): His Life and Influence*. Fearn, Scotland: Christian Focus, 2012.

———, ed. *Matthew Henry's Unpublished Sermons on the Covenant of Grace*. Fearn, Scotland: Christian Focus, 2002.

Henry, Matthew. *The Communicant's Companion*. Philadelphia: Presbyterian Board of Publication, 1843.

———. *The Complete Works of the Rev. Matthew Henry*. 2 vols. Grand Rapids: Baker, 1979.

———. *Experiencing God's Presence*. New Kensington, Pa.: Whitaker House, 2002.

———. *Family Religion: Principles for Raising a Godly Family*. Fearn, Scotland: Christian Focus, 2008.

———. *Matthew Henry's Commentary*. Peabody, Mass.: Hendrickson Publishers, 2003.

———. *The Pleasantness of a Religious Life*. Morgan, Pa.: Soli Deo Gloria, 1996.

———. *The Quest for Meekness and Quietness of Spirit*. Morgan, Pa.: Soli Deo Gloria, 1996.

———. *The Secret of Communion with God*. Grand Rapids: Kregel, 1991.

———. *A Way to Pray*. Ed. O. Palmer Robertson. Edinburgh: Banner of Truth, 2010.

Joo, Jong Hun. *Matthew Henry: Pastoral Liturgy in Challenging Times*. Eugene, Ore.: Pickwick, 2014.

Williams, John Bickerton. *The Lives of Philip and Matthew Henry*. Edinburgh: Banner of Truth, 1974.

Jonathan Edwards

Carr, Simonetta. *Jonathan Edwards*. Christian Biographies for Young Readers. Grand Rapids: Reformation Heritage Books, 2014.

Crampton, W. Gary. *Meet Jonathan Edwards: An Introduction to America's Greatest Theologian/Philosopher*. Morgan, Pa.: Soli Deo Gloria, 2004.

Dodds, Elisabeth D. *Marriage to a Difficult Man: The "Uncommon Union" of Jonathan and Sarah Edwards*. Philadelphia: Westminster Press, 1971.

Edwards, Jonathan. *Altogether Lovely: Jonathan Edwards on the Glory and Excellency of Jesus Christ*. Morgan, Pa.: Soli Deo Gloria, 1998.

———. *Charity and Its Fruits*. Edinburgh: Banner of Truth, 1988.

———. *The Freedom of the Will*. Morgan, Pa.: Soli Deo Gloria, 1998.

———. *A History of the Work of Redemption*. Edinburgh: Banner of Truth, 2003.

———. *The Life and Diary of David Brainerd*. Grand Rapids: Baker, 1989.

———. *The Religious Affections*. Edinburgh: Banner of Truth, 2001.

———. *The Works of Jonathan Edwards*. 2 vols. Edinburgh: Banner of Truth, 1974.

———. *The Works of Jonathan Edwards*. 26 vols. New Haven, Conn.: Yale University Press, 1957–2008.

Gerstner, Edna. *Jonathan and Sarah: An Uncommon Union*. Morgan, Pa.: Soli Deo Gloria, 1995.

Gerstner, John. *Jonathan Edwards: A Mini-Theology*. Wheaton, Ill.: Tyndale House, 1987.

Hart, Darryl G., Sean Michael Lucas, and Stephen J. Nichols, eds. *The Legacy of Jonathan Edwards: American Religion and the Evangelical Tradition*. Grand Rapids: Baker, 2003.

Hosier, Helen K. *Jonathan Edwards: The Great Awakener*. Uhrichsville, Ohio: Barbour, 1999.

Kling, David William and Douglas A. Sweeney, eds. *Jonathan Edwards at Home and Abroad: Historical Memories, Cultural Movements, Global Horizons*. Columbia: University of South Carolina Press, 2003.

Lawson, Steven J. *The Unwavering Resolve of Jonathan Edwards*. Orlando: Reformation Trust, 2008.

Marsden, George M. *Jonathan Edwards: A Life*. New Haven, Conn.: Yale University Press, 2003.

Murray, Iain H. *Jonathan Edwards: A New Biography*. Edinburgh: Banner of Truth, 1987.

Najapfour, Brian G. *Jonathan Edwards: His Doctrine & Devotion to Prayer*. Caledonia, Mich.: Biblical Spirituality Press, 2013.

Nichols, Stephen J. *Jonathan Edwards: A Guided Tour of His Life and Thought*. Phillipsburg, N.J.: Presbyterian and Reformed, 2001.

Ortlund, Dane C. *Edwards on the Christian Life: Alive to the Beauty of God*. Wheaton, Ill.: Crossway Books, 2014.

Smith, John R., Harry S. Stout, and Kenneth P. Minkema. *A Jonathan Edwards Reader*. New Haven, Conn.: Yale University Press, 1995.

Story, Ronald. *Jonathan Edwards and the Gospel of Love*. Boston: University of Massachusetts Press, 2012.

Strachan, Owen and Douglas A. Sweeney. *The Essential Jonathan Edwards: An Introduction to the Life and Teaching of America's Greatest Theologian*. Chicago: Moody, 2018.

Sweeney, Douglas A. *Jonathan Edwards and the Ministry of the Word*. Downers Grove, Ill.: InterVarsity Press, 2009.

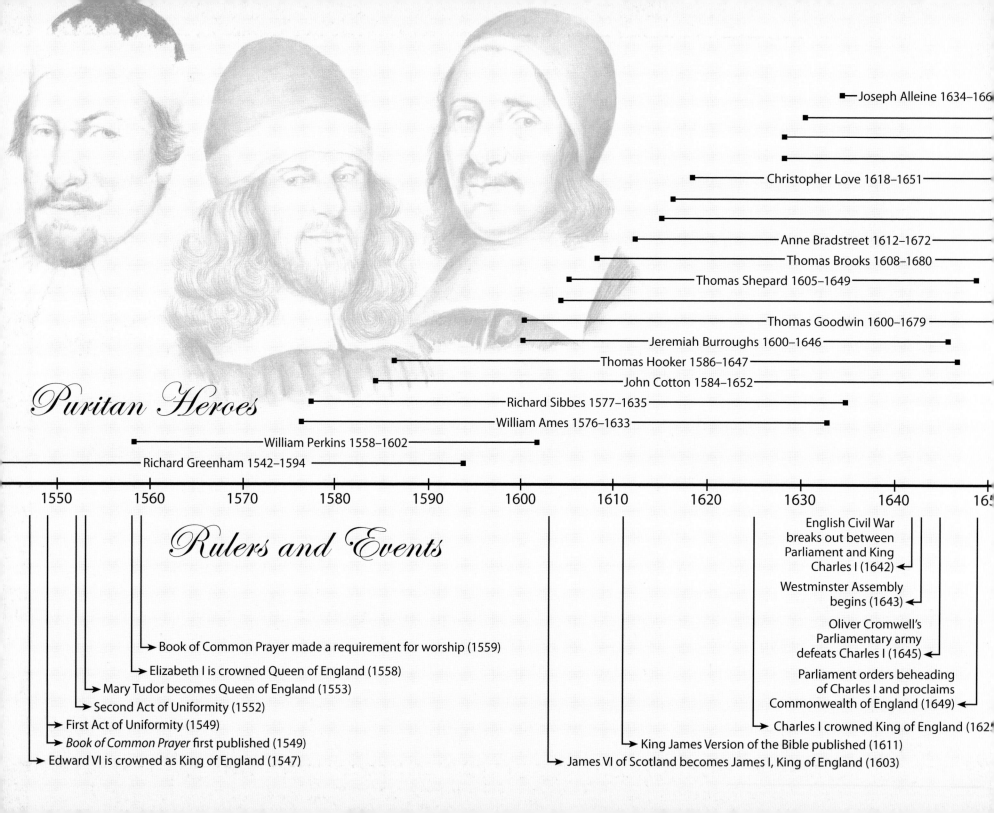

Puritan Heroes

Joseph Alleine 1634–166[6]

Christopher Love 1618–1651

Anne Bradstreet 1612–1672

Thomas Brooks 1608–1680

Thomas Shepard 1605–1649

Thomas Goodwin 1600–1679

Jeremiah Burroughs 1600–1646

Thomas Hooker 1586–1647

John Cotton 1584–1652

Richard Sibbes 1577–1635

William Ames 1576–1633

William Perkins 1558–1602

Richard Greenham 1542–1594

1550 1560 1570 1580 1590 1600 1610 1620 1630 1640 165[0]

Rulers and Events

English Civil War breaks out between Parliament and King Charles I (1642)

Westminster Assembly begins (1643)

Oliver Cromwell's Parliamentary army defeats Charles I (1645)

Parliament orders beheading of Charles I and proclaims Commonwealth of England (1649)

Book of Common Prayer made a requirement for worship (1559)

Elizabeth I is crowned Queen of England (1558)

Mary Tudor becomes Queen of England (1553)

Second Act of Uniformity (1552)

First Act of Uniformity (1549)

Book of Common Prayer first published (1549)

Edward VI is crowned as King of England (1547)

Charles I crowned King of England (162[5])

King James Version of the Bible published (1611)

James VI of Scotland becomes James I, King of England (1603)